THE BLACK AND WHITE RAINBOW

AFRICAN PERSPECTIVES
Kelly Askew and Anne Pitcher
Series Editors

The Black and White Rainbow

Reconciliation, Opposition, and Nation-Building in Democratic South Africa

Carolyn E. Holmes

University of Michigan Press
Ann Arbor

For questions or permissions, please contact um.press.perms@umich.edu

Published in the United States of America by the
University of Michigan Press
Manufactured in the United States of America
Printed on acid-free paper
First published October 2020

A CIP catalog record for this book is available from the British Library.

Library of Congress Cataloging-in-Publication Data

Names: Holmes, Carolyn E., author.
Title: The black and white rainbow : reconciliation, opposition, and nation-building in
    democratic South Africa / Carolyn E. Holmes.
Description: Ann Arbor : University of Michigan Press, 2020. | Series: African
    perspectives | Revision of author's thesis (doctoral)—Indiana University, 2015. | Includes
    bibliographical references and index. |
Identifiers: LCCN 2020018396 (print) | LCCN 2020018397 (ebook) | ISBN 9780472074631
    (hardcover) | ISBN 9780472054633 (paperback) | ISBN 9780472127177 (ebook)
Subjects: LCSH: Nation-building—South Africa. | Democratization—
    South Africa. | Nationalism—South Africa. | Post-apartheid era—South
    Africa. | Reconciliation. | South Africa—Social conditions—1994- | South Africa—
    Politics and government—1994-
Classification: LCC DT1971 .H648   2020 (print) | LCC DT1971 (ebook) |
    DDC 968.07—dc23
LC record available at https://lccn.loc.gov/2020018396
LC ebook record available at https://lccn.loc.gov/2020018397

Publication of this volume has been partially funded by the African Studies Center,
University of Michigan.

Cover image by MG Drachal, Shutterstock.

To my mom, who took me to the library,
and to my dad, who always let me choose my own pumpkin.

ACKNOWLEDGMENTS

This book is the culmination of years of work, and I have so many people to thank for their support, encouragement, and tolerance during the course of research, writing, and publication. I owe a huge intellectual debt to my advisors from my time at Indiana University. First, I would like to thank my fantastic mentor, Dr. Lauren Maclean, who has tirelessly read multiple drafts of this work and contributed in so many ways to making it better. Her help and support throughout my time in graduate school and afterward have been absolutely crucial to my development as a scholar and a teacher. I owe Dr. Jean Robinson a profound debt of gratitude for the support and guidance she has given me in terms of writing and professional development. My sincere thanks go to Drs. Alex Lichtenstein and Gardner Bovingdon for the many insightful and theoretically important conversations we have had during the development and execution of this project. I also want to thank the leadership of the African Studies Program at Indiana University, especially Drs. Maria Grosz-Ngate, Patrick O'Meara, and Samuel Obeng, who supported my work both intellectually and materially. My graduate school colleagues, especially Beth Easter, Emily Hilty, and Katie Scofield, were some of my best first readers and critics, as well as friends.

The fieldwork for this book was carried out thanks to the generous funding provided by the Andrew W. Mellon Foundation and administered by the Institute for International Education. During the course of my fieldwork, I was hosted by the Department of Political Studies and Governance at the University of the Free State in Bloemfontein. My most sincere professional admiration goes to Profs. Theodor Neethling and Hussein Solomon, who were instrumental in guiding and assisting my research during my time in the Free State. My thanks also go out to the wonderful scholars formerly of the University of Pretoria, and now of the University of Fort Hare, Dr. Irma du Plessis and Prof. Andries Bezuidenhout, whose contributions have been influential in shaping how I ask questions and investigate the answers. I want to also say a word of thanks to the Department of Sociology at the University of Pretoria, especially the department chair, Prof. Debby Bonin, for their continued affiliation with me as a research associate, and their support for my ongoing research. I am also deeply indebted to the fabulous crew of friends and colleagues I had while conducting my fieldwork, including Dr. Muziwandile Hadebe and Ms. Sidisiwe Lekoba in Durban, as well as to my Afrikaans teachers in Bloomington, Heila and Madeleine Gonin. My thanks also go out to the 110 South Africans who took time out of their lives and gave generously of their opinions to a virtual stranger about important and sensitive matters. For ethical reasons, they remain anonymous.

I would be truly remiss if I did not also thank my fantastic family. My father, D. Peter Holmes, to whom this book's dedication refers, has been an incredible source of support and encouragement throughout this process. Although my mother, Barbara Bibbs Holmes, is not still with us, her memory, and the vocabulary quizzes she gave during breakfast, have informed my approach to life in too many ways to count. My fantastic sisters, Emily and Elizabeth, their husbands, Andy and Matt, and their wonderful children, have been a source of inspiration regarding how to live well and be kind to others even when times are trying. My daughter has been a wonderful balance to the stresses of book writing, and a constant reminder of the importance of both work and play. Last, and most consistently, I want and need to thank my husband, Dr. Vasabjit Banerjee, for teaching me so much in this process: persistence in the face of obstacles, tenacious courtesy to others, the superpower of friendliness, and bravery above all.

CONTENTS

Digital materials related to this title can be found on the Fulcrum platform via the following citable URL: https://doi.org/10.3998/mpub.11518321

CHAPTER 1

Introduction

Remembering and Forgetting in Democratic South Africa

Down a gravel road, nearly fifty kilometers east of the nearest town of Dundee, two museums sit on opposite banks of the Ncome River in an otherwise empty field. The museums commemorate the battle of Ncome/Blood River, fought on 16 December 1838 between Afrikaner Voortrekkers and regiments of the Zulu Empire. Although strategically peripheral, the battle is part of the bedrock of Afrikaner nationalist history. Largely forgotten until the early twentieth century, the battle was recast as the keystone in the mythology of divine election of the Afrikaner people and their place in South Africa, along with the historical reconstruction of the Voortrekkers as a unified, cause-driven population (Crampton 2001; Murray 2013). While the battle looms large in Afrikaner nationalist history, the river—which such accounts say ran red with the blood of slain Zulu warriors[1]—is little more than a muddy stream.

The museums, standing across the river and memorializing different sides of the battle, are themselves curiously martial in posture and architecture. On the west bank of the river stands the Bloedrivier Museum, which is home to a set of sixty-four life-size bronze recreations of the Voortrekker wagons, arranged in a circular formation, or *laager*. This daunting installation is located, according to museum staff, on the very site where the Voortrekkers circled their wagons to fight with Zulu warriors. Emerging victorious despite being vastly outnumbered, the Voortrekkers are said to have taken this as a sign of their divine election and rightness of place in South Africa. Dedicated in 1947, during the ascendency of the Afrikaner nationalist cause, the Bloedrivier Museum commemorates the military victory of the Boers. Private donations make up the majority of the museum's operating budget.

Directly opposite the *laager*, on the east bank of the river, stands the

Ncome River Museum. Founded in 1998, this museum commemorates the sacrifice of Zulu warriors who died in the same battle. Funded by the government, the museum seeks to offer a "positive reinterpretation of the 1838 war and Zulu culture in general" (Dubin 2016, 187). The building is shaped as a concave arch, arrayed with *izihlanu* (shields) from each of the regiments of the Zulu kingdom that fought in the battle. The concave shape of the building evokes the "bull horn" (*impondo zenkomo*) formation of the Zulu regiments and stands, according to museum staff, on the site where the Zulu warriors arranged themselves for battle when their calls for parley with the Boers went unanswered. Frozen in concrete, bronze, and collective memory, the two sides still stand, poised for combat.

These museums, sitting just across the river from one another, commemorate two vastly different interpretations of a single battle, each sympathetic to its own group. Each side claims that the other was treacherous, and that each was acting in self-defense. Each side claims their rightness of place, through divine election of the Afrikaners or through the indigeneity of the Zulus. Both sides, in other words, claim the moral high ground, in victory and defeat. The "mutually annihilating truths" of each institution, to borrow a phrase from Rian Malan (2009),[2] exist alongside each other.

On the day I visited, local groups were visiting each of the museums. The visitors, children from an Afrikaans-medium primary school at the Bloedrivier Museum, and young local artists painting a mural in the Ncome River Museum, said that they had known about the museums for a long time. When asked whether they would cross the river and visit the museum on the opposite bank, the artists laughed, and the children's teachers asked why they should. Both the teachers and the artists could see the museum other bank of the river, but could not imagine viewing the battle from the other side. Even now, nearly 180 years after the battle, visitors are choosing sides.

Public figures, such as former president Jacob Zuma, have said that the coexistence of the museums is evidence of the power of the newly democratic South Africa to bring together formerly warring factions and build a rainbow nation that represents the interests of all citizens (Dzanibe 2014). But does the parallel existence of discrete interpretations of history indicate the emergence of a newly unified nation? While there is a kind of balance in telling the story of both sides of the battle, it is a balance of peaceful coexistence of discrete groups (Girshick 2004, 34), rather than a meaningful integration of narratives, or space, or history, or people.

To address these contradictions, the South African government dedicated funds to open a bridge connecting the two sites. In 2013, then-president Zuma presided over the commemoration of the bridge at the Ncome River Museum in a ceremony marking the 175th anniversary of the battle. The bridge was intended to literally and figuratively connect the two museums and provide a path to reconciliation. The sign explaining the bridge proclaims that it "was constructed to symbolize the removal of racial and social barriers by connecting two institutions built on one battlefield, narrating the same story . . . from two different perspectives. This bridge moves beyond linking these two institutions to connect and unite citizens through shared history, heritage and values towards unity in diversity and nation building."

The reconciliation bridge, however, was a source of conflict from its inception (Coan 2013). At the commemoration of the sign quoted above, state dignitaries standing at the Ncome River Museum campus were greeted with apartheid-era flags flown in protest at the Bloedrivier Museum campus (Dzanibe 2014). The sign itself, situated on the Ncome River Museum grounds, is decorated with the same Zulu shields that adorn the museum building. Like the museum that houses it, the sign signals its allegiance in design, location, and content. The protests against the bridge signaled their own partisan leanings, evoking symbols of Afrikaner power, such as the old regime's flag and the apartheid anthem. The bridge, while physically linking the two banks of the river, has not spanned the metaphorical distance between the two institutions and their constituencies.

Perhaps most remarkable of all, the bridge itself is literally inaccessible. It is gated and locked on both sides. The Ncome River Museum staff hold the keys. The Bloedrivier Museum site is surrounded by razor wire, which prevents visitors from approaching the bridge at all. While the reconciliation bridge exists, it is not possible for most visitors to actually traverse the distance between the two museums. Those metaphorical barriers, which led the schoolteachers and the artists to dismiss my question about visiting the other museum, are recreated in physical form on the bridge that was supposed to overcome them.

The reasons behind the closure of the bridge are somewhat unclear. There have been some reports of vandalism, as well as security-based objections to "uncontrolled access" to the museum campuses (Coan 2013). Representatives from each of the museums have also cited the lack of funds for maintenance and security as a major barrier to the bridge's use (Department of Arts and Culture, Republic of South Africa 2016). Similar efforts to bridge disparate institutions have come to the same end. The "reconciliation road" linking

Freedom Park (a post-apartheid monument to the anti-apartheid struggle) and the Vootrekker Monument (an apartheid-era memorial commemorating the Voortrekers) outside of Pretoria was closed indefinitely in 2015, due to budgetary and security concerns (Alfred 2015).[3]

The bridge and the road, however, are not simply infrastructural connections. They were constructed to be symbolically resonant. Their existence was meant to indicate the possibilities of the new, democratic order to create connections that could not have existed under the old regime. While building new institutions, such as Freedom Park and the Ncome River Museum, was a critical part of the redress of past injustices, the symbolic and literal bridge-building was, in many ways, the central feature of the transition. These bridges, whether the literal, concrete ones, or the symbolic ones—like the new multilingual, multimelody national anthem, the 1995 Rugby World Cup, or the Truth and Reconciliation Commission—were meant to reconfigure what it meant to be South African. Leaders of the transition, from Nelson Mandela to F. W. De Klerk and Desmond Tutu, called these efforts "reconciliation." The hallmark of the negotiated transition was not only the justice of majoritarian democracy, but the institutionalized attempts to remap the social and political sphere to overcome the divisions made and sustained by previous regimes.

At their core, such efforts were aimed at nation-building, attempts to create a community of sentiment that meaningfully mirrored the new multiracial community of free and equal citizens. While representation of previously disenfranchised people was key to making the new democracy meaningfully multiracial, the attempts to connect previously separated communities were central to the very idea of building a new South Africa. The transition did not just mean that a new museum would be built,[4] but that it would be connected to the extant museum, telling both sides of the battle and encouraging the conversation.

The closure of this bridge is, then, a kind of allegory of South Africa more than two decades after the transition from apartheid to democracy. While the implementation of institutionalized democracy has been largely successful—characterized by a strong and independent judiciary; free, fair, and regular elections; and protections of civil rights and liberties—there are signs that the nation-building aspirations of the transition have become tarnished. These divergent fates are, in part, because the two projects—establishing democratic institutions and nation-building—are distinct and sometimes have opposing incentives. Nation-building imperatives compel citizens to focus on what makes them similar and what binds them together, forgetting what makes them different. In other words, nation-building asks citizens to look at their bridges, and then forget that the river ever separated them in the first place. Democratic institution–building, on the other hand, requires fostering opposition through conducting multiparty elections and encouraging debate. Leaders of democratic factions, such as parties or interest groups, can consolidate their power by emphasizing difference. The conduct of elections, then, may incentivize leaders to remind citizens to look at the museums, and turn away from the bridge.

But when held in tension, these two impulses—toward remembering difference and forgetting it, between focusing on unity and encouraging division—are both elements of sustainable democracy. Both are necessary to build sustainable peace after periods of conflict. Democracies fundamentally require sentiments of unity to be sustainable. Such sentiments underpin peaceful transitions of power, allowing tolerance for dissent and electoral losses and protections of minority rights (Levitsky and Ziblatt 2018). Unchecked nationalism is almost inevitably undemocratic in practice, veering into xenophobia and violent exclusion. Without a community of sentiment, a democracy is profoundly volatile. Without democratic debate and institutionalized checks on power, national unity often devolves into tyranny. Holding these forces of unity and division in balance is the key to creating and sustaining peace in postconflict situations.

The project of postconflict peace-building often pairs these two imperatives because of their potential synergies, especially in the case of negotiated transitions (Beall, Gelb, and Hassim 2005; Linz and Stepan 2011). In such situations, newly constituted (or reconstituted) central authorities undertake the process of framing a new government and using various initiatives, from redistribution to truth commissions, to redress the histories of conflict. The state, in other words, is tasked with building a nation.

This is a peculiarly modern scenario, in which already established central authorities attempt to build from groups of former combatants a community of sentiment that resembles the community of citizens. Such an arrangement stands in opposition to the ways in which many theorists of nationalism understand the emergence of national communities.

Many theorists of nationalism, including Renan and continuing through Anderson and Hale, have assumed that the nation chronologically, or at least sentimentally, precedes the creation of the democratic state. This arrangement is the basis on which the defining characteristic of national groups, self-determination, is legible. A nation, as a defined group of people united by shared traits and the "belief in the right to territorial self-determination" (Barrington 1997, 713), must demand the creation of an authority that governs them and the territory in which they live.[5] The state emerges as the consequence of the nation's demands.

Other theorists, such as Wimmer (2012) and Tilly (1994), have argued that state-building, the creation of strong central authorities, gives rise to the possibility of nationalist sentiment through the role of political entrepreneurs. In this version of nation-building, it is the emergence of the capacities of the state, such as public education, urbanization, industrialization, and public commemoration, that allows the identity of the nation to be formulated and disseminated. The nation, then, emerges from the creation of the state.

However, postconflict transitions do not really accommodate either of these theoretical trajectories. In many cases, as was certainly the case in South Africa, central state authority is already well established and often quite strong. While the transition from apartheid to multiracial democracy did involve negotiations around the electoral system (Lodge 2003), the allegiance and composition of the security forces (Friedman 1993), and the allocation of powers to different levels of government (de Haas and Zulu 1994), much of the structure and function of the South African government remained the same, as did the individual people working in the jobs, at least through the period of the Government of National Unity (GNU) (Pottie and Hassim 2003). The major challenge in the South African transition was to transform a government structured to serve the minority of citizens to one that would serve all citizens. The particular challenge in postconflict scenarios such as South Africa's is to try to leverage extant authority to create a community that legitimizes that self-same authority within a defined territory and population.

As such, many multiethnic or multiracial states do not necessarily create national identities that supplant or supersede other sectarian affiliations such as religion, caste, ethnicity, or race. These "state-nations" can protect and value multiple, complementary forms of identity (Stepan, Linz, and Yadav 2011). However, even in these cases there is still enormous political value in states fostering the creation of a community, based on a sense of belonging, that "engender[s] strong identification and loyalty from their citizens" (Linz and Stepan 1996, 27; see also Linz and Stepan 2011). In such situations, it is not about necessarily forgetting difference, but de-emphasizing the metaphorical rivers and keeping the bridge open.

The South African transition from apartheid to democracy presents a fascinating case of both the implementation of democratic state institutions and conscious efforts at nation-building in the wake of minority rule, violence, and repression (Shoup and Holmes 2013). As part of the transition process, the Interim Constitution established the GNU to bring all major political parties into government, and to promote "reconciliation" and "national healing." As such, the GNU was tasked with creating a newly united national community under their own leadership (Wilson 2001). These strategies of community-building and self-legitimation were also paired with party-based considerations. Such pressures ultimately led representatives from the National Party, the erstwhile architects of apartheid, to leave the GNU for status as an opposition party.

Yet despite dire predictions of civil war before and during the transition (Horowitz 1991), the advent of multiracial democracy in South Africa was largely peaceful.[6] The elections in 1994 were hailed as a "political miracle" (Lewis 1994), in part because of the ways that former adversaries had committed to work together not only to build democratic institutions but to try and create a new community. This transition has become a model for similar transitions from repressive rule to fully fledged democracy in other postconflict societies (Mamdani 2015; Graybill 2002; Adler and Webster 1995).

Yet the optimism of the transitional period faded rather quickly. The promise of a newly formulated "rainbow nation" that brought together previously divided communities in a newly reconciled society had dimmed by the turn of the century. Despite the nation-building aspirations of the transition, Zapiro, a prominent South African political cartoonist, published a piece entitled "The Black and White Nation" in 2000 (fig. 1).

The cartoon, which plays on South Africa's "rainbow nation" moniker, shows an older man speaking to a boy, looking at a rainbow that has only two stripes: one black, one white. The multicolored rainbow of the transition, the old man implies, was "just a temporary illusion." The rainbow nation, as a metaphor for, and symbol of, the new multiracial dispensation in South Africa, signaled hope and change, whereas the black and white rainbow shows the speaker (and potentially the artist and his audience) to be resigned to and disillusioned by the continued primacy of race as a governing logic, even after the official systems of apartheid had been dismantled.

The persistence of race as the "common sense" of social identity in South Africa (Posel 2001; Maré 2005; Sallaz 2010) is evident in myriad social contexts. Racial labels and attributions continue to be the source of conflict in schools (Dolby 2001; Teeger 2015; Mangcu 2017), in the delivery of public

Fig. 1. The Black and White Nation, Zapiro, 2000. (© 2012 Zapiro; All Rights Reserved. Used with permission from www.zapiro.com)

goods (Patel 2016; McClendon 2016), within and between political parties (Ferree 2010), in the renaming of public spaces (Duminy 2014), and in the management of public monuments (Marschall 2004; Coombes 2005; Holmes and Loehwing 2016). The experience of transitional justice, in the form of the Truth and Reconciliation Commission, in some cases seems to even have strengthened the salience of sectarian racial and ethnic identities (Gibson 2004), and negative attitudes about the commission seem to have intensified over time (Backer 2010).

While political science research does not often have to explain continuity, in the case of the celebrated (and emulated) South African transition, it is remarkable. The transition was laudable because it was supposed to be a break with the past. Yet the troublesome divisions created and sustained by the prior regime still divide the post-apartheid, democratic society. Scholars such as Jeremy Seekings and Nicoli Nattrass have argued that it is the persistence and growth of economic inequality, which coincides to a startling degree with the racial categories established by the old regime, that explains the endurance of identity from the old regime to the new (Seekings and Nattrass 2008; Seekings 2008; Nattrass and Seekings 2001). Economic grievances have inspired social movements aimed at demanding redistribution of goods and delivery of services such as reliable electricity, formal housing, and piped water (Ballard et al. 2005; Zuern 2011; De Juan and Wegner 2019). While the lack of economic transformation in South Africa since apartheid can certainly account for some of the persistence of racialized social cleavages, social and political processes recreate and sustain the divisions created by the colonial and apartheid governments.

Non-class-based senses of self, place, alienation, and belonging play a critical role in both supporting and undermining the project of South African nation- and democracy-building. Aside from the pressing material dimensions of social division in South Africa, social and political dynamics are also associated with both the functioning of democracy and the practices of community-building. Like material inequality, which has its roots in the apartheid era but has been exacerbated since 1994, the social and political divisions that lead South Africans to see the "black and white rainbow" are partially the product of the past, but are also recreated by individual and collective choices made in the post-apartheid era.

These divisions, and the processes that make them relevant and quotidian even in the absence of state-sponsored segregation, highlight the tensions between building a democracy and building a nation. While the political transition from apartheid to multiracial democracy involved unprecedented efforts to build a national community, the divides of the past have proven resilient, in part because of the ways that democratic systems have calcified around these same divisions.

The argument presented here, in being informed by ethnographic and interpretive approaches, is not mechanistically causal. Because it delves into the meanings, actions, and interpretations of research participants in research settings, the contribution of this book is in what Schwartz-Shea and Yanow have called "constitutive causality," in which actors and their contexts create and recreate codes of meaning that are logically contingent on one another (Schwartz-Shea and Yanow 2013). As such, it fits in well with the kinds of arguments often presented in the field of nationalism studies, which are informed both philosophically and empirically but examine the historical and contextual development of particular cases to develop a theory of how and why an "imagined community" (Anderson 2006) or "story of peoplehood" (R. M. Smith 2003) arises.

NATION-BUILDING AND DEMOCRACY: MEMORY AND FORGETTING

Nations, as communities of sentiment, are built through emphasizing similarities and understating difference. Whether those are the stable, innate similarities of primordialist thinkers,[7] or differences between communities emphasized by elites for political ends as in the instrumentalist school, or long-term social and political processes emphasized by constructivists, the idea of nationhood is fundamentally about emphasizing what ties a community together and sidelining or sublimating internal diversity. The creation of a national community, whether of a nation-state or a state-nation, is premised on a collective, and selective, forgetting.

Stemming from the writings of Ernest Renan, who asserted that forgetting was "a crucial element in the creation of nations" (1882, 11), Michael Billig argues that

Mamdani

> Every nation must have its history, its own collective memory. This remembering is simultaneously a collective forgetting: the nation, which celebrates it antiquity, forgets its historical recency . . . once a nation is established, it depends for its continued existence upon a collective amnesia . . . Not only is the past forgotten, as it is ostensibly being recalled, but so there is a parallel forgetting of the present. (Billig 1995, 37–38)

Whether it is forgetting local dialects, as in Anderson's *Imagined Communities* (2006), or remembering the patriotic "stories of peoplehood" for Rogers Smith (2003), nationalism is premised on selective histories and on disregarding difference. Even in the primordialist school, the construction of "Ethno-history," which "harks back to one or more 'golden age,'" is a critical feature of the transition from prepolitical *ethnie* to nation, as "these ages have become canonical; they epitomize all that is great and noble in 'our community,' now so sadly missing, but soon to be restored with the nation's rebirth" (A. D. Smith 2010, 151–52).

Gellner (2008) calls this process "social entropy," wherein information is selectively lost in the process of modernization and nation-building through the industrial age. By forgetting their differences, people in newly formed and forming urban classes, drawn from different places, can peacefully associate and form communities. The loss of information with the passage of time and policy interventions aimed at creating a new class of citizen is crucially important to underpin nationalist sentiments. Whether it is the loss of information through building history of heroes as in Smith (2003) or Renan (1882), the dissemination of a common language to eclipse local dialects as in Anderson (2006), economic transformation as for Gellner (2008), the emergence of a powerful central authority in the state that propagates a common identity as with Wimmer (2012) or Tilly (1994), the loss of information is critical in the process of national coherence.

Theorists of nationalism disagree on how this loss of information comes about. Under what conditions are differences forgotten, and to whom is the duty of emphasizing similarity attributed? In some accounts, it is the conscious propagation of a version of history consonant with leaders' goals (e.g., R. M. Smith 2003) or a heroic sense of past (e.g., Renan 1882) that grounds the national community. For others, state-sponsored activities such as the proliferation of banal symbolism (e.g., Billig 1995) or the drawing of strong borders (Laremont 2005; Kedourie 1993) help to differentiate nations from outsiders and emphasize internal cohesion. Some theorists, by contrast, understand the loss of information to be the inevitable outcome of long-term social processes such as industrialization, economic development, and urbanization (Gellner 2008; Robinson 2014), or the codification of language and its relationship to power (Anderson 2006). The common thread, however, is that nations and nationalism depend on a community of sentiment whose construction, and constituent parts, must obscure the fact of themselves. This is because, as Suny points out, "Identities might in fact be fluid, but in the real world of politics the players act as if they are immutable, both for strategic reasons and emotional satisfaction" (Suny 2004, 7). The emotional draw of nationalism is in the perceived naturalness of the community that it constructs, a community based on forgetting internal diversity.

There are two complementary sides of this forgetting: the writing of a consonant national history of the unifying events of the community, and the selective erasure of the things that have divided the community. The creation of national communities has been premised on strategic ignoring of the past in large celebrations in Gabon (Fricke 2013), Ethiopia (Orlowska 2013), and former Soviet states (S. J. Cohen 1999). In these cases, leaders commemorate, or attempt to create, a community with relatively shallow references to history. Other empirical cases demonstrate the importance of writing authoritative nationalist history to help ground the community in a narrative of their own inevitability. This narrative can involve nationalist symbols, such as the flag in India (Roy 2006); public celebrations and school curricula, as in Eastern Europe (Esbenshade 1995); or diplomatic and international relations (He

2007). In all these cases, after a significant conflict, the goal of establishing nationalist history and myth is to ground the community in whatever history can serve to unify it. Often, this has meant ignoring contentious aspects of prior conflicts, papering over social divisions, or raising a set of historical figures to national prominence. The precondition for such myth-making is the selective erasure of the contentious past.

However, newly emerging democratic systems, like South Africa in the mid-1990s, prevent at least some of the information loss that is involved in writing nationalist history. As parties arise, they seek to consolidate their voter bases by drawing on extant social cleavages (Chandra 2007; Zielinski 2002). In drawing on these cleavages, parties consolidate their voting bases and reinforce divides in society, both directly and indirectly (Ferree 2010). Many of those pieces of social information, which Gellner says are inimical to the emergence of nationalism, are preserved and made important through the processes of democratic contestation. While the emergence of nationalism requires selective forgetting, it is often advantageous for individuals and political parties to remind constituents of salient political divides to distinguish themselves from their opposition and build support (Reilly 2006).

In short, while the building of nationalist history asks community members to forget their differences, democratic functioning seems to incentivize remembering and recreating division. It is not that democratic contestation is inimical to the formation of nationalist sentiments. Rather, this book argues that deeply divided communities, whose divisions are mutually reinforcing and codified in a political party system, have difficulty in forming new modes of citizen association that mitigate inherited divides. The iterative competition between factions in the form of democratic contestation of elections can therefore have the effect of recreating the same divides and impeding the creation of nationalist sentiments.

Although social divides between citizens are inevitable in large democratic systems, the sustainability of democratic political contestation relies on the presence of divides that allow people to cohere with others in a variety of different ways. Cross-cutting cleavages are centrally important in creating stability in ethnically, linguistically, or religiously divided societies (Dunning and Harrison 2010; Gubler and Selway 2012). The process of nation-building is intimately connected with the formation of cross-cutting cleavages, insofar as they promote identities that undermine the salience of conflict-era divisions (Hayner 2002, 161; Verdeja 2009, 3). These networks of intersecting social divisions allow citizens to be active and politically engaged without their group identities threatening the political system. If social divides coincide with one another, they become more profound. When these mutually reinforcing cleavages are represented in the form of political parties, the social divides they represent are consistently recreated (Mozaffar, Scarritt, and Galaich 2003). In the wake of political violence, drawing out social cleavages that cut across, rather than reinforce, the identities associated with the past struggle allows for robust political contestation to occur sustainably (Goodin 1975; Simonsen 2005).

Creating and sustaining meaningful modes of democratic contestation in young democracies is a vital part of the process of consolidation. As explained in detail in chapter 4, the mechanisms of institutionalized opposition in South Africa, particularly political parties and opposition groups, are linked closely with racialized labels and racial identities. Although it is not necessarily true that voters' preference for parties is linked directly to their racial identity, the racialized labels of the various parties contesting elections are central to the ways individuals choose the parties they support (Ferree 2010; McLaughlin 2007). As early as the second democratic elections in 1999, South African scholars were calling for a newly conceptualized mode and vocabulary of opposition, which could help distance the country from the racialized divides of the past, strengthen the hand of the opposition, and provide a greater challenge to the African National Congress (ANC) (see, for example, Habib and Taylor 1999). Later scholars have argued that this new mode is largely absent (Maré 2005; Habib and Herzenberg 2011).

Despite the massive effort to promote interracial reconciliation and to form a single, inclusive South African identity, "the available evidence suggests that the 'new South African' remains a decidedly incomplete democratic animal" (Mattes 2011, 93). Clear majorities of the South African population expressed the desire to suppress the political expressions of their ethnopolitical opponents, even those within the mainstream of the political spectrum (Gibson and Gouws 2003, 56–61). Afrobarometer surveys in 2018 indicate that 41 percent of South Africans do not trust opposition political parties at all, and an additional 29 percent trust them "just a little" (Afrobarometer n.d.). Intolerance is widespread, especially of immigrants but also of political opponents, and it is not generationally confined (Mattes and Richmond 2014).

This book undertakes a thematic exploration of how the social divides of the past, specifically those of race, are being re-inscribed in democratic South Africa, and looks at attempts to bridge those divides. Each of the chapters, discussed in detail below, examines a facet of national and democratic life, such as the integration of public space or the development of a national symbolic repertoire, to understand how the post-apartheid, democratic order is shaped by reminders and re-inscriptions of the past versus efforts to promote unity and redraw social relations.

In examining these questions of memory and forgetting, some scholars of South African democracy have focused on the transformation (or its lack) in museums and monuments (Murray 2013; Marschall 2004; Coombes 2005). Such works examine authoritative public choices on the management of public space and collective memory, and in some cases, citizen responses to them (Witz, Minkley, and Rassool 2017). This book, by contrast, seeks to examine how individual citizens, as well as subnational groups, construct their senses of place and identity within the democratic state.

Because nation-building is a multifaceted enterprise, this book takes a thematic approach in each chapter to try to understand the complexity of the lived experience of social relations in South Africa. The themes are drawn both from scholarly work on nationalism and democracy as well as from interview participants' accounts and fieldwork, as discussed below. Each thematic exploration is an attempt to grapple with the complex forces that shape the politically relevant "we-groups" that constitute either the complementary network of multiple identities that make up modern South Africa, or that challenge the formation of broader senses of community.

RESEARCH DESIGN AND METHODOLOGY

This book is underpinned by data collected and created during fieldwork that I conducted from June 2012 through May 2013. The data, from interviews, participant observation, newspapers, and other documents, was assembled primarily in the cities of Bloemfontein (from June to December 2012) and Durban (from January to May 2013), with trips to Pretoria, Eshowe, Dundee, Utrect, Ulundi, Centurion, and Johannesburg for participant observation, specialist interviews, and notable events. While in Bloemfontein, I was affiliated with the University of the Free State, Department of Political Studies and Governance, within the Faculty of the Humanities. I received funding in support of this research from the Andrew W. Mellon Foundation and the Institute for International Education. The collected data fall broadly into three categories: interview transcripts, ethnographic observation, and collected documents. The data were collected among two populations defined linguistically: Afrikaans and isiZulu speakers. To conduct this research, I undertook several years of language study in both isiZulu and Afrikaans, including a summer of language study at the University of KwaZulu-Natal in Pietermaritzburg funded by Fulbright Group Projects Abroad, as well as through the Indiana University African Languages Program.

Case Selection—South Africa

In the South African case, the issues of democratic consolidation and nation-building loom large, in part because of the country's prominence in the literature on transitional justice and postconflict transitions away from authoritarian regimes. However, much of the literature on the South African transition from apartheid to multiracial democracy discusses the negotiations, the execution of the process of transitional justice, and the first round of inclusive elections in 1994. By limiting the time frame of the analysis in this way, scholars, decision-makers, and popular audiences are "are overwhelmingly enamored with the 'miracle' of South Africa and the TRC's perceived role as midwife to that miracle. Many countries consider the TRC to be a model for how to facilitate transition from authoritarian rule to democracy" (Cole 2009, 124). This level of fame has led to a debate in the scholarly literature on the South African transition about whether the process of transitional justice, and the transition away from apartheid more generally, can be seen as a "miracle" or a "model," with some scholars arguing that it was, in fact, both (Graybill 2002; Shore 2009). If, indeed, these are the only two options, then the process of nation-building and democratic consolidation in South Africa can be considered a fait accompli. But, there are reasons to believe that the nation-building project has stalled, in no small part because of both the continuities with the apartheid regime that are evident after twenty years of democracy, and the ways that those social divides are being recreated through contemporary social and political practices.

In addition to its prominence as a case, South Africa is currently undergoing a massive demographic shift that makes evaluating the process of democratic consolidation and nation-building even more pressing. In the 2014 (national) and 2016 (municipal) elections in South Africa, voters who were born just before or after the end of apartheid were the single largest potential cohort in the electorate. The so-called "born-free" generation, those who have no memories of the apartheid system and who have come of age under an ANC-led democratic government, were eligible to vote in large numbers in 2014, although they had relatively low voter turnout compared to other age cohorts (Independent Electoral Commission of South Africa 2014). But interestingly, despite not having apartheid as a reference point, the born-free generation is not significantly more racially tolerant (and in some samples is less tolerant), and it is markedly less committed to democracy than older age cohorts (Lefko-Everett 2012; Mattes 2012). This apparent inheritance of intolerance and distrust of democratic functioning seems to indicate that the simple passage of time will not produce a more tolerant, democratic, or inclusive South Africa, and demonstrates the continuing and re-inscribed salience of divides associated with race and ethnicity.

Case Selection—Afrikaans Speakers and Zulu Speakers

Both of the groups with whom interviews were conducted have historically grounded claims of belonging to the country and the land. The two groups, as opposed to other domestic groups such as British South Africans or Xhosas, have had historically strong nationalist sentiments, as well as claims to self-determination. The Afrikaners are a "sociologically indigenous" deep-settler population who severed their ties to Europe centuries ago and created an identity around *hiervandaan* or being *from here* (Stone 1986). Afrikaner group identity, which from the 1940s to the early 1990s was closely bound with the National Party, reached a point of crisis during the period of transition away from apartheid. Memoirs from and about that time by noted Afrikaans-speaking authors, such as Antjie Krog (2000), Breyten Breytenbach (1993), Rian Malan (1990), and At Van Wyk (1991), are filled with reflexive examination of self and place, attempts to process the information that was surfacing about the horrors of apartheid and the guilt associated with what had been done in the name of this group of people.

By contrast, Zulu *izibongo* (families or clans) have claims to indigeneity that go back a thousand years, having arrived in Southern Africa sometime around the ninth century, although their formation as a more-or-less cohesive nation dates only to the early 1800s (Hamilton 1998). Some scholars have argued that, as a politically salient identity, *ubuZulu* only emerged in the early twentieth century in response to government policies defining so-called "native reserves" (Wright 2009). During the time of transition, the Inkatha Movement organized paramilitary forces and engaged in a paramilitary ground war in KwaZulu-Natal and Gauteng. This apparent surge of violent nationalism dissipated quickly after the first democratic elections, the Inkatha Freedom Party (IFP) has shrunk as a politically salient force, and since the transition away from apartheid in the mid-1990s, many public manifestations of Zuluness that were associated with the transitional period have faded (Carton 2009). Yet some scholars have observed a newer manifestation of Zulu nationalism emerging that is disconnected with the ethnic entrepreneurs of the transition period and closely aligned with the ANC and the administration of then-president Jacob Zuma, who defines himself as proudly Zulu (Ndletyana and Maaba 2010).

Bloemfontein and Durban as Research Sites

The two cities in which this research was primarily conducted were Bloemfontein and Durban. These cities, demographically, historically, and in terms of public culture, were well suited to target the ethnolinguistic populations that this project concerns, and to provide scholarly resources to aid this research. Each city is home to monuments significant to the subpopulations I was seeking to study, and has significant media outlets—television, radio and newspapers—in the target languages, as well as sports teams.

Bloemfontein, the capital city of the Free State province, is the eighth-largest city in South Africa. Called one of the "firmest bastions of Afrikaner power under apartheid," (Verwey and Quayle 2012, 557), it has a reputation for being relatively conservative in the post-apartheid period. Serving as the judicial capital of South Africa, Bloemfontein also houses several museums, including the National Museum. Additionally, the city is home to the National Women's Monument, discussed in chapters 2, 4, and 5, which is a significant artifact of the Afrikaner nationalist period. First-language Afrikaans speakers are a plurality in the city of Bloemfontein, with 42.53 percent of the population. The city is also historically important as the place where both the South African Native National Congress (later the ANC) and the National Party were founded, in 1912 and 1915 respectively.

Durban is South Africa's third-largest city, and home to the largest concentration of Zulu speakers in the country, who make up a plurality of the city population, about 33 percent. The capital of KwaZulu-Natal, Durban also houses significant museums, such as the KwaMuhle Museum. The city itself is closely identified with Zulu culture, especially since the end of the apartheid era, and it is also home to the offices of several political parties, such as the ANC and the IFP.

I supplemented work at these sites with observations and interviews in a variety of other locales, urban and rural, to address the shortcomings of their situation. However, each of these cities, while providing access to key populations as well as public spaces for observation, also presents limitations for the present study. The most obvious limitation is that the racial makeup of the subpopulations under study was, in important ways, set by the contexts in which interviews were conducted. The South African government categorizes the vast majority of Zulu-speakers as black African, regardless of where they reside, and this is certainly true in Durban. The Afrikaans-speaking population in South Africa is more diverse, and geographically dispersed. While the vast majority of the people with whom I spoke in Bloemfontein would be classified as white (though many declined to adopt that moniker themselves when discussing identity politics), nonwhite Afrikaans speakers are the demographic majority of the linguistically defined population. Geographically concentrated in the Cape Region, so-called "Coloureds" (historically mixed-race or Creole populations) make up the slight majority of first-language Afrikaans-speakers.

However, for both practical[8] and theoretical reasons, situating my research outside of Die Kolonie—a somewhat unflattering moniker for the Cape Region often used by Afrikaans speakers in the Free State and other Northeastern regions of the country—was advantageous. First, I could target the populations of Afrikaans speakers who were themselves the potential constituents of some of the most strident attempts to derail the transition process of 1994. Second, Afrikaans speakers support a wider variety of political parties outside of the Cape region, which helps to inform the variety of political stances reflected in this research. Third, while somewhat unrepresentative of the Afrikaans-speaking population as a whole, the Afrikaans-speaking population of Bloemfontein is demographically similar to the Afrikaans-speaking population in the non-Cape regions of the country (Statistics South Africa 2012). Fourth, because primary or home language is relatively less subjective, and certainly less controversial, than race as a label, recruitment of participants was somewhat easier, as well as being less difficult to define. Lastly, by identifying language as the defining feature of the populations under study, even if race was an influencing factor, it allowed the issue of race to come up in organic ways during the course of interview conversations.

Interview Methodology

Interviews with South African citizens of voting age formed a key part of the data that underpin this book. Interview participants were recruited for interviews through written correspondence, or occasionally over the phone after formal, written invitations had been issued using IRB-approved invitation language. Throughout the course of twelve months of fieldwork, 109 individuals volunteered to sit for individual or group interviews, which ranged in duration between forty-five minutes and nearly seven hours. The average interview lasted about ninety minutes. Interview participants ranged in age from nineteen to eighty-six, and were nearly balanced between men (54 percent) and women (46 percent). Interview participants were eligible for participation if they were South African citizens, over the age of eighteen, and primarily spoke either Afrikaans or isiZulu at home, and/or considered the language their primary or first language. Interviews are identified in the text with a three-digit code, which can be cross-referenced with the interview index in the appendix that includes demographic and voting information for each participant.

Interview participants were recruited primarily through snowball sampling, largely using referrals from participants to find additional potential participants, with an emphasis on making the sample demographically representative of the target population in terms of age and gender. I also recruited people to participate through public flyers and email contact. Snowball sampling is particularly useful when discussing sensitive topics (N. Cohen and Arieli 2011), and to get a sense of the interactions within a given community (Noy 2008), both of which were advantageous to my overall study. Given the reticence of many South Africans to engage in political discussion, either within or across racial communities, snowball recruitment was particularly effective at establishing legitimacy in new research sites. Individual invitations were sent to key figures, such as politicians, journalists, and NGO and activist leadership, as a way to try and capture more engaged members of the political class, but most of these went unanswered. Where relevant, quotes from elites are mentioned as such in the text. The sample was tabulated against the 2011 census along the two major dimensions, and corrections were made accordingly after two months, and again after four months in each field site. No compensation was given for participation. There is a slight undersampling of both populations in the over-sixty age category because of difficulties in recruitment, as well as no representation in the under-eighteen category for ethical reasons. All anonymized interview details are included in the appendix. Darkened rows are for interviews in which the participant did not fit within the defined populations. Where multiple rows are merged, it indicates a small focus group or multi-participant interview.

A central limitation to the interview methodology was probably imposed by the effects of perceived shared racial identity with Afrikaans speakers, versus its absence with Zulu speakers. Because I present and identify as a white woman, there were probably familiarity effects within the Afrikaans community, which as stated above was almost exclusively white. Such effects, which research suggests may prompt different responses (Adida et al. 2016), are difficult to counteract in the context of a single interviewer. However, where appropriate, I tried to mitigate such effects through other kinds of signaling, like relying on snowball sampling, using culturally respectful Zulu honorifics to older participants, speaking Zulu with the greatest degree of fluency I had at my command (after more than seven years of study), and inhabiting spaces in which I was introduced by familiar community figures. While this is not an exhaustive list, and certainly did not completely neutralize the effects of shared racial identity, I believe that these interventions did help overcome some of the barriers with Zulu-speaking interview participants.

All interviews were conducted via in-person interactions, in which individuals were given consent briefings and asked to fill in identification sheets with basic demographic information, including their age, employment status, home language, and whether they had voted in the last national and municipal elections. The interviews were notated by the author and transcribed soon thereafter to maintain the maximum degree of clarity and accuracy of the accounts provided. In general, interviews were structured around standard questions supplemented by follow-up questions or clarifications when the author deemed it necessary or interesting.

Ethnographic Methods

A second methodological arm of this project was attending cultural and political events in the places where I was living, as well as writing field notes on ordinary daily occurrences. These notes are supplemented by photography of the spaces and events that I visited. These observations and photos are scattered throughout the various empirical chapters.

The special events that I attended included the Vryfees music festival in Bloemfontein, which lasted from 10 through 15 July 2012, the Day of the Vow service in Pretoria on 16 December 2012, an ANC centenary rally in Durban on 8 January 2013, the Reed Dance in Ulundi on 1 September 2012, and a variety of church services in both Bloemfontein and Durban. In addition, I went to various museums, including the *Erfenissentrum* (Heritage Center) at the Voortrekker monument in Pretoria, the Talana Museum and the battlefield memorials at Blood River/Ncome, Isandlwana, Rourke's Drift, and Spionkop. I also wrote extensive ethnographic notes on various shopping centers in and around Bloemfontein, Pretoria, and Durban, because shopping centers have proven to be an important aspect of semipublic but also securitized space in the post-apartheid landscape. Ultimately, only a fraction of these notes became part of the text of this book, but they provided important pieces of ambient information that undergirds this analysis.

Other Methods Employed

Other significant data were collected from printed materials. The first collection, mostly used for evidence in chapter 7, was the compilation of newspaper articles from the primary non-English-language newspapers in Bloemfontein, *Die Volksblad* in Afrikaans, and in Durban, *iSolezwe* in isiZulu. Nearly every day, before any interviews were possible, I would purchase a copy of the newspaper in Afrikaans in Bloemfontein and in isiZulu in Durban, and read through the front-page news and any additional political coverage, in addition to reviewing the English-language news. This practice contextualized the comments of some interview participants, and prevented me, as the interviewer, from missing some of the references made by interview participants. For the analysis presented in chapter 8, newspaper articles were compared and supplemented by news sources in other cities, such as Cape Town and Pretoria, via online archive.

The other print materials collected included brochures from museums, political party paraphernalia, church bulletins, maps, playbills, and magazines. For the most part, this collection of materials was not used directly to support this research, but rather gave context to the interpretation of interview quotes and gave background to both references from interviews.

STRUCTURE OF THE BOOK

Each chapter adopts a theme and a central research question aimed at addressing a different aspect of national or group identity in South Africa. The chapters concentrate both on factors that remind South Africans of their social divisions and on those that point to a unified nation that have been created and sustained in the post-apartheid period. Although interconnected, the chapters draw evidence from different sections of the interview questionnaire, distinct collections of documents, or discrete episodes of ethnographic observation. The themes of the chapters were developed through a grounded theoretical approach, but are by no means exhaustive. Certain themes that could have been included, such as the influence of religious communities or the role of urban/rural positionality, were not, either because they did not often come up in the course of conversations, or because of ethical or practical concerns. The thematic explorations of each of these chapters emerged from the standard interview questionnaire (included in appendix 2) and associated conversations that took place over the course of my research time.

While scholarly explorations of nationalism, as discussed above and in the introductions to the individual chapters, informed the questionnaire and the interpretation of the evidence, the thematic collection of the chapters emerged from manual qualitative coding of the interview transcripts and other evidence after the conclusion of the fieldwork. This combined grounded and deductive theorizing regarding identity-based issues positions this work to contribute to scholarly discussions of nationalism and democratization, and to avoid overdetermining elements of identity that were important to participants. Each of the themes in the chapters is discussed in terms both of the scholarly understanding of its contributions to nation-building and democratization, and of how and why participants discuss the theme in their own words.

Chapter 2 is an analysis of the historical trajectory of identity politics in South Africa. By examining how group identities have been constructed, and some of the political ends that they have served, this chapter seeks to ground later chapters. This chapter argues that the landscape of identity politics in South Africa predates the existence of "South Africa" as a category. The subtitle of the chapter, "Forming a State, Building a Community," emphasizes how South Africa, as a point of national imagination, has evolved from one predicated on the notion of exclusion based on race to one in which, at least nominally, all citizens belong.

By shifting the understanding of racial politics from the deterministic, almost biological language employed in so many interview quotes later on, this chapter seeks to frame the readers' understanding of identity as a constructed and malleable phenomenon in South Africa. As such, it posits that the point of national identification, of being "South African," has indeed served as a reference point historically, but a contested one. The opening of the chapter argues that indeed, for decades, governmental exhortations have sought to make the category of "South African" a meaningful one. Yet the category, like many other points of identification, contends with other identities that have been built and sustained through conflict, expansion, struggle, and material circumstances. This chapter traces the evolution of ethnolingustic cleavages, and the attempts to overcome them, in South African history.

Proceeding out of the discussion over history, chapter 3 discusses the ways that the political transition utilized history to create a newly united South Africa. Contrasting the Truth and Reconciliation Commission (TRC), with one of the key symbols associated with the project of reconciliation, the idea of South Africa as the Rainbow Nation, the chapter argues that both ahistorical and historically reconstructive symbols—associated with remembering and forgetting—were utilized as techniques of nation-building during the transition. The chapter draws extensively from interview data, specifically questions about participants' recollections about and evaluations of the TRC, as well as their connections to the "rainbow" symbol.

Because nation-building took the form of both historical erasure, as with the rainbow symbolism, and historical reconstruction, as with the TRC, many interview participants felt ambivalent about how the transition figured within their own understanding of their history. What emerged from interview evidence was a divided picture, one in which South African nation-building could be pursued either by "moving on" or by "not forgetting," the former largely advocated by Afrikaans speakers and the latter by Zulu speakers. This division, then, is a product of the transition but coincides with other politically and socially meaningful cleavages.

Chapter 4 deals with how democratic contestation in South Africa serves to flag difference or build national coalitions. Contestation, which is critical to the practice of democracy, is examined through the lenses of party politics, as well as extra-institutional forms of dissent, such as exit. Stemming from a rich literature on race and vote choice in South Africa, these sections of the chapter take on the ways in which voters expressed party preference, and how their decision to support or oppose given parties is linked to their identity politics. Additionally, in the last decade or so, the efforts of the ANC to undermine opposition have manifested themselves in a particular language for speaking about democracy and opposition, which has filtered out in many ways to their constituents.

The final section of the chapter deals with the ways that exit forms an important repertoire of opposition in South Africa. In the first half of the section, civil-society organizations directly involved with politics are the basis of inquiry, because so many of them reject the labeling of their activities as "political." The widespread characterization of politics as a dirty, negative, or degrading activity seems to indicate a rejection of democratic contestation as a method of resolving problems. This exit from "politics," while engaging in political activities, is often accompanied by a condemnation of electoral democracy as insufficient, ineffective, or troublesome. The other form of exit examined in this section is the phenomenon of emigration from among the community of Afrikaans speakers. Since 1994, a significant percentage of white Afrikaans-speaking South Africans have left the country. While not necessarily an outright rejection of multiracial democracy, this phenomenon poses an interesting opportunity to examine Afrikaans-speakers' understandings of the future of South Africa and their place in a multiracial community.

Chapter 5 deals with nation-building as a project that is visceral and intimate, played out by embodied individuals. As such, this chapter asks how threat perception and the ways it is conditioned by race and gender serve to remind people of social divisions. The chapter proceeds from interview-based evidence about the ways race and gender interact in the project of nation-building now, and how bodily discomfort and threat are understood as barriers to nation-building. There are interlocking, but also distinct, solidarities and notions of threat associated with raced and gendered identities. By using ethnographic data, the chapter attempts to understand how identities are enacted outside of the constructed space of the interview. The final empirical section of the chapter recounts a difficult encounter I had after concluding an interview. In so doing, the chapter draws attention to the ways in which the raced and gendered orders of apartheid and colonialism are being recreated in the present democratic era.

Chapter 6 examines the ceremony and performance of group and national identities. These ceremonies are examined in the context of three categories: exclusive, nominally inclusive, and truly inclusive. The first category, which takes as case studies the Day of the Vow celebration in Pretoria and the Reed Dance in Ulundi, are those ceremonies whose audience and participant pool are based on a strict definition of ethnic identity. Such ceremonies have remained resilient, and grown, in the context of a democratic South Africa. The most striking growth in participation, however, has been in the category of nominally inclusive performances and ceremonies. This category of ceremony includes the Afrikaans music and culture festivals that have sprung up since the mid-1990s across South Africa, as well as the experience of the spectator in a sports stadium. Although framed as events that are inclusive, or based on associative identities, such gatherings are, de facto quite homogenous spaces. The final category, truly inclusive ceremonies, examines the new holidays the government has recognized. The argument of this chapter is that although strictly defined ethnolinguistically homogenous spaces are common in the new South Africa, in general, the events that have the largest pool of supporters are those that are nominally inclusive and based on identities framed as affiliations. These spaces are not more integrated in practice, but are framed as potentially more inclusive. Drawing from ethnographic observations and field notes, as well as interview data, this chapter attempts to give the reader a sense of the ways in which performances are enacted, and also to allow interview participants to give their opinions.

Chapter 7 addresses the ways that the politics of place and space are playing out in the post-apartheid state. Emerging from decades of segregation and control over space in the colonial and apartheid regimes, many places are still characterized by profound separateness in South Africa. The chapter argues that, in important ways, many spaces are still unshared in South Africa, twenty years into democracy. Looking at both public and private space, this chapter delves into the idea of space, land, and ownership as being central to the communal imagination of both Zulu and Afrikaans speakers. The public spaces examined in this chapter—neighborhoods and monumental architecture—demonstrate a remarkable degree of change in the democratic era. Newly integrated neighborhoods and newly erected statues point to meaningful change in the landscape of democratic versus apartheid South Africa. Private spaces, like individual homes and patterns of land ownership, are less transformed, and are often deadlocked by communities' perception of space and ownership as constitutive of belonging. In the case of land ownership, threats of land reform are often seen as indicating a broader kind of hostility against Afrikaner farmers by the government. For Zulu speakers, by contrast, the lack of movement on land reform signals an unwillingness on the part of the government to engage in meaningful economic reform. The final section of the chapter, which addresses the national territory of South Africa and its contestation through separatist "cultural" communities of Afrikaners, demonstrates how contestation over space is also a dispute over the symbolic boundaries of the nation.

The connections between language and identity are the subject of chapter 8. It discusses how interview participants spoke about language and used language identity as a proxy for both race and ethnicity in their own speech. In addition, language has, according to some participants, come to serve a role as a socially acceptable mode of segregation, especially in Bloemfontein and at the University of the Free State. This chapter also considers a case study of newspaper coverage of a key event from my fieldwork in South Africa—the violence at the mines in Marikana—and analyzes how different language media covered the event. This event, the largest and most deadly use of police force against civilians in the post-apartheid era, left 34 miners dead and more than 200 wounded. The accounts that emerge in the coverage of the violence immediately afterward vary significantly between isiZulu and Afrikaans newspapers.

The chapter concludes that, although language cleavages correspond to other kinds of divisions, such as class, race, and location, they represent a peculiar and iterated kind of division within South Africa. The fact that, for example, different-language-reading publics in South Africa were presented with such vastly different interpretations of the Marikana narrative, or that different language classes at the University of the Free State or the University of Pretoria present such distinct educational opportunities, the everyday affiliations of language reproduce and subtly widen gaps by introducing new vocabularies to talk about events and distinct spaces within a community.

The concluding chapter serves to wrap up the analysis presented in the empirical chapters of this project. Also included are suggestions for further research, the policy implications of this study in terms of institutionalist approaches to the study and practice of nation-building, and some very basic projections about the future consolidation of South African democracy.

CHAPTER 2

South Africa

Forming a State, Building a Community

Do South Africans exist? Have they ever? In a place that has, for more than 350 years, defined itself through territoriality and the exclusion of one or another group from its boundaries or the privileges of belonging, it is difficult to find a clear accounting of what could constitute the basis of a national identifier. According to one pre-apartheid account from English émigré to South Africa, journalist, and author G. H. Calpin,

> The worst of South Africa is that you never come across a South African. There is no surprise in the discovery that the United States produces Americans; or Siam, Siamese; or Lapland, Laplanders. The naturalness of so natural a condition does not strike one until its exception appears. The exception is South Africa. You may travel the thousands of miles of Garden Route from Cape Town to Durban, and thence along the white-lined road fringed with white-washed boulders to guide you through the night; or you may leave the highways that radiate from the City of Gold; and never, at petrol bowser, hospitable farm, the ubiquitous tea room, or gaunt hotel, meet a South African. Turn to any of the newspapers . . . and you will soon be persuaded, by the number of editorial exhortations to their readers to think and act as South Africans, of abundant proof of the rarity. The term South African has no significance outside of South Africa, and only there because of a widespread ignorance. (Calpin 1941, 9)

This question of whether anyone might be South African in a meaningful sense has been debated since the very beginnings of South Africa's existence as a single territorial-administrative unit. It has been asked and answered in the titles of multiple scholarly works (e.g., Calpin 1941; Hancock 1966; Chip-kin 2007; Chipkin and Ngqulunga 2008; Norris et al. 2008) as well as in con-ferences ("Identity: Are There Any South Africans?" 2010) and popular media (Gumede 2013; McKaiser 2010; Pennington 2012). It has been complicated by internal wars and a succession of complex political arrangements, and by the linguistic, cultural, ethnic, and racial diversity within its borders. Internal divisions and "ongoing animosities emanating from fractious identity pol-itics of dominance and suppression" that predate the territorial unification of South Africa have meant that "the Union [of South Africa] remained a body whose validity to exist was as contested as the politics that sustained it" (Alden and Schoeman 2015, 190). The question of how people with South African citizenship could/should/will cohere into a single, affective national unit was even the subject of a national conference, sponsored and spear-headed by the presidency to evaluate the "health of the nation" postapartheid ("Social Cohesion and Social Justice in South Africa" 2012).[1]

This central question—who and what is a South African?—has been asked throughout the twentieth century. Attempts to construct that category—erasing distinctions seen to be "internal" while emphasizing those that are "external"—have been deeply political projects that have attempted to build a national community to a political end: supporting the legitimacy of a state, a cause, or a political party. The apartheid state, in encouraging the unity of whiteness, sought to soften the previously contentious Boer/Briton divide (Rassool and Witz 1993). The Black Consciousnesses Movement in empha-sizing the unity of blackness was actively dismantling the racial categories of the apartheid state (Hirschmann 1990). The attempts to nation-build post-apartheid have taken on distinctly partisan (Abrahams 2016) or nativist (Ndlovu-Gatsheni 2009) tones, in defining who can be part of the national community.

Indeed, nation-building has been a central political imperative, and a way to manage dissent, in South Africa for nearly the entire history of its exis-tence. The contestation over the boundaries of the national community, those who could claim the title "South African," has been a leitmotif in the country.

The same constant policing and rearticulating of group boundaries has also taken place at the subnational level. Throughout the twentieth century, both Afrikaans and Zulu leaders have expressed the need to write and rewrite history, to articulate both the things that tie groups together and the need to forget their own internal divisions. Both groups have made claims to indige-neity and exclusive belonging in the national community, while also articulating the basis on which others should be excluded or have their claims to national or group belonging marginalized. Therefore, starting from early history, this chapter traces the historical context that produced the subnational identities with which the nation-building project in post-apartheid South Africa contends, and the ways in which they articulate both the basis of internal cohesion and the external boundaries of the national community. In addition, by tracking the historical trajectory through which South Africa has been defined through exclusion, this chapter also addresses the ways that inclusionary counterclaims, based on territoriality, fairness, and integration, have tried to challenge these narratives.

NO SOUTH AFRICANS BEFORE SOUTH AFRICA

The state of South Africa, and the subsequent possibility of national identification with it, can only date back to 1910, with the unification of British colonies, the annexed Boer republics, and land claimed by black African leaders into a single administrative unit. However, many of the contestations over group identities and boundaries took place during the early 1800s because of migration, conflict, and economic pressures throughout what is now known as South Africa.

Starting from around 1800, and lasting until the genesis of the Anglo-Boer War decades later, violent confrontations between the Afrikaners, the British, and African leaders such as Moshoeshoe I of the Basotho, Dingane of the amaZulu, and Mzilikazi of the amaNdebele began to calcify divisions among groups. The previously diverse coalition of Dutch farmers, French Huguenots, and German settlers began to crystallize into a group, calling themselves Afrikaners by the end of the eighteenth century.[2]

Complementary narratives of the early decades of the nineteenth century loom large in Afrikaner and Zulu nationalist historiography of South Africa: the *Mfecane* and the Great Trek. These two events, which are understood as founding the Afrikaner and Zulu nations, are both contested in scholarly histories, but remain vital to understanding the development of group identity throughout the late colonial and early apartheid eras.

The story of the *Mfecane*, a great imperial war and military revolution led by Zulu patriarch Shaka, constitutes a founding myth of the Zulu nation. It is largely accepted that the group that would adopt the moniker "Zulu" began to coalesce around its patriarch, Shaka Zulu, in the early 1800s through wars of conquest (Hamilton 1998). The narrative of the *Mfecane* as a foundational myth emphasizes the military prowess of Zulu leadership under Shaka, and the massive social and political disruption caused by these innovations, including huge migrations north and eastward of refugees and defeated peoples and the conquest and political consolidation of the Zulu Empire (see for example Omer-Cooper 1966). Several decades of scholarship have debated the extent and importance of these conflicts. Contemporaneous documentation of the conflict is largely limited to missionaries' accounts and traders' diaries that record only second-hand information (e.g., Etherington 2004; Hamilton 1995; Hamilton 1998). The emergent trade in slaves from the Delagoa Bay, rather than an imperial urge, may have also spurred a defensive militarization among the Zulu (see for example, Wright 1995; Eldredge 1992). Nonetheless, the rhetoric of violence and the understanding that it had shaped society pervaded South African historiography for decades, as well as fundamentally framing the contemporary understandings of Trekboere and English colonials (Etherington 2004). Post-1994, neither the massive conflict nor the pre-existing peaceful equilibrium that it supposedly interrupted has been verified by scholarly historians. The dearth of hard evidence of conflict has led some historians to conclude that the *Mfecane* is "fundamentally, and essentially no more than a rhetorical construction—or, more accurately, an abstraction arising from a rhetoric of violence" (Wylie 2000, 194). The leadership and military prowess of Shaka are, however, a useful set of founding myths, because they found the nation after the conglomeration of Ndwandwe, Hadebe, Mthethwa, and other chieftaincies, thereby obscuring in-group diversity. By making Shaka the patriarch, and founding the Zulu nation during and after conquest, it is easier to erase the internal diversity that characterizes the group "Zulu."

By contrast, Afrikaner nationalist historians establish many of their national myths in the Great Trek. This movement of Afrikaners from the Cape, according to these accounts, coincided with the advent of British colonialism in the early 1800s, because the Afrikaners of the Cape saw serious challenges to their way of life. Seeking freedom from British rule that, they saw, had upset their land tenure and forced the emancipation of their slaves and indentured workers, thousands of Afrikaners elected to leave the territory controlled by the British and set up independent Boer (Farmer's) republics in the interior of the country (Thompson 2001). While some historians, such as Giliomee, contend that these events catalyzed a sense of peoplehood and divine election for many of the Voortrekkers, especially in regard to their military victories over the local leaders (2010, 165–66), others argue that the unifying mythos of the Trek itself is a later invention of nationalist historians, which was turned into a keystone of the narrative of Afrikaner nationalism (e.g., Etherington 1995). Whether understood as a cohesive movement or a fragmentary migration, however, the clash between the British notion of liberal trusteeship and the Afrikaner's notion of *baaskap*[3] proved to be critical insofar as it gave later justification of the Boer republics as a response to and rejection of the British. As with the Zulu founding myths, the Afrikaner nationalist accounting of the Great Trek once again founds the group after the amalgamation of Dutch, French, and German settlers. They are a group characterized by their opposition to the British, but also by their own internal (albeit newly formed) unity. Once again, diversity of origins is deemphasized in favor of common ground.

These narratives are complementary because they reinforce the claims of one another. The Zulu military decimation of the interior territories of South Africa supposedly set up the Boers to enter terra nullius in their northeastern expansion, justifying their claims to land and rightness of place. By contrast, the encroachment of the Voortrekkers and British colonists into territories claimed by skilled Zulu warriors defending an ascendant nation set up the conflicts between these groups as part of larger trajectory of power and expansion (Carton, Laband, and Sithole 2009). What is uncontested in this period, however, is that the wars fought over territory and control served to shore up divisions between groups, and the clashes helped to define the later project of group-building, and the erasure and forgetting of the internal divisions within each group. The framing of these conflicts, especially later in the service of nationalist projects, in terms of immutable difference and divine ordination simply furthered the cause of group unity and distinction (Ramutsindela 1997).

UNITY THROUGH SEGREGATION:
MID-NINETEENTH TO EARLY TWENTIETH CENTURY

By the mid-nineteenth century, administrators of both the British colonies and the Boer republics began to define land within their territories that would serve as "native reserves" separate from the areas where white residents of the country would live. Following from the approach of Sir Theophilus Shepstone, secretary of native affairs in Natal, reserves would be established to minimize contact between white and black citizens (Giliomee and Schlemmer 1985, 41; Guy 2013). Even at this early stage of radical territorial segregation, the reserves were impoverished and largely invisible to the white population (Thompson 2001, 97, 100, 154–55). Distinct from the *baaskap* relations that tended to pervade the Boer republics' large farming areas, the reserves were an extension of the trustee liberalism embraced by the British and in many ways reproduced the systems of domination already present, though they also served as reservoirs of command labor for white farmers (Keegan 1997, 292–93).

Conflict over trade routes and mineral deposits fractured the tenuous peace that had held between the Boer republics and the British Empire since 1881, and war broke out in 1899. The conflict itself was perceived in racialized and nationalistic terms, with differences between Briton and Boer understood to be insurmountable and innate (Calpin 1941; Giliomee 2010, 35). Indeed, even in the design of later institutions and architecture, the racial nature of the conflict between Britons and Afrikaners was memorialized. The Union Buildings, designed in 1913 and still home to the executive branch of the South African government, have two wings meant to represent the two races of South Africa: the Briton and the Boer (Bremner 2016).

In the post-Anglo-Boer War years, certain appeasements were made to mitigate the complexities of the power struggle between the British, Afrikaner, and black African elites. The unification of the two Boer republics with the British colonies and a number of other land holdings produced the unified South African state, but in seeking stability in the newly unified republic, the British made concessions to incentivize collaboration from the Boer-Afrikaners at the expense of black Africans.

Through a policy of appeasement of white agitators after the Afrikaner's military defeat, the British made the foundation of the South African nation coterminous with the politics of racial domination. By appeasing violent and organized opposition by the Boer-Afrikaners, the relatively more liberal English governors of the Dominion of South Africa abandoned the cause of black enfranchisement and citizenship, in favor of the project of white unity (Marx 1998, 2). In so doing, they minimized the importance of the Boer-Briton divide, emphasizing a white in-group as opposed to racial others.

From 1910, the Union of South Africa excluded the majority of the people who lived within its borders from participation in politics in a full or equal sense. Although there were debates over issues of enfranchisement and citizenship in the Union, ultimately the laws adopted were similar to those in the

Boer republics that completely excluded nonwhite residents from any participation in or consideration from the state (Johnson 2004, 111). Such laws, in addition to shoring up racial solidarities, served to solidify mining capital elites, and to secure a pool of inexpensive and accessible laborers (Wolpe 1972). Nation-building through the exclusion of racial others was used to promote social cohesion among whites, across the previously contentious Boer-Briton divide. The price of this unity was the exclusion of nonwhites from political, social, or economic equality.

Around the same time, leaders within the black African community also began calling for and organizing around the cause of unification within and between their communities. In 1912, the South African Native National Congress (SANNC)—later renamed the African National Congress (ANC)—was established. The goal of the Congress was to advocate for the rights of black Africans within the new state, in part through reference to colonial subjects throughout the British Empire (see for example South African Native National Congress 1914). In the lead-up to the conference that would form the organization, a founding member and later president of the organization, Pixley ka Isaka Seme, addressed the conflicts and fissures within the black African population. He urged that these communal divisions be overcome, saying, "The demon of racialism, the aberrations of the Xosa-Fingo feud, the animosity that exists between the Zulus and the Tongaas, between the Basutos and every other Native must be buried and forgotten; it has shed among us sufficient blood! We are one people. These divisions, these jealousies, are the cause of all our woes and of all our backwardness and ignorance to-day" (Seme 1911).[4] Such calls for unity and the measures undertaken to secure buy-in from conflicting communities, whether Boer/Briton, amaXhosa/amaFengo, or vaTsonga/amaZulu, were present at the genesis of nation-building in South Africa. Encouraging people to "bury" their divisions, nationalist entrepreneurs sought to build new identities through the forgetting of difference and emphasis on bridging or commonality.

THE RISE OF AFRIKANER NATIONALISM AND THE HARDENING OF LEGAL SEGREGATION

Despite efforts to legislate where races could live, by the 1920s the patterns of hierarchy and separateness that had been solidified in the post-Anglo-Boer War period were being threatened by multiracial slums that had grown in the cities in a rapid wave of industrialization and urbanization, connected with the growth of the mining sector. Emergent class politics, including violent strikes, also threatened the case for white solidarity, insofar as there were anxieties among a number of leaders over whether class alliances across racial boundaries could supersede the politics of racial domination. The settlement that arose out of this violent period, especially in the wake of the 1922 Rand Rebellion, cemented the coalition of "white labor and Afrikaner nationalism" that would reinforce the color bar in hiring practices and pay grades, as well as protecting the interests of the white working class as a racial and class group that superseded the divisions within the white community (Hazlett 1988, 92–93).

In response to the perceived racial and moral contamination taking place in the slums and to the threat of cross-racial class alliances, the Dutch Reformed Church and Afrikaner politicians undertook a massive campaign of socioeconomic uplift for the white poor, vested in organized labor and parastatal cooperatives,[5] aimed at providing employment and better wages and conditions for the white working class (Adam and Giliomee 1979, 146–48). This campaign was undertaken in the name of racial purity, and to help to cement white identity and superiority and prevent racial mixing (Bottomley 2012). Often addressed in terms of the "poor white problem," or *armblankev-raagstuk*, the moralistic, politico-racial imperative to improve the lives of the white poor was characterized in a National Party circular in 1924 as

> a question which not only concerns the poor; it affects the whole white civilisation of this country. It confronts us with the question whether we, the descendents of the staunch old pioneers, will maintain their civilisation and hand it over to our children. . . . It may be asked whether there is poverty only in South Africa and whether other countries do not suffer from the same thing. There are poor people everywhere, but the circumstances in South Africa are unique. . . . *In this country, there is a small number of whites against the natives, a few civilised people against uncivilised hordes, and for that reason it is so important that not a single white person should be allowed to go under*. . . . There is no greater problem than this, because the existence of the European civilisation in this country hinges on it. (From Hansard, House of Assembly, 12 August 1924, col. 429–32, cited in Seekings 2007, 382, emphasis added)

By the mid-1920s, one quarter of the Afrikaner population, or 15 percent of the total European population, was classified as "poor white" (Bottomley

1990, 353; "The 'Poor-White' Problem In South Africa" 1933). The calls to save them, from literal poverty and the metaphorical contaminations associated with it, were again framed by the unity of the white cause and the threat of "others" (Bottomley 2016).

Hostile divisions between British and Afrikaner South Africans remained and were reinforced through labor disputes and disparate standards of living. Although the first prime ministers of the Union of South Africa, Louis Botha and Jan Smuts, called for "unity and cooperation" between the two white communities in South Africa, the popularity of their rivals, led by J. B. M. Hertzog,[6] testified to the enduring salience of differences in "historical background, culture and language, economics, and the bitterness engendered by the war" between the English and Afrikaners (Feinberg 1993, 71–74). Increasing reliance on claims to autochthony and demands by Afrikaners for assimilation by the British, coupled with their demographic and numerical dominance of politics, solidified a coalition in the 1930s that eventually served as the voting bloc that propelled the National Party to power in 1948 (Thompson 2001). According to a 1941 issue of *Die Transvaler*, a morning newspaper closely aligned with the National Party, "We completely and totally reject the notion that all South Africans must be counted together as one people: Afrikaners are, for us, the nation of South Africa, and the rest of South Africa, as far as those who are white, are either potential Afrikaners, or aliens" (Hancock 1966, 16, translation by author). These calls to assimilate or be alienated were central to the consolidation of white nationalism, which in the eyes of its proponents, was synonymous with South African nationalism.

Yet the majority of people who lived in South Africa were, of course, black Africans, and while they were excluded from membership in the white national community, they were still under the jurisdiction of the South African state. Throughout this period, the boundaries of "native reserves" that had been established as early as the mid-nineteenth century began to be codified and strengthened. The Land Act of 1913 set boundaries of black movement and land ownership in South Africa until its repeal in 1991.[7] Black African elites expressed their frustration with and alienation from the central South African state and from the nationalist community, in reaction to these and other measures that curtailed their movement and claims to land. Sol Plaatje, founding member of the South African Natives National Congress, summed up the feeling of the time in his 1916 treatise arguing against the Land Act, when he said "South Africa has by law ceased to be the home of any of her native children whose skins are dyed with a pigment that does not conform with the regulation hue" (Plaatje 1916). Further legislation, such as the Native Affairs Act of 1920 and the Natives (Urban Areas) Act of 1923, cemented the idea of pervasive, countrywide racial segregation in South Africa.

The projects of segregation and "separate development,"[8] although potentially different in degree and market orientation, were not different with regard to the idea that South Africa, as such, was reserved for a white population.[9] The differences lay later in history with the development of separate Bantustans, which were justified through a rhetoric of "independence" and "self-governance" that further fractured the idea of South Africanness. The fiction of Bantustan independence, although generally regarded as such by both domestic and international audiences, was nonetheless an important move in understanding "South Africa" as being reserved for only white citizens, with black citizens belonging, or being forced to belong, elsewhere.

THE GRAND APARTHEID ERA

With the rise to power of the National Party government after 1948 and the genesis of the formal policies of apartheid, the rhetorical boundaries of South Africa had shifted. Apartheid, and especially the focus on "multi-nationalism" within South Africa "sought to keep blacks and whites as neighbours but not fellow countrymen" (Ramutsindela 1997, 102). The Bantu Homelands Citizenship Act of 1970 reclassified all black Africans as foreign nationals within South Africa, with primary citizenship in their Bantustans (homelands), although none of the entities at that time were formally independent. As early as 1963, there were "citizens" of the Transkei who had dual citizenship in South Africa, and were officially referred to as "expatriates" in South Africa (see for example Hancock 1966, 19).

The Bantustan experiment culminated in the formal granting of independence to the Transkei, Bophuthatswana, Venda, and Ciskei in the mid-1970s and early 1980s, with limited autonomy granted to other homelands such as KwaZulu and QwaQwa (Lipton 1972; Dugard 1980). The Bantustans, given their differing levels of autonomy, funding, resource endowments, governing capacity, and territorial fragmentation, had different capabilities in the administration of citizenship or enforcement of (limited) sovereignty within their boundaries (Giliomee and Schlemmer 1985).[10] By defining and legalizing the boundaries between groups and reifying the importance of traditional leadership in the homelands, the National Party government formalized divisions between ethnic groups in South Africa, and sought to categorize people according to the homeland, and hence the "tribe" to which they belonged.

The National Party election in 1948 and the subsequent enactment of major legislative planks of apartheid, including the Group Areas Act and the Suppression of Communism Act, drew widespread criticism from religious groups, intellectuals, groups such as the Black Sash, and a new generation of leadership of the African National Congress. The 1952 Defiance Campaign, which was spearheaded by the African National Congress, the South African Indian Congress, and the Coloured People's Congress, engaged in passive resistance exercises in response to the National Party government's programs. As a coordinated effort by organizations representing different constituencies, it was an important step in the establishment of a nonracial struggle against apartheid.[11]

The Defiance Campaign was a direct precursor to the formation of an umbrella group of protest organizations, called the Congress Alliance, which adopted the Freedom Charter in 1955. Present were the executive committees of the African National Congress, the South African Coloured Peoples' Organisation, the South African Indian Congress, and the Congress of Democrats ("The Freedom Charter" 1987, 676). Interestingly, the Congress Alliance, despite being a nonracial movement, was comprised of organizations with distinctly racialized constituencies.[12] The state-sponsored logic of racialism proved to be a difficult one to overcome, even within a movement that sought to dispense with such categories.

The Freedom Charter called for nonracial democracy and the instantiation of a government of all the people. The famous opening lines state "We, the People of South Africa, declare for all our country and the world to know: that South Africa belongs to all who live in it, black and white, and that no government can justly claim authority unless it is based on the will of all the people"; these lines were often invoked during the following decades of the anti-apartheid struggle. This conception of South Africa, as a nation whose enabling conditions of existence were territorial boundedness and the fact of cohabitation, provides a rather thin basis for the cohesion of a singular will of the people (Ndlovu-Gatsheni 2007; Ndlovu-Gatsheni 2009). Given the time and place in which the document was crafted, however, the National Party government saw these basic calls for integrated nationhood as subversive. Within a year of its adoption, 156 people, many of whom had a hand in the drafting and adoption of the charter, were put on trial for treason ("The Freedom Charter" 1987).

Nonracialism became an important principle within the struggle against apartheid, and was espoused by many prominent struggle organizations. As a guiding principle, however, it was not associated with well-defined objectives, aside from the removal of discriminatory barriers, and it did little to deconstruct the ideas of race and racial categories within South Africa as fundamental defining features of the political arena (Maré 2003). Additionally, the term lacked substantive content, or contained inconsistent meanings (Maré 2001; MacDonald 2006). While associated with a staunch opposition to apartheid, some scholars have alleged that the object of nonracialism—whether the state, the individual, or the public at large—remained unclear throughout the anti-apartheid movement, and that the conflation of the phrase with terms such as *interracial* and *multiracial* further confused the issue (Everatt 2010). Yet nonracialism is cited as a founding value of South Africa in the 1996 Constitution, and persists as a slogan of the ANC, and even as the "official credo of the South African state" (Sharp 1998, 243).

The nonracial stance of the ANC was what prompted a group of more militant African nationalists to break off from the organization and form the Pan-Africanist Congress (PAC). The newer organization, which wanted to represent those whose "primary loyalty" was to Africa, promoted Africanist ideology in order to achieve liberation (Marx 1998, 200). This fracturing, ultimately, resulted from yet another framing of the national community: as racially inclusive or exclusive, based in claims to autochthony and colonial history. After the banning of both the ANC and the PAC in 1960, however, the latter organization faced crises over leadership and funding, as well as internal disputes that ultimately undermined its power.

The vacuum left by the banning of major struggle organizations in 1960, in concert with the official policies of territorial separate development and the formalization of Bantustans, allowed for a new generation of leaders to come to the fore. Black-Consciousness thinkers in the late 1960s began to assert blackness as a rallying point, defined in opposition to the apartheid state and its discriminatory policies and articulating a new kind of belonging and community. One of the key innovations of the Black Consciousness Movement was in defining blackness as a source of unity, but also in "reject[ing] all value systems that seek to make [the Blackman] a foreigner in the country of his birth and reduc[ing] his basic human dignity" (cited in Karis and Gerhart 1997, 100, 482). This assertion of the illegitimacy of the apartheid state's definitions of citizenship and belonging made the student activism of the 1970s critical in the continuing debate over the boundaries, as well as the meaning and content, of the national community.

Biko and other Black Consciousness leaders distanced themselves from white liberal organizations and leaders who had participated in the nonracial initiatives of earlier decades of the struggle.[13] Drawing on thinkers such as Frantz Fanon, Malcolm X, and Léopold Sédar Senghor, Black Consciousness thinkers emphasized the shared nature of subjugation based in blackness and overcoming the "inferiority complex—a result of 300 years of deliberate oppression, denigration and derision" that characterized the mind of the black person in South Africa (Biko 2002, 21). The definition of "blackness" for Black Consciousness thinkers was capacious, including all groups the apartheid government designated as "non-white," and those who stood up to white supremacy with dignity, in spite of the degrading circumstances that apartheid had created.

However, it was fundamentally still based on the racialized rhetoric of the apartheid state, with blackness being formed from a coalition of black African, coloured, and Indian people, in opposition to unity of whiteness that was represented by the interests of the state.[14] The racialized categories of the state and the prior generation of coalition organizations were collapsed into a single black-white division, but the major cleavage emphasized by Black Consciousness thinkers was still a racial one. By using the lived experience of discrimination at the hands of the apartheid state, Biko and his contemporaries were compelled to invert, but not undermine, the state-sponsored racial categories and hierarchy that dominated the lives of people in South Africa.

The rhetoric of Black Consciousness merged with school-based student activism in June 1976, when students in Soweto took to the streets to protest (Karis and Gerhart 1997, 156–75; Marx 1998, 202). The protests spread quickly and elicited violent repression from the apartheid state. Black Consciousness leaders, following the uprising, became more closely aligned with the ANC in exile (Marx 1998, 202–3; Karis and Gerhart 1997, 279–80).

The unity of blackness inspired by Black Consciousness thinkers, in connection with the activities of the ANC and the UDF in the 1980s, led to a successful boycott of limited reforms of the apartheid system by Prime Minister P. W. Botha. The elections for a proposed tricameral parliament—with separate and subordinate houses representing both coloured and Indian voters—were largely ignored by eligible voters, principally because of the success of multiracial campaigns calling for the boycott (Seekings 1992). Boycotts, strikes, and mass mobilizations became more and more frequent throughout the 1980s. The opposition of black protesters (in the capacious sense of the unity of blackness inspired by the Black Consciousness movement) to the white state meant that the violent episodes of protest in the 1980s were mostly interpreted through a bilateral racial framework. This lens shored up support in both self-consciously black and white groups (Marx 1998, 204).

The 1983 founding of the United Democratic Front (UDF) signaled the return of nonracialism to the struggle against apartheid. While endorsing the Freedom Charter and including members of the ANC, the UDF declared the need for "unity in struggle through which all democrats, regardless of race, religion or colour shall take part together" and called for the abolition of the homelands and group areas (South African Institute of Race Relations, Survey of Race Relations, cited in Thompson 2001, 229).

There were groups that by the 1980s were alienated from the project of the ANC and Black Consciousness. The Inkatha movement, led by Mangosuthu Buthelezi, the premier of the homeland of KwaZulu, although originally ANC-aligned, broke ties with the ANC in 1979 (Gerhart and Glaser 2010, 29–30). The leadership of the "independent" homelands also opposed the new incarnation of the struggle against apartheid because of their entrenched interests and ties with the apartheid state (Karis and Gerhart 1997, 226–29).

The intensity and breadth of protest against apartheid increased steadily throughout the mid-1980s, and in 1985, state president P. W. Botha instituted a state of emergency. This declaration was cemented in Botha's declaration that South Africa was "crossing the Rubicon," which referred not, as would be expected, to reforms of apartheid the system, but to the government's resolve to restore order (Omer-Cooper 1994, 238). While the state of emergency led to myriad human rights abuses,[15] it did briefly restore an uneasy order in the country, but the peace was short-lived. The tide of public opinion among white South Africans had begun to shift away from the National Party to both the right-wing Conservative Party and the reform-minded Progressive Party. Coupled with demographic changes—including the urbanization of the Black African population and the proportional decrease in the white population—and international shocks such as economic decline and the collapse of the Soviet Union and hence disappearance of the *Rooi Gevaar* (Communist Threat), the National Party's hold on power was weakened.

The political resolve to suppress opposition at any cost seemed to leave the party leadership with Botha's exit in 1989. In 1990, Botha's successor, F. W. de Klerk, announced the un-banning of the ANC, PAC, and other organizations, and the release of political prisoners. In a speech on 2 February 1990 in Parliament, de Klerk opened the door for talks between the apartheid government and anti-apartheid struggle organizations.

NEGOTIATING THE END OF APARTHEID:
NATION-BUILDING AND DEMOCRATIZATION

Negotiating the end of apartheid and the creation of a new political order was a difficult prospect for all involved. The participation of so many different organizations, and the boycotting of these negotiations by others, threatened the prospect of a negotiated settlement. However, in a 1992 referendum among white voters, 68.6 percent of voters accepted the negotiations and voted for them to continue (Jung 2000, 136). In the same year, violence, especially the Boipatong Massacre, led to the termination of negotiations. Yet, by November of 1993, an interim constitution was ratified by Parliament, and a timeline for the first truly majoritarian election in South Africa was established.

When voting to elect a government in the new democratic dispensation in April 1994, the citizens of South Africa embarked on a project that had never really been tried in the country: the election of a government to represent the interests of all citizens equally. Yet, at the heart of this moment lay a deeper question: what was the basis of national unity in South Africa in 1994? In the words of Ivor Chipkin, reflecting on the event,

> The South African people lacked national marks. It was only really clear who they were not. They were not the South Africans of old: those who had perpetrated and endured the injustices of the past. They did not speak any particular language, nor did they follow any one faith. They had neither a common culture, nor race. Despite this, the first democratic election proceeded as if they had; as if, nonetheless, it made sense to include them in a single demos. (Chipkin 2007, 174)

In the new South Africa, still divided by the cleavages of colonialism and apartheid, the power dynamics of privilege and class, and the persistent segregation of living spaces that these social phenomena had created, people voted together. Overwhelmingly, individuals who were surveyed at the time expressed enthusiasm for, and connection to, an inclusive national community (Møller, Dickow, and Harris 1999). Although the election of 1994 marked an important step in the road toward building a democratic South Africa, it could not be expected to complete the process. According to one anti-apartheid struggle activist at the time, "In South Africa, building a nation has to be a conscious process; it won't just happen. . . . Previously no government tried. To the contrary, they divided. . . ." (Marx 1998, 213).

Qualifications to the "miracle" narrative of South African nation-building were rife, and deeply connected with the ways that groups opposed the transition or the ANC's role in it. There were outbreaks of political and ethnic violence, especially in northern KwaZulu-Natal and in hostels that were home to migrant workers in Gauteng and other mining areas, allegedly sponsored and encouraged by apartheid state security forces and their allies among Bantustan elites (Taylor 2002; Donham and Mofokeng 2011). Voters largely voted along ethno-racial lines, which some took as a shortcoming of the quality of the new democracy (Ferree 2006). Corruption within and violence against the police service compromised law enforcement (Thompson 2001, 272–73). Levels of social and economic inequality among citizens were extremely high ("Poverty and Inequality in South Africa: Final Report" 1998).[16]

These deep cleavages were recognized by the newly elected ANC government, which took steps to implement various programs aimed at nation-building, both socially and materially (Shoup and Holmes 2013). The aptly named "Promotion of National Unity and Reconciliation Act of 1995" (RSA Legislature 1996 n.d.) established the Truth and Reconciliation Commission (TRC) in a conscious attempt to construct a sense of peoplehood through writing and broadcasting a common national history. By creating a forum in which the previously unacknowledged brutality of the apartheid regime could be documented and made public, the TRC set out to fundamentally undermine the ability of South Africans to disregard or ignore their history, and to discourage nostalgia and any return to the brutalities of the past (Wilson and Hamber 2002). This shared history would, it was posited, help build a foundation for the legitimacy of the new state (Boraine 2001), but also as the basis of an identity for South Africans, despite their cultural, linguistic, religious, or racial differences (Chipkin 2007, 173–74). As explained in chapter 3, there are genuine and important questions about the extent to which the history told by the TRC accomplished any part of these lofty goals.

The newly formed South African government of 1994 undertook myriad nation-building projects, but what of the cultivation of opposition through democratic channels? The ANC-led government, in the wake of the adoption of the new constitution of 1996, signaled at their national conference a broad tolerance and support for opposition in their resolutions, saying

In general terms, an opposition that pays allegiance to the constitution and the country's laws and seeks to modify the programmes of transformation or even to express a retrogressive school of thought shared by a given constituency, is a legitimate actor in the contradictory process of change. Indeed, such forces should be treated as legitimate expressions of the country's social contradictions. (50th National Conference 1997)

Yet within ten years, the overall tone of the dominant ANC had changed. In their 2007 national conference, the ANC said of opposition parties,

> The ANC must continue to exercise maximum vigilance against forces which seek to subvert social transformation. Indeed, there are continuing attempts by forces connected to the old apartheid order and international reaction to undermine the state and to disorganise, weaken and destroy the liberation movement through clandestine means, including all kinds of manipulation within and outside its ranks. In addition, marginalisation and destitution inherited from apartheid and the kind of greed represented by organised crime do create fertile ground for lumpen elements whose actions can have counter-revolutionary implications. (52nd National Conference 2007)

This turn away from the acceptance of opposition and toward the need to maintain unity signals that the intervening years had changed the tone and content of democratic opposition to the majority party. In both forgetting difference and emphasizing unity, in looking to the museums and the bridge, the posture of South Africans had changed in the first two decades of the post-apartheid era.

CONCLUSION

The notion of a national community in South Africa has been contested and redefined by a variety of communities, throughout the history of South Africa's existence as a unified country; multiracial democracy is a relatively new intervention in this effort. Whether exclusivist claims were based on assumptions about divine election, as with Afrikaner Nationalist definitions, or on inclusive definitions based on the spatial principles put forth in the Freedom Charter, the essential contestation over who can or should be part of the nation has been a major theme of successive movements in establishing and resisting apartheid. The nation-building project of the transition from apartheid to multiracial democracy did not end such conversations. Instead, it reframed and intensified the contestation over South African nationalism and its relationship to the past, both in remembering and forgetting the lines that have divided South Africa for so long. It also raised questions about the legitimacy and place of opposition parties, especially those who stood in ongoing opposition to parties that had framed themselves as the moral and political heirs of the anti-apartheid struggle.

So the question remains, what does the term "South African" mean in the post-apartheid era? Who uses it, and for what purposes? And how is the national community contested through the practices of democracy? The fact that these questions continue to be asked seems to point to the persistence of the cleavages discussed above, despite efforts to bridge these divisions, or indeed to channel them through democratic institutions. The historical trajectory of South Africa, comprised as it is of so many efforts at segregation and separateness, seems to militate against efforts to build a more cohesive national identity or a single, representative democracy.

What a historical survey reveals, however, is that like so many other identities, the racial and ethnolinguistic identity politics of South Africa are the direct result of intensive social engineering, and were created and amplified to serve a variety of political causes: imperial, capitalist, and supremacist. The question then arises as to whether these ethnolinguistic or racial identities persist as complementary to, or in competition with, a broader sense of community, and how they interface with democratic functioning and political contestation. The variety of thematic approaches in the following chapters ask about the relationship to memory and forgetting to the building and quotidian management of South African national identity, and how the conduct of elections consolidates and challenges the way that national signifiers are deployed.

CHAPTER 3

Reconciliation and Rainbows

Symbols With and Without History

The elections of 1994 were a momentous occasion for South Africa. With news media from around the world watching, people stood in long lines, waiting to vote in the first meaningfully multiracial elections. For many, it was the first time voting. The occasion was accompanied by a surge in nationalist pride, based on this expectation-defying achievement: peaceful, multiracial, democratic elections as the outcome of a negotiated transition away from apartheid. Through these elections, an African National Congress–led government came to power, Nelson Mandela having been elected as the first president of the new South Africa. On the occasion of his inauguration, he gave a speech, declaring

> We have triumphed in the effort to implant hope in the breasts of the millions of our people. We enter into a covenant that we shall build a society in which all South Africans, both black and white, will be able to walk tall, without any fear in their hearts, assured of their inalienable right to human dignity—a rainbow nation at peace with itself and the world. (Mandela 1994)

The rainbow-nation image, as a symbolic invocation of both the diversity and unity of the new South Africa, was used first by Archbishop Desmond Tutu, but became a key component of the nation-building rhetoric of the transition for Mandela and other leaders. It symbolized a break from the past, with Judeo-Christian echoes of the Genesis flood narrative. The rainbow nation, like the biblical covenant after the flood's devastation, was forward-looking, marking the beginning of a new era in South Africa. Such symbolism was highly resonant, with public opinion polls conducted in 1994 showing that about 65 percent of South Africans supported the idea of a rainbow nation (Møller, Dickow, and Harris 1999). This largely ahistorical approach, through which a new South Africa would be built starting with the advent of democracy and almost without regard to the past, was espoused by Mandela, along with Archbishop Desmond Tutu, as a way to heal the country in the wake of the brutalities of apartheid and the violence of the transition.

In 1996, these same nation-builders also took an alternative approach. The Truth and Reconciliation Commission (TRC) established by the newly elected multiracial parliament was tasked with uncovering the neglected and obscured histories of the brutality of the apartheid period. Both designers and commissioners framed the TRC mandate as one of creating shared history through forensic and historical investigation, as well as contextualization of these revelations within a broader context of apartheid (Boraine 2001; Witz, Minkley, and Rassool 2017). To uncover previously disregarded or obscured history, the TRC was divided into three committees: the Human Rights Violations Committee, tasked with investigating abuses; the Reparation and Rehabilitation Committee, tasked with creating and implementing proposals aimed at promoting reparation; and the Amnesty Committee, which examined applications for amnesty by individuals who had perpetrated crimes or human rights abuses.

By creating a forum in which the previously unacknowledged brutality of the apartheid regime, as well as the civilian casualties of the anti-apartheid movement, could be documented and made public, the TRC set out to fundamentally undermine the ability of South Africans to ignore or idealize their history (Gibson 2006, 158). It was supposed to be the sheer weight of evidence—of police brutality, anonymous killings, state-sponsored violence, and of civilian casualties—that would change how South Africans understood themselves and their history. This history was not the nationalist narrative of victorious heroes, but the gritty details of violence and violation, often told by bereaved victims or their surviving relatives. This rewritten history of South Africa would thereby form the basis of a new national community, collectively mourning past violence and healing together.

In this process of transition, then, there were opportunities for both the recall of the past and its erasure—a symbolic repertoire that emphasized a break with the past, and a commission that emphasized how South Africans were products of their most contentious history. The transition from apartheid to multiracial democracy emphasized both memory and forgetting. Although often contradictory, these two tactics were advanced by the same people, and to the same end. Given these divergent approaches, how are the symbols associated with the transition from apartheid viewed after twenty years of multiracial democracy? How do South Africans connect with the symbols of the nation-building project, and talk about history with regard to their national community?

This chapter argues that there is a deep-seated ambivalence about both the historical nature of the TRC and the more ahistorical rainbow-nation symbols. Both nation-building with reference to history, as in the TRC, and nation-building through breaking with the past, as with the rainbow-nation symbolism, were seen as alienating by interview participants, though for different reasons. Although interview participants did, by and large, support the idea of multiracial democracy, the symbols of the transition had been tarnished by the intervening years. While the TRC and the rainbow symbolism were meant as nation-building tools, neither resonated as a potential bridge between communities. Both symbols were reinterpreted as either potentially divisive—with the rainbow being composed of distinct and separate colors akin to the apartheid logic, and the TRC being characterized as a "witch hunt"—or symbolic of unfulfilled promises or disappointed optimism. This chapter explores the various interpretations and evaluations of the nation-building symbols of the transition from apartheid to democracy, and how they were discussed in the course of interviews twenty years later. The evaluation of both the TRC and the rainbow symbolism as nation-building tactics also serves as a kind of referendum on the present state of the nation-building project in South Africa.

RAINBOW NATION SYMBOLISM

The term "rainbow nation" has come to symbolize South Africa and is almost as common as the national flag in tourism and national promotional activities. It is used in both political and commercial campaigns, as well as in national-level sporting and other public events (Møller, Dickow, and Harris 1999, 246). The rainbow symbol, as a national point of reference, resonates with the national motto, "unity in diversity," as well as the idea of reconciliation and healing after trauma. While the rainbow of Noah accompanied the receding floodwaters as a symbol of the end of the destruction in the biblical version of the rainbow narrative, some cautious observers worried that the "rainbow" unity of the South African transition, with its implications of finality, could not sustain the agonism of democracy (Habib 1997). Given that much of the work of democratization and nation-building occurred after the transition from apartheid to multiracial democracy, how is the symbol of the transition viewed twenty years into democracy? Is the notion of the rainbow nation resonant either now or as a reflection of the period of transition from apartheid?

Unsurprisingly, South Africans have varied reactions to this symbolic repertoire, and their reactions coincide with their broader views of the transitional period and the promises made at that time. The responses can be broadly broken down into four categories. First, there are those participants who view the rainbow symbol as an accurate representation and positive symbol for South Africa in the democratic era, which denotes a break from the past. Although in a distinct minority, these "tempered optimists" often reference the diversity of languages and cultures in South Africa to explain their support. The second group are those who see the rainbow symbol as representing an "unrealized ideal" left over from the optimism of the transition but unfulfilled in the post-apartheid era, largely because of how the transition was marked by continuity with the past. These participants tend to see the "rainbow nation" as a set of disappointed expectations, and are largely disenchanted with or alienated from the current politics of South Africa. The third category is comprised of those who see the rainbow-nation rhetoric as cynical, disingenuous, or unfounded, for whom the transition no longer represented a new start. The final group, those whom I have classified as the "rainbow segregationists," is heterogeneous in their immediate reaction to the question about the rainbow nation. What ties them together as a group is their support for ethnolinguistic and/or racial segregation in their social spheres. These are people who directly challenge the symbolic unity of the rainbow nation, in favor of an interpretation of the rainbow that allows for parallel and separate lives.

These categories, in themselves, are mixed. None of these categories are inhabited exclusively by either Zulu speakers or Afrikaans speakers, or by men or women, and they do not seem to be related in any obvious way to the age of the participants. Yet each category provides a different way to understand how the rainbow symbol fares in the post-apartheid era as a barometer of South African nation-building and the reconciliation project.

Tempered Optimism

During the course of interviews, a minority of participants expressed positive associations with the term "rainbow nation" as a description of South

Africa. For these participants, the term emphasized diversity and accurately described the ethnolinguistic constellation of South African society. According to one Afrikaans-speaking respondent, "[the rainbow nation term] is appropriate and accurate. We are a diverse country with many cultures and languages. I like the description. It emphasizes diversity" (045). In general, the Afrikaans-speaking participants who identified positively with the concept of the rainbow nation were likely to identify with the diversity of a rainbow, rather than its unity.

For Zulu-speaking participants who had positive associations with the term, the rainbow nation was a symbol of the potential for all people in South Africa to be considered South African. Rather than the separate development of the rainbow segregationists, the rainbow in this sense was the fulfillment of the Freedom Charter's opening stanza.[1] One Zulu-speaking participant noted her support for the concept of rainbow unity by saying, "We are embracing [the Rainbow Nation]. We are accommodating of it. For the first time after apartheid, we can say we are all South African. Before, the government saw me as an immigrant" (093). Although accepting of the rainbow-nation rhetoric, she is skeptical about how South Africa had made progress on the themes of reconciliation or inclusion. She suggested that "maybe in two or three decades . . . we will see the new South Africa, the rainbow South Africa. Maybe the new generation will enjoy things that we cannot see right now" (093).

The positive associations with the concept of the rainbow nation, then, among participants in my interviews, were overwhelmingly tempered with a sense that although some symbolic change had happened, there was still a long journey ahead to realize the promises of the political transition.

Unrealized Ideal

For many participants, the rhetoric of a rainbow nation signaled the gap between their expectations at the point of transition and the present reality. The loss of a more idealistic time or the sense of disappointed expectations came up with both Afrikaans and Zulu speakers.

The major difference in these expressed senses of lost optimism was in whether—and where—blame was assigned. In the case of Afrikaans speakers, most blamed "the government" or "the ANC" when expressing who was at fault. According to one participant, "["rainbow nation"] refers to the multiple ethnic, cultural and language groups in the country living harmoniously together. . . . [It is accurate] regarding the multiplicity of our society. However, the present government has alienated the minority groups in the country with their race politics" (022). The expressed feeling of alienation, or the idea that the rainbow does not have space for some people, came up repeatedly in interviews. Another Afrikaans speaker in Bloemfontein, when asked what she thought of the idea of South Africa as a rainbow, said "It is supposed to be that way. But not all of the colors are represented. There was supposed to be a place in the sun for everyone. We all fought for freedom. Why can we not all just be here?" (043).

In response to the question of what things make her feel as if she does not have a place, she responded, "We have security systems, dogs, burglar bars, all of that. Even then, I do not feel safe. Why live like that? Just because people do not accept me? This happens because they do not think I belong. The government does nothing. Black criminals, white victims. The government does not want to execute 'their own' people" (043). Although not directly attributing her alienation from South Africa to the work of the government, she does imply that the government's inaction on crime is a result of a calculated policy to protect "their own," a community of which she is not a member.

One Afrikaans-speaking participant implied that although the politics of the rainbow were appealing in the immediate aftermath of the transition to democracy, the luster of the rhetoric had largely worn off: "That is an old story, that Rainbow Nation stuff. We believed it when Tutu said it, but we do not believe it anymore. We wanted it, but we have not achieved it. Race is everywhere" (036–037). This feeling of continuity with, or even of backsliding into, a time when race was the primary determinant of social life in South Africa was expressed as a disappointment for Afrikaans speakers who thought of the transition itself as a break from the past.

For Zulu-speaking participants, there was also a visceral feeling of lost optimism in discussions about the rainbow symbolism. The major difference was that there was not an obvious target for anger or blame in these accounts. According to one Zulu-speaking participant, "[The rainbow nation] is the correct thing to aspire to. Not that we have arrived there, but we are trying. . . . We had high expectations post-1994. Everyone waited for manna from heaven. Then, we became despondent, because there were no quick solutions without hard work. [The transition] was a process, but we thought it would be an event" (099). Another Zulu-speaking participant, although very willing to criticize the government on a variety of matters,[2] did not assign blame to them in the project of national unification. She said, "It is true. We have all kinds of people. It is a good description. Yeah, we have whites, coloureds, everyone. But in terms of unity, it is not there so much" (095). These interpretations of the rainbow symbolism emphasize the shortcomings of the current situation compared to the sense of optimism that people had at the time of transition. Although not outright condemnations, as those below are, this category of responses is characterized by a sense of disappointment.

Disassociation

Most of the interview participants did not express a positive association with the idea of a rainbow nation. One particularly terse Afrikaans-speaking interviewee simply answered my question about what the rainbow symbol meant by saying "It is bullshit" (007).[3] This view seemed to be shared by many participants, both Afrikaans and Zulu speakers. The question itself was often greeted by a palpable sense of anger or even sardonic laughter.

The rainbow symbolism question opened up many other avenues of conversation and tapped into a variety of related political and social issues, such as a lack of de facto integration, the politicization of education, and the invocation of race by leaders for political gain. Others said that political rhetoric kept the rainbow from becoming the reality. In the words of one Afrikaans-speaking young woman, "I just do not feel welcome here. Especially with the political leaders talking about 'Kill the Boer.'[4] The Rainbow Nation just does not exist. The fact is that people will always clash" (020).

For many Zulu-speaking participants, the rainbow rhetoric was thrown into harsh relief when they looked at the continuity of their own circumstances before and after the transition, especially with regard to race relations, socioeconomic status, and privilege. For one Zulu-speaking young woman, the fact of de jure equality was difficult to celebrate when she lived with prejudice and racism on a daily basis:

> There is a lot of baggage with being South African. We carry a lot of historical baggage. You try to place yourself within a society that says racism no longer exists, but everything reminds you that you are black. . . . We are bombarded with information about how much we have changed, but I do not live in a place that has changed. . . . We are telling the world that we are rainbow nation, but we are constantly reminded of just how far we are from that. . . . The rainbow nation is just a catchy phrase. It was put on us. It is not really there. Fine, the constitution says that we are equal, but mostly we are not. (105)

Another Zulu-speaking participant, when asked whether he thought the rainbow-nation rhetoric was a good fit for the country, responded by saying

"We see that Mandela has danced with the widows of our opposition. He has danced with the people who killed us. But all this while, the gap between the rich and the poor has grown" (108). This level of negativity, springing from a sense that not much has substantively changed in the first two decades of democracy, presents a real challenge to the project of nation-building in South Africa. Among participants in this group, there was a sense that too much time had passed and too few promises of the transition had been fulfilled, for a substantive sense of community based on the rainbow-nation symbol.

Segregationists in the Rainbow

The idea of the rainbow has for some people come to stand more for the idea of ethnic federation than for cross-racial unity. For this group, the stripes of a rainbow came to stand for separate communities, with no need to integrate more broadly, although this is not a direct product of a relationship to memory or forgetting. When one Afrikaans-speaking participant was asked how he felt about the term "rainbow nation" to describe his country, he said,

> It is nice. It recognizes the colors and creeds in our country. We have white, black, like pitch black, Coloured and Indian. We are all belonging here. We are all playing a part. . . . I still believe in separateness. I believe in marrying people of your own race, and things like that. Yes, I do have black friends and neighbors. But I believe we still have a choice. I decide who I want in my own home. . . . God created people differently. (077)

Other Afrikaans-speaking interview participants also acknowledged this interpretation of what the rainbow could mean. The metaphorical rainbow nation could stand in for a segregated social sphere where one could choose to associate mostly (or exclusively) with people from backgrounds similar to one's own. In the vivid words of one Afrikaans-speaking young man,

> From the outside, everything seems fine. But when we go home, we are all in our own bubble. We will not go out to *braai*[5] or party with black people. We sometimes mix with English white people, but not with blacks. . . . I definitely would never invite a black person into the house for coffee. . . . There is always suspicion. We do not trust black people. You can never tell if they are just planning the break-in. Are they there just to do recon on your house? Interra-

cial relationships too. I just do not like them. It does not look right. If people would just stay with their own, it would be better. . . . People just should not mix. It is against my religion.[6] (034)

Although there was little outright support of hardline separate development or segregation, many interview participants expressed an acceptance of or support for de facto segregation in social life, roughly along ethnolinguistic lines. As with a Zulu-speaking woman, who claimed that sitting with white people was uncomfortable (095), and the young man above who will not socialize with black people, many others simply suggested that it is easiest and most comfortable to live a largely segregated life. Another young man in Bloemfontein said, "When your own people are harmed, you get very defensive. If things go downhill, I will stand in defense of my people. It is like a war zone now. . . . We annoy them as much as they annoy us. We do not want to listen to *Kwaito*.[7] They do not want to listen to Steve Hofmeyr.[8] Some students even go so far as to build a wall in the middle of an 'integrated' hostel"[9] (026). This lived level of segregation was addressed by one man in Bloemfontein, who acknowledged, "On the surface, it is peaceful, but when you look a bit deeper, there are no friendships across racial lines. . . . We live in little pockets. There is no real integration" (070).

Zulu-speaking interview participants were often equally disenchanted with the rainbow rhetoric. The gap between the rhetoric and the reality of the transition was particularly palpable for many Zulu-speaking participants in the ways that racism continued to manifest itself.

When our children are playing in the park, they move around together like it is not a big deal. But white children are eventually told not to mix with *kaffirs*. . . . You will still find people who do not think that we belong here. There are still white people who will tell their children to be careful of the *kaffirs*. . . . I was working as a teacher at Rhodes. The reaction of white people just shows you that you are not welcome in their halls. They still have the word *kaffir* in mind when they see you. (089)

It was easier, then, for this man and his children not to associate with white people. The puzzling part of these responses is not the anger or the sense of bitterness, it is that they were elicited by a question about the relevance of a national symbol.

Nation-Building without History

For many of the people above, the relevance of the rainbow symbolism went much deeper than whether the framing of the nation in those terms resonated with them. Many interview participants took the question to be about the status of nation-building post-apartheid, and the change that had been brought about by the transition from apartheid. Opinions on the rainbow, ultimately, can be understood through the lens of continuity or change, and the extent to which the transition itself represented a new era for South Africa. The fact that most interview participants were disillusioned with, or rejected, the symbolism of the new covenant promised by the rainbow after twenty years of democracy shows that this approach to nation-building as a new start has not had durable resonance in the post-apartheid era. For many of the interview participants, the continuities with the apartheid era, or the return to them after a brief interlude, eclipsed the promises of rainbow-nation symbolism.

These varied reactions, all given in response to questions regarding the resonance of the rainbow symbolism twenty years after the political transition, shed light on how the ahistorical nature of the transitional symbolism left open the possibilities for interpretation. While many interview participants did see the optimism and transformative potential of the rainbow symbolism, most were disappointed in some way with the unfulfilled nature of the promises they believed to be inherent in such rhetoric. The first three categories—the tempered optimists, the unrealized idealists, and those who disassociate from the symbol—saw the history of South Africa since the transition as largely falling short of the nation-building ambitions of the rainbow ideal.

Perhaps most interestingly, however, is the way the rainbow symbol's ambiguity and ahistoricity have opened up the possibility of such vastly different interpretations. The rainbow segregationists, seeing the symbol as permission to have parallel lives akin to apartheid in the new dispensation, have reinterpreted the symbol, marking it as a sign of core social continuities in the midst of political change. The break represented by the newness of the rainbow nation was fundamentally about the structure of governmental participation and institutions, rather than a newly reformed national community.

Perhaps these shortfalls have occurred because, while the transition was an unexpected reconfiguration of large parts of the governmental structure in South Africa, it was not a postdiluvian restart of the world or of history. The continuities between the apartheid nation and the rainbow-democratic one, which led some participants to express frustration and anger, have eclipsed the promises of a new start. The rainbow promised a clean slate, but the contentious history of the anti-apartheid struggle, and the socioeconomic continuities between that time and South Africa today, loom large and threaten to eclipse the rainbow.

THE TRUTH AND RECONCILIATION COMMISSION: NATION-BUILDING THROUGH HISTORY-TELLING

The Truth and Reconciliation Commission, unlike the rainbow-nation symbolism, was a project that was deeply concerned with the reconstruction of apartheid history. The primary tasks of the three-pronged commission included investigating alleged human rights violations, processing applications for amnesty and hearing testimony from applicants, and formulating proposals for reparation and rehabilitation based on victims' and perpetrators' accounts. The causal assumption inherent in the commission, including in its name, was that exposing the history of brutality under the apartheid regime would provide the basis for national healing, or reconciliation. The truth-telling of the TRC was meant to simultaneously destroy the nationalist history of apartheid, including the mythologies of separate development as a benign devolution of power and autonomy, and to reconfigure the historical points of identification by airing individual trauma on a national stage. The nation-building aspirations of the TRC were in deconstructing apartheid-government histories and rebuilding a new, inclusive history of South Africa that would provide the basis for newly formed associations. These associations, ostensibly based in shared trauma, would help to promote national healing.

To do this, the TRC conducted interviews and subsequently selected some interviewees for public hearings, whether those hearings were of the Human Rights Abuses Committee, which focused on victims, the Amnesty Committee, which focused on perpetrators, or most spectacularly but least commonly, both victims and perpetrators in pseudo-confrontation. The committee also did less-public work through the Reparation and Rehabilitation Committee, designed to provide both interim and long-term interventions aimed at restoring the dignity of victims.

Given the enormity of the task, it is hardly surprising that the TRC inspired assessments of its practices and mandate. The TRC received scrutiny and criticism from a variety of scholars, who raised a number of issues: the insufficiency of the reparations process (Stanley 2001); the fact that the TRC did not provide the basis for substantively ending violence (Hamber 1998); the demand, especially in public hearings, to tell a compelling narrative of trauma rather than focusing on the victims' experiences (Krog, Mpolweni, and Ratele 2009); the overreach of amnesty rather than focusing on justice for victims (Mamdani 2002); and the fact that spectacle seemed to be of paramount importance in the proceedings (Msimang 2017).

Additionally, large-N survey work, conducted by scholars such as Amanda Gouws and James Gibson, has questioned whether truth is either necessary or sufficient to create a sense of tolerance, promote interracial contact, or develop the legitimacy of the post-apartheid state (Gibson 2006; Gibson and Gouws 2003). Ultimately, Gibson concludes that such historical investigation can be effective in creating the basis of tolerance and community-building if the histories recorded are complex and if the truth offered "tends to challenge dogmatic assertions about the virtues of the parties engaged in the struggle over apartheid" (Gibson 2006, 330). It is the complexity of the newly rebuilt history that has the potential to contribute to nation-building, by giving people the chance to imagine themselves as part of a common history.[10]

For many people with whom I spoke, however, the narratives remembered as coming from the TRC were not characterized by complexity. They did not bridge boundaries or help to resituate people in the world. Rather, these stories combined to build a history that simplified both the apartheid regime and resistance to it. Both Afrikaans- and Zulu-speaking participants in my interviews explained their reactions (and objections) to the TRC in terms of very simplistic good/bad, black/white, victim/perpetrator narratives, not in terms of the challenging history proposed by Gibson. As such, the history and the truth offered by the commission were weaponized to reinforce communal divides. Rather than providing a heroic history of struggle, loss, and triumph in which all South Africans could find their place, as in the nationalist histories of Billig and Renan, the history presented by the TRC was simplified, and thereby turned into demands for or resistance to the idea of apologizing for the past.

Many Afrikaans speakers saw a clash, between their own experiences and those of their loved ones, and the history offered by the commission, which they construed as a personal accusation. For many Zulu-speaking participants, the history told by the TRC was resonant, but the granting of amnesty and the apparent lack of sanction of perpetrators meant that the new narrative offered little comfort. For some, this disconnect between the narrative of the barbarisms of apartheid failed to match their families' personal histories. As explored by Jacob Dlamini, this nostalgia, even in the face of the crimes of apartheid, makes the history-building exercise of the TRC one that is fraught with contradictions (Dlamini 2009). The exercise in nation-building through historical retelling, then, fell short of delivering a basis on which South Africans could re-imagine their relationships to one another.

Interview Participants' Reflections on the TRC in Practice

During the course of interviews, participants were asked about their personal recollections of the TRC process, and their evaluations of the commission's impact after twenty years. For many participants, the historical narrative produced by the TRC was personally situated in terms of their own and their families' experiences under the apartheid regime. Their recollections of the TRC's history were not often complex, but rather simplistic narratives of whites as perpetrators and blacks as victims. Because of the mix of this version of TRC history with their own family experience either of involvement with or resistance to the apartheid regime, the history provided by the TRC was not the moderating force that Gibson prescribed, but rather conveyed a polarizing sense of whose stories could belong in new South African history.

Among the Afrikaans speakers who objected to the TRC, the term "witch hunt" came up as a common descriptor, with interview participants referencing the idea of indiscriminate group culpability. In one dual interview, a twenty-three-year-old woman—a very young child when the TRC was happening—reported her impressions of the TRC, saying "My father and brother were in the South African Defense Force. So, the experience of the TRC was very negative for me. . . . Of course, there were things that were not right [with apartheid], but the TRC was a witch-hunt. They really should have focused more on both sides" (051–052). Another middle-aged Afrikaans-speaking woman, in an unrelated interview on a separate day, echoed much of the same rhetoric. In response to the same questions, she said, "For whites, it felt like a witch-hunt. Everyone we knew was being blamed" (027). Or in the words of another middle-aged, Afrikaans-speaking woman working in Bloemfontein,

> I knew about [the TRC], but it was nonsense . . . it was just a waste. The people who needed to benefit did not. The people who went to the TRC were also

one sided. Poor, innocent black victims, never poor white people. Not our people. Our people were pushed to one side. . . . People really were oppressed. That is true for both sides, but they only listen to one side. Why can they only hear about one side's troubles? (043)

Yet others, like one Afrikaans-speaking older man, while not using the same terminology, saw the commission in the same light, as prosecuting a group, and dealing with only one kind of history. He said

[The TRC] was a good thing. All of this would have been worse without it. Most people would say that they did not really know about all of these things before. I was against apartheid from my student days. I always had read the alternative press. . . . But this TRC, this reconciliation must also be balanced. Black people also did bad things. In the 1980s, we had a small congregation. Seven members were killed by the MK[11] and APLA.[12] That did not come out enough. Innocent, good people were murdered, but those stories are not told. (078)

Although the narratives recounted by Zulu speakers were different in many respects, they were often just as simplistic. According to one Zulu-speaking man, "I followed as much as the media gave us with the TRC. But, you know, it failed. It failed because it protected whites as the perpetrators of violence. It stopped short. . . . Something else should have been done" (088). When asked to clarify or expand on what more could have been done, he demurred. Perhaps the most succinct summary of the TRC offered by an interview participant came from a Zulu-speaking man in his mid-30s, when he said "When we first heard of this thing [the TRC], you know, everyone thought, ha! Now! Mandela is giving us the chance to expose these people. People wanted to get satisfaction. Some did, but many did not" (094).

These interpretations of the TRC led many interview participants to feel a deep anger and resentment about the entire process, in part because their reaction to the newly presented evidence was preconditioned by their racial and ethnic identities. This was true for interview participants from both Afrikaans- and Zulu-speaking backgrounds, across the age spectrum. In one focus group of Afrikaans speakers, both men and women, ranging in age from twenty-eight through fifty-two, the participants responded to the question of their impressions of the TRC by saying

There was quite a lot of media coverage, but it did not really make an impact. . . . There were a lot of issues that were not dealt with. There was no closure. By the end, everyone was angry. There was lots of truth, but not much reconciliation. It is a harsh truth. Even now . . . it is painful. . . . How can you reconcile when you know how someone killed your father? How can you reconcile with that person, ever? (057–060)

A forty-year-old Zulu speaker, in her upscale office in Durban, offered much the same evaluation of the TRC. When asked what she remembered of the commission, she said "I saw it on TV when it was happening. It was very traumatizing, quite emotional. To know what happened to relatives, to see them burying your relatives, that is very hard. But really, no, it was not good for the country. We were looking for answers, but it did nothing except bring tears to our faces. People were interviewed just to get parole" (097).

Many interview participants used simplified tropes rather than complex narratives to talk about the TRC. But additionally, most interview participants understood the TRC in ways conditioned by their position within family structures, as mothers, brothers, daughters, and fathers. The revelation of some incidents of violence on the part of perpetrators brought shame on an entire family. For the white women, whose husbands and fathers and brothers had fought in the Border War or worked in the security forces, the reception of the TRC was not one of relief, but of disenchantment. In the words of one interview participant, "For these women, who had idealized their husbands and fathers and sons in the police and the army, it was difficult to reconcile the images. The levels of brutality, of violence; this was dishonorable. They could not feel proud anymore. They lost their honor" (032). For those Afrikaans families whose patriarchal structure prescribed reverence for the father figure, the TRC's revelations were not about the creation of a unified national history, but rather the destruction of their understanding of honor and sacrifice. The loss of their personal understanding of their own history was perceived keenly, and met with some resistance.

Reconciliation as Apologies

Given this simplified narrative structure, and the connections to personal history, interview participants often simplified the process of reconciliation, and thereby belonging in the new national history, into an issue of group or personal apologies. Yet like the reactions to the historical narratives presented above, the issues of guilt and blame were also conditioned by autobiography. Accusations that one group or another had apologized or had failed to apologize came from both sides. In two separate interviews, conducted months apart, with two professional men of roughly the same age, each accused "the other side" of failing to apologize, and thereby hindering the process of reconciliation. The Afrikaans-speaking interview participant, in an interview in Bloemfontein, said

> We must remember that we were in a war with the ANC and the UDF.[13] It is not internationally recognized, but it was a war. . . . As a white man, I know that we killed. We murdered family members. Then we asked for forgiveness, but it is not like that with the ANC or the UDF. Whites are asking for forgiveness, but not the other way around. It's all one way. (073)

His Zulu-speaking counterpart, in an interview in Durban, said:

> [The TRC] was a part of the negotiated settlement. The condition was, if you told us everything, we would give you amnesty. We were meant to forgive and forget. We were supposed to move forward peacefully. [author's follow up: Has that happened?] Eish,[14] you know, reconciliation must be between two people. With only one, it cannot be reconciliation. It is just conciliation. It must be about coming together. I am not saying that all white people should apologize now, but they did not apologize in the first place. Whites need to take responsibility and apologize. The people responsible did not come forward. That is an insult. It is an insult to us and to our attempts to make things better. (108)

These accusations, about whether one side or the other apologized sufficiently, or for the correct reasons, or at the right time, undermine the history-building mandate of the TRC by reinforcing, not the complex history that might serve as the basis of community building, but the simplistic and identity-based understanding of apartheid and the resistance to it. Yet this equation, of reconciliation with apologies, was present throughout the majority of my interviews.

Enmeshed as many of the interview participants were in the simplified narratives of black victims/white perpetrators, many Afrikaans-speaking participants had strong opinions about whether they were willing to offer apologies. In one memorable tandem interview, the male participant, when asked what reconciliation was and whether it was important, responded by saying "Reconciliation is just white apology. But many whites will not say sorry. In 1994, whites lost the sense of guilt. They became more conservative. There was suddenly a sense of 'we created it and we stopped it.' So, it was done" (024–025). When I asked the woman participant if she had anything to add, she responded by giving me a withering look and by saying "You are full of s**t, you know. I will not apologize" (024–025). When asked to elaborate, she refused.

Although less adamant, other Afrikaans-speaking participants echoed the sentiments above. One respondent said, "I will not apologize for the past, but other people ask me to apologize. I was not a part of apartheid, or the past. There has been damage caused, but I was not a part of that. I will not apologize because some politicians did things to the country" (077). Another young woman Afrikaans-speaker in Bloemfontein recounted the following story:

> I had a black student . . . who basically implied that I need to apologize to him because I am white. He called that reconciliation, which I found very offensive and very unfair. If I did something to somebody personally, I will always try and reconcile with that person, but I just feel that if you are going to keep something against the race as a whole, against the white people, we will never be able to reconcile anything. (005)

Reconciliation, then, is reduced to apologies, and the roles of those interactions are pre-determined based on race.

The issue of apologies, as linked to the nation-building process, is starkly displayed in two popular pieces written by Afrikaans-speaking artists. The first, by Antjie Krog, published at the end of the 1998 edition of her book on the Truth and Reconciliation Commission *Country of My Skull*, is a highly emotional poem, in which Krog as the speaker celebrates the calming effects of the TRC in South Africa, acknowledges her own transformation, and asks for forgiveness.[15] Six years after the publication of that book, an Afrikaans pop-punk band called *Klopjag*, released a best-selling song called *"Nie Langer"* or "No Longer." The lyrics, which acknowledge both the past and the need for certain kinds of redress, also proclaim that it is time to move on, and that both individually and collectively, the band members and their constituency will no longer apologize.[16]

This focus on apologies could in fact stem from the framing of the issue of reconciliation by the TRC commissioners themselves, because they focused on the importance of interpersonal reconciliation between perpetrators and victims within individual cases. The reluctance (some might say recalcitrance) on the part of the perpetrators to offer apologies, however, was also present at that time. Apologies, or their absence, took center stage from the beginning of the process. However, with the simplification of the TRC narrative, the issue of apology has transitioned from one of being based on the *actions* of an individual to the *identity* of an individual. Hence, the reception of the history presented by the TRC is deeply conditioned by the positionality of the person being asked to reflect on it. The question about reconciliation becomes almost indistinguishable from an accusation. It is this conflation of apologies and identity that forms the nexus around which much of the resistance to the TRC has hardened.

Reconciliation as an Ongoing Process: Relating to the TRC after Twenty Years

The historical practice of the TRC is, of course, distinct from the ongoing ambitions of nation-building through historical retelling. Because of how the TRC was perceived as polarizing in the historical sense, many interview participants reported negative associations with the aspirations of nation-building and "reconciliation" in the present. The majority associated the reconciliation process with divisive forces such as hatred, anger, and conflict, mirroring their views of the historical construction mandate of the commission. There were even some interview participants, mostly Afrikaans-speaking, who saw the reconciliation process as a kind of state-sponsored discrimination against white South Africans. In this view, the reconciliation that was meant to be offered through the history-building exercise of the TRC and affiliated nation-building social programs (Shoup and Holmes 2013) worked against nation-building.

The majority of interview participants, when asked what they thought about reconciliation in practice, expressed views ranging from indifference to hostility. The question was even sufficient to incite some to anger. For one young Afrikaans-speaking man, the question provoked an angry response. He raised his voice when saying

> I was not part of apartheid. What do you want from me? Nowadays, we are forced to be racist. When you deal with the government, when you go to the shops, you get slow, bad service. . . . Look at the people who commit murders.

I have never heard of a white hijacker, have you? It is always whites being attacked by blacks. . . . Now, if there is an argument, it is always about race. People assume that whites are racists. I do not want to be a racist, but these things, the crime and that, change the way I think. (034)

Another Afrikaans-speaking young man, in his mid-twenties, also responded to the question angrily. In response he snapped, "Reconciliation? Of what? How many years have passed? Who do you want to reconcile? Shouldn't people be doing it on their own? . . . You cannot force people. If you don't like others, you do not like them" (054). For both of these young men, the question itself seemed to be tantamount to an accusation. Rather than seeing their place in the historical narrative provided by the commission, they saw themselves as being accused, and were thereby alienated.

A Zulu-speaking interview participant, a fifty-three-year-old woman, echoed this conception of reconciliation. When asked if it was still important to address the subject nowadays, she responded:

Reconciliation now is not an easy thing. It might lead to war if we talk about it too much. It is very sensitive. There are many things to address. Even issues then were not properly done. Things are coming up now, like with Winnie Mandela, that prove that how it was done back then was not right.[17] There was a lot of information that was left untackled. Are you asking should that be started again? [interjection by author, "well, not exactly . . ."] Eish, but that would be difficult. It would be impossible. It would be war. (103)

The last category of responses to the idea of reconciliation, linked to the reactions to the TRC discussed above, is that the reconciliation project implies in itself a kind of reversal of the direction of discrimination. Some participants went so far as to equate reconciliation and the process of the TRC as constituting "reverse apartheid," wherein they were targeted as guilty or deprived of their full citizenship by the process. A twenty-year-old Afrikaans-speaking young woman said, "Now, on paper, we have equal opportunity. We have democracy. But, things are turning around now. It is like apartheid in reverse" (020). Another young woman said of reconciliation, "Before 2000, it was still important, but now it has been a long time since apartheid. Now we have BEE, which is unfair. It is apartheid in reverse. Now we need reconciliation again, in reverse. People are angry all over again. Reconciliation is about trying to make everyone equal, but now we have black-on-white racism" (016). These participants, all from among the group of Afrikaans-speakers in Bloemfontein and Pretoria, expressed their alienation from and disgust with the project of national reconciliation, and programs and policies that they associated with it.

The Unbearable Heaviness and Lightness of Remembrance

Whether understood as biased, incomplete, insufficient, or irrelevant, interview participants' understandings of the history-telling of the TRC were shaped by their autobiographical and positional histories. While an average white South African, having benefitted from the governmental policies of the apartheid regime, may have experienced the history uncovered by the TRC as a revelation, it is far less likely that a black South African would have been surprised by the orientations of the past government or the revelations of the commission. The average white respondent, who was given the rights and privileges of a full citizen under the apartheid regime, and was spatially and mentally distant from the most intensely inhumane aspects of apartheid, would have had a very different relationship to the truth revealed at the commission than the average black respondent. Accepting the history built by the commission involved not only acknowledging the facts of apartheid, but destroying the myths of place and space that supported apartheid, and potentially the admission of personal privilege and advantage that apartheid bestowed on the white population at the expense of populations of color. In other words, to imagine themselves as part of the history, or to understand that history as part of their autobiography, interview participants had to travel very different paths.

These differences, in themselves, do not negate the possibility that the TRC could serve as an effective nation-building tool. If, as Gibson notes, the history were told and recalled in a complex way, it could serve as a bridging, and indeed unifying history. The complicated histories of the violence of apartheid and resistance to it could have been a way for all South Africans to imagine themselves as products of collective trauma. But for the majority of interview participants, the TRC was primarily recalled in terms of attributions of blame and demands for or resistance to apologies. The history built by the TRC, and interpreted through the individual experiences of the South Africans with whom I spoke, served to shore up communal boundaries.

MEMORY AND HISTORY IN NATION-BUILDING
AND NATIONAL SYMBOLS

Because the transition from apartheid to multiracial democracy contained efforts to nation build through both memory and forgetting, the role of history in building a national community is fundamentally contested in post-apartheid South Africa. Those who would prefer to move on from the apartheid era, seeing the transition as a break with the past, have access to one symbolic repertoire, while those who see history-telling as key to a reconciliation process have access to another. Perhaps unsurprisingly, these two camps are not randomly distributed. Among the people with whom I spoke, the Afrikaans-speaking participants in Bloemfontein and Pretoria on the whole advocated moving on, while Zulu-speaking participants in Durban and Pretoria were strong proponents of remembrance as facilitating nation building.

The Zulu-speakers who insisted that history and telling about the atrocities of apartheid were central to the process of nation-building used a remarkably consistent vocabulary to describe their position. Centered around the idea that you cannot demand that those people who suffered under apartheid forget their trauma, Zulu speakers, both men and women and from across the age spectrum, asserted that history and memory were essential to the reconciliation process, and hence, the nation-building effort. In the words of one middle-aged Zulu-speaking man, "You cannot demand forgetting with [reconciliation]. It is not fair to ask people to move on from the trauma" (092). Another young man said, "[Reconciliation] is still important. . . . But before that happens, we need to sit down and you must confess and I must accept. You cannot ask for forgetting" (101). Another Zulu-speaking woman said "Reconciliation is not really happening. The TRC tried, but things are still missing. . . . There is a lot of resistance from the people who enjoyed the apartheid system. They want us to forget" (099). This insistence on memory and not-forgetting constituted a fundamental plank of the nation-building-through-reconciliation process, even if interview participants did not have uniformly positive reflections on the history-building process of the TRC.

On the opposite side of the spectrum, among Afrikaans speakers, there was an insistence that the only way to create a national community was to "move on" from apartheid. One middle-aged professional woman in Bloemfontein, while acknowledging that there was a need to build a national community through reconciliation, said that the time for such things had largely passed. She said "Unless we draw a line through it, if we keep it alive . . . then we influence a whole new generation and make them angry. We need to draw a line. We need to bury it. They are always looking back, not forward. We need to go forward" (071). Another Afrikaans-speaking professional man agreed that reconciliation was important, but insisted that "the way it is done now is not really right. They use the past as an excuse for bad behavior. They use reconciliation to keep uneducated people loyal to the ANC. Malema says land was stolen by the whites from blacks. He gets people angry and calls it reconciliation. It is important to talk about it, but not the way it is talked about now. We must move on" (076). A twenty-four-year-old Afrikaans-speaking woman, asked about the TRC and its effects, said "I do not have any real impressions of the TRC, if I am honest. I did not even remember it. The big problem now is that people are still bringing it up. . . . Now, we have to look to the future. They are making real hate by still talking about it. They are bringing some of the hate back in" (072). Like Zulu speakers, these Afrikaans speakers were from diverse backgrounds, but unified around a common theme: moving on from apartheid.

This clash between memory and forgetting is played out most starkly in perceptions of governmental programs aimed at redressing past socioeconomic injustices and building capital among previously disadvantaged South Africans. Such programs were part of the nation-building project (Shoup and Holmes 2013), which sought to ameliorate the long history of discrimination based on race. However, because of the possibility of associating the transition from apartheid with a new beginning, many Afrikaans-speaking interview participants saw such programs as unjust and benefitting racially defined population groups based on apartheid-style logic. Various participants identified redress programs specifically as a problem. A twenty-year-old Afrikaans-speaking young woman said "Now, on paper, we have equal opportunity. We have democracy. But things are turning around now. It is like apartheid in reverse" (020). Another young woman said of such redress programs, "Before 2000, it was still important, but now it has been a long time since apartheid. Now we have BEE [Black Economic Empowerment], which is unfair. It is apartheid in reverse" (016).

One Afrikaans-speaking man who owned his own business was particularly bothered by these policies, which he saw as a direct threat. He said, "Just after 1994, people were thinking about the country. It started back with the apartheid thinking under Mbeki. BEE is the clearest form of reversed apartheid you have ever seen" (049–050). Another woman echoed many of the same sentiments, although she was positive about the reconciliation process.

> I did not grow up during apartheid, and neither did they. They have all the luxuries now. . . . If I say I do not like it, the way things are now, then I would be a racist. White South Africans have bent over backwards. We made a big change. Now it is the reverse of what it was. White men cannot find jobs now. It would be so much better to take the person who can do the job, rather than this BEE. (074)

Like the man quoted above, a middle-aged Afrikaans-speaking woman echoed the sentiment that race relations had gotten worse since 1994, but also reinforced the idea of white alienation as a direct result of the reconciliation process. When asked about reconciliation, she replied, "We are more divided than before. . . . White people feel alienated in their own country. Most people I know feel that way. The shoe is on the other foot now. . . . We are going back into our race camps. . . . If push comes to shove, we are on our own and so are they. . . . We are *moedeloos*[18] now. . . . If you want to understand us, you have to understand that people are losing hope" (056).

Some interview participants also called for another reconciliation commission, aimed at eradicating corruption and bringing to light the abuses of the ANC government. One young man, advocating this strategy and focusing on "minority rights," said when asked about reconciliation "At this rate, in another 50 to 100 years, *we* will need another Truth and Reconciliation Commission to deal with the abuses perpetrated on minorities in the current government" (014). In the words of another young man, "Reconciliation now is in the past. As of 1994, we are all equal. Now the scale is tipping the other way. *We* will be previously disadvantaged. *We* will then need reconciliation. It will go on and on" (047). And another, focused on the economic abuses of corruption and mismanagement, said

> Reconciliation is not important anymore . . . perhaps we should start it again, really, in parliament. . . . They must ask forgiveness for stealing money, preventing education, healthcare and water. In the last seven years, a lot of money has gone missing. With that money, they could have built 900,000 houses. That is forty-five whole new towns. They want to talk about apartheid, but what about corruption? We need reconciliation for that. Where is that money? (073)

What these discussions of reconciliation ultimately reveal is that many interview participants use reconciliation not only as a byword for building a national community, but that there is an implicit assumption that the process of reconciliation is based on the recording of history. Because the extant history-building exercise of the TRC was alienating, they seem to claim, they will need an additional commission of their own. The history that was built by the TRC would need an accompanying history of what they perceived to be their own struggles. This orientation toward the history built by the TRC, that it is not inclusive and would need a similarly sympathetic pair to achieve something like nation building, sends the project into a potential infinite regress, wherein each commission calls forth another. This obviously unsustainable outcome is almost diametrically opposed to the nation-building ambitions of the history built by the TRC.

RAINBOW FORGETTING OR COMMISSIONED REMEMBERING

The transition in 1994 from the apartheid government to a majoritarian democracy, made with comparatively little violence and witnessed by numerous international observers, was an occasion for celebration. The extent to which this momentous occasion represented a new start, or another step in the process of the history that produced both apartheid and resistance to it, was then and is still today under intense debate. This debate is partially spurred by the fact that two distinct symbolic repertoires were pursued during the transition and immediately after it that utilized national history in two very divergent ways. While the rhetoric of the rainbow nation presented an approach to understanding the nation-building project in South Africa as fundamentally starting anew with the transition to multiracial democracy, the Truth and Reconciliation Commission was primarily concerned with a detailed reconstruction of history that would then provide the basis for a new community.

But these two approaches are, in many ways, incompatible. How is it possible to see the transition from apartheid as both continuity with the past and a break from it? Put another way, how can the contentious past be both remembered and forgotten in the building of a national community? The difficulty in utilizing these strategies simultaneously is that both those who seek to remember the past and those who would rather move on are accommodated. But with reference to programs aimed at reparation of past injustices, these two attitudes come into conflict. If the transition was a break from the past, then the clean slate provided by this change means that little needs to be done to create a newly equitable country. If, by contrast, the project of the transition was in retelling and affirming the wrongs of the past, then such injustices need to be reckoned with to create the new order. Consequently, there is an ambivalence regarding the ways in which national history and symbolism can be deployed for unifying purposes. While the complex narratives originally offered by the TRC and the unity implied in the rainbow-nation rhetoric both have the potential to be fruitful symbolic repertoires of nation-building, interview participants rarely saw them in that light.

CHAPTER 4

Opposition and Party Politics in Democratic South Africa

Multiracial democracy in South Africa has been in practice for just over two decades. Voter registration is consistently high, with 76.7 percent of potential voters registered and eligible to vote as of the 2011 census and the 2014 national election, and voter turnout has consistently exceeded 70 percent in national-level elections (Independent Electoral Commission of South Africa 2014), with the exception of the 2019 general election.[1] But elections have a longer tradition in the country, with the colonial and apartheid governments holding whites-only polls for more than a century. Although elections were marred by limited suffrage and vast inequality of rights, the apartheid government was elected in twelve consecutive national elections, which were contested by opposition parties and took place according to a transparent set of rules. Apartheid was domestically legitimized through elections (Adam 1971). Because of the importance of elections, a central point of the anti-apartheid struggle was, simply, the establishment of democracy for all South Africans, rather than just whites (Maré 2001; Binns and Robinson 2002).

However, it can also be said that almost no one currently alive in South Africa has participated in a national election in which the outcome was truly uncertain, or that brought about a change in leadership, with the possible exception of the 1992 referendum on ending apartheid.[2] Although the 1994 elections brought the ANC to power, it was widely assumed before the date of the election was set that the ANC would win by a substantial margin. The election of 1994, while absolutely preferable to the violent alternatives so many feared, had the effect of exchanging one dominant party system for another. Additionally, many scholars of South African politics have argued that indicators of democratic stability seem to be lacking, as evidenced in increasing inequality, a tendency toward centralism and securitization within the ANC, declining voter turnout among key constituencies, and a seemingly unsupportive political culture among supporters of losing parties (Mattes 2002; Rich and Holmes 2016; Oyedemi and Mahlatji 2016).

Given the dire outcome that so many scholars had predicted coming out of the anti-apartheid struggle, the fact that free and fair elections are a consistent part of politics in South Africa is certainly a positive result. The question, then, is how do elections help to remind people of the divisions of the past, or obscure them? This chapter investigates this question in three thematic sections: Race and Elections, Opposition Politics, and Exit from Politics. In the first two sections, using interview evidence, this chapter argues that the ongoing practice of elections has served as a reminder of the racial divisions within the national community, because of both the ways that voters identify with parties and the conduct of political parties themselves. Voters, in identifying racial exclusivity as the primary push factor away from parties such as the ANC or the DA, are often siloed into racialized constituencies that reinforce such divisions and limit community-building possibilities. Additionally, the efforts of the ANC and other parties to challenge opponents in racialized terms undermine public cultures of tolerance for opposition parties. The last section looks at the ways key constituencies, especially young voters, poor South Africans, and Afrikaans speakers, discuss their perceived alienation from politics. This section argues that exit from political participation because of disillusionment, through either nonvoting or emigration, poses challenges for nation-building through the practice of procedural democracy.

RACE AND ELECTIONS

Early analysis of multiracial voting concluded that elections were largely a "racial census" in which citizens supported the party that most closely demographically represented them, with black voters supporting the ANC, white voters supporting white opposition parties, and Coloured and Indian voters supporting parties catering directly to those communities (Giliomee, Myburgh, and Schlemmer 2001; Maylam 2001; Friedman 2009). In this theory of voting, elections are merely a tool for counting the numbers of voters belonging to each group. Rather than relying on information about parties' stances on issues, voters would simply choose a demographically representative party. Vote choice, then, was not a choice at all, but rather an assumed outcome.

Another, contemporaneous strand of research suggested that the contribution of racial identity to vote choice is a largely incidental phenomenon, either as a heuristic or a secondary factor that was outweighed by policy preferences (Mattes and Piombo 2001; Mattes 2004; Mattes and Christie 1997). In this vein, it was the lack of voter information on opposition parties that kept voters supporting the ANC in the face of declining approval ratings, rather than some kind of misplaced racial solidarity. In this theory of vote choice, race is one of many heuristics, and need not be central to the analysis.

Yet more recent, survey-based work has revealed a subtler take on voter choice. Voters in general have become more uncertain about parties in South Africa over time. However, those who do identify with a party tend to see it as inclusive, while they see other parties as exclusive, almost always based on race (Habib and Herzenberg 2011, 203). Support for the idea of inclusive politics as the primary positive that draws in voters undermines the idea of racial census voting, but the view that other parties are exclusive based on race seems to indicate that race is still central to the calculus of voter choice (see for example Ferree 2010; Vincent and Howell 2014). But party labels, as inclusive or exclusive, are key in understanding voter choice through racial heuristics. Because voters perceive certain parties as racially exclusive, they feel they cannot support them. The converse of these sentiments also holds true, insofar as voters, when asked, tended to rank whatever party they allied with most closely as the most racially inclusive, and therefore the most desirable party (Ferree 2010).

National Elections and Identity Politics

In their analysis of the 1999 national elections, Giliomee, Myburg, and Schlemmer argue that "Despite the non-racial banner the ANC waved during the liberation struggle it was quick after the 1994 election to call for 'black unity,' emphasizing that black South Africans retain a 'common interest'" (2001, 163). Race is constantly being re-inscribed through the process of electoral politics, in part through the ways that parties campaign for office, and especially the ways in which opposition is framed. In a 2012 campaign, the Democratic Alliance Students' Organization, a wing of the DA, circulated a poster as part of a student campaign, which depicted a naked couple embracing—a white man and a black woman—with the tag line "In OUR future, you wouldn't look twice." The furor over the poster spanned the political spectrum, from those protesting the implications of miscegenation to those who rejected the claim that it was the DA alone that could bring about a nonracial South Africa (Vincent and Howell 2014, 88–89).

The material realities of race, combined with racialized party labels, result in South African elections looking much like a "racial census," as noted above, in large part because of the perceived racial exclusivity of parties. This viewpoint was reinforced by many interview participants, who when asked about which parties they supported, or which parties they believed spoke for them in the realm of politics, reverted to simplistic notions of race to talk about their participation or support. One interview participant, a Zulu-speaking woman in Durban, when asked about what she thought about the present government, expressed frustration when she said "They are comfortable. They have forgotten about us. Now, it is just about self-enrichment. They have forgotten about how they got there" (095). But when she was asked about the parties of the opposition, she said "In the opposition, they are definitely still stuck with apartheid. If the DA were in power, that would be fine. But, as a black lady, I cannot support them" (095).

Another woman, also a Zulu speaker, said much the same thing in a later interview. When asked what she thought of the government, she said, "Our government is very corrupt. If you are in a workplace and if you do not know people, you cannot get ahead. If you want to get ahead, you better have relatives in top positions" (096). A standard follow-up question asked if she thought that there was anyone working to fix these problems. She responded by saying "It is a general problem. Even if the DA wins, they will think about whites like Zuma thinks of blacks. Everyone thinks of their own. I am happy that [Zuma] is there. He always thinks of and understands black people" (096). Another Zulu-speaking participant characterized the same sentiment in terms of ethnicity, when he said of the 2009 election of Jacob Zuma,

> The Zulus said, "enough is enough." We had white presidents, then we had Xhosa presidents. Enough. We need a Zulu president. So, we put in a Zulu president. The Zulus will not elect a Sotho or an Indian president. Zuma is bringing our Zulu premier to him.[3] Most of his ministers are Zulu. They are there supporting a Zulu president. It is Zulus, Zulus, Zulus, all the way down [laughs]. If they change Zuma and put in an Indian president, then it would be Indians all the way down. But that will not happen. (094)

These seemingly contradictory statements, dissatisfaction with the ruling party and its leadership but still rejection of opposition-party options, confirms Ferree's large-N results. The push factor of parties' perceived racial exclusivity is more important in vote choice than the pull of racial affiliation, or even efficacy. For these two women, although they are disappointed in the ANC's performance, the DA is unacceptable because they are a party that caters to white interests. Such interests are fundamentally divorced from their own.

Afrikaans-speaking interview participants in the Free State echoed many of the same perceptions of parties, but from the other side of these constructed lines. When asked "Is there anyone currently in politics who you believe speaks for you?" one Afrikaans-speaking man responded "The DA, maybe . . . a bit. But the conundrum is that if they chase the majority, if they go for the black vote, then they cannot represent minorities like me" (069). An Afrikaans-speaking woman, in a separate interview, echoed many of the same sentiments, saying

> If [the DA] want[s] to take over the country, they need 9 million black votes. But a white woman[4] will never get nine million black votes. That is just true. It is not possible for DA to fight for Afrikaans schools, street names, buildings, monuments, culture. If they want those votes, they have to be concerned with the issues of other cultures as well. They cannot speak for the Afrikaner. (011)

Another older Afrikaans-speaking man who was directly involved with electoral politics and affiliated with a smaller opposition party said:

> We do not oppose the present government, because there is no way we can be as the majority in this government. But we say we want to cater for the interest of the Afrikaner because the ANC, who is the government at this time in South Africa, caters for the Zulus and the Sothos and the Tswanas and their people, and there must be a political party that is catering for the interests of the Afrikaners. (004)

When speaking about the practice of voting, one young Afrikaans-speaking woman, who identified herself as a supporter of the DA, said "No, it is not effective [to vote], but . . . I cannot complain without voting. Here in the Free State there is a big base for the ANC. The majority votes for them. But I do not vote for the ANC. I will always be outnumbered" (023).[5] A young Afrikaans-speaking man put the same issue more plainly. When asked about voting, he said that yes, he did vote regularly, but added "You know, there are more black people to vote for the ANC in the Free State than there are people to vote for the *Vryheidsfront*.[6] I know we cannot win" (046). This man, however, did say that he voted regularly and was proud of that fact.

An older Zulu-speaking woman, a staunch ANC supporter, when asked what she thought of the current government, echoed many of the same themes. She responded to the question of how the government was doing by saying "There is an acceptance of the new order. Now, the ruling party is predominant. African people are in power. We have the majority in government, and we are the majority of people" (093).

Some other Afrikaans-speaking interview participants did reference the issue of race and party choice in order to distance themselves from it, or to refute what they assumed was my understanding of their vote choice. One young woman, in response to the question of whether she thought anyone spoke on behalf of her interests, said

> I believe in Helen Zille, but not because of color. She has proven herself to be a good leader. She keeps delivering services. She is lifting up the people. She is having a hard time though. Voters do not believe in the person, they only believe in the culture . . . In this country, there are minority and majority groups. We vote in groups. People vote for the ANC because it was the party that got us out of apartheid. They fear that if they vote for the whites, the history would repeat. (029)

In a two-person interview, a young Afrikaans-speaking woman and man agreed, "People vote for parties without knowing what the party does. People feel like they have to vote for the party because of loyalty. But white people do the same" (051–052).

In different ways, then, these women disavow racialized voting in terms of their own decision calculus but recognize its importance for others. The second woman, however, suggests that the Democratic Alliance, a traditionally white party of the opposition, could with some change in its leadership profile, appeal to a multiracial audience. Yet, as referenced above, for many Afrikaans-speaking DA supporters, such a shift would signal the end of their representation within the party. The continual reference to race, even as a push factor away from parties, is a re-inscription of the logic of race as a way to make sense of politics. The references mean that election campaigns serve as reminders of communal identity, with alienation from some groups serving as a primary logic driving vote choice.

Race and Opposition within Political Parties

Data suggest that the intolerance of political opponents in South Africa is fairly widespread (Rich and Holmes 2016). Many scholars of South African political culture have pointed to a distinct lack of public support for democratic institutions, especially multiparty democratic institutions (Friedman 2009; Giliomee, Myburgh, and Schlemmer 2001; Mattes 2002). James Gibson concluded that in general, there is not widespread support for multiparty democracy in South Africa (Gibson 2003, 796).[7]

Additionally, the ruling ANC has been intolerant of opposition, in terms of both rival parties that are perceived to be gaining strength, and internal opposition. ANC leadership has been at pains to describe both internal and external opposition as counter-revolutionary, traitorous, or associated with the apartheid regime. Party leadership has been fractured in part because of what Beresford (2015) has termed "gatekeeper politics," in which patronage politics has led to factional struggles because of the ways that power positions ensure access to key resources, which not only hampers internal debate but reduces the ANC's ability to have regular turnover in leadership.

These characteristics were especially pronounced under Jacob Zuma's leadership of both the party and the country, which was marked by personalistic leadership and public corruption (Lodge 2014). Zuma's rise, following the procedurally unprecedented unseating of then-president Thabo Mbeki, was fueled by factional support and internal contestation (Giollabhuí 2017), and characterized by increased antagonism to democratic opposition (Booysen 2015, 2–3). Doling out private goods from the public treasury, and making accusations of corruption both founded and baseless, were ways to both buy support and undermine opposition under the Zuma administration (Beresford 2016, 61–62).

Under the Zuma administration, the ANC also frequently sought to undermine leaders of opposition parties with racial epithets (Bosman and Du Toit 2011, 220–21). Though not a new strategy—white opposition leaders, even those firmly left of center, were frequently accused of being Nazi or apartheid sympathizers, or of committing treasonous acts by criticizing the ANC (Maré 2001a), and the ANC often sought to define all "robust opposition" as "illegitimate" (Southall 2001, 2) since the earliest days of democracy—it became a more common one under the Zuma administration.

Many Afrikaans-speaking interview participants referenced these kinds of accusations in the course of interviews. A standard interview question was "What do you see as the major political challenges facing South Africa right now?" Many Afrikaans speakers, after giving an account of what they saw as the most pressing political challenges, would revert to a kind of defensive position, saying that their criticism was not coming from a place of racism. One Afrikaans-speaking man, in response to that question, said,

People who are not in government are the ones who are working to fix things. . . . Now, we have people in the ANC appointing family and mates. That is the ANC in the majority. But saying that makes me come across as racist or unpatriotic. But the question is, should I be keeping quiet, just because I am white? I do not think so. We have to appoint people to do jobs who are qualified to do them. (066)

One particularly upset interview participant did not wait to be prompted regarding her evaluations of the political system. Instead, during the opening of our interview, she asserted:

I am not a racist. I have had and I still have friends in other cultures. But when the ANC came to power, we were pushed aside. We have to make a place for ourselves now. . . . I am not a racist because I do not believe in the ANC. But they do not care. They welcome violence. They want to get rid of us. They want South Africa to themselves. This is my country as much as it is theirs. I belong and they belong. The ANC makes promises, but they do not deliver. The world just sees the promises and is impressed. That is not the way it is. (043)

The accusations of the ANC against opposition parties, of racial exclusivity or even of illegitimacy, have filtered down to the parties' constituencies, and made some of their voters defensive about their speech in criticizing the ANC. This stance toward opposition, from both ANC members and party leadership, was a source of anxiety for many supporters of opposition parties. But in many ways, this is a strategic position taken by the ANC and has been effective in maintaining vote share, as well as in delegitimizing opposition parties (Holmes and Shoup 2013; Shoup and Holmes 2013).

Among Zulu-speaking ANC supporters with whom I spoke in interviews, the party's view of the opposition, as largely unproductive or counter to the well-being of the post-apartheid state, was commonly expressed.[8] When asked what he thought about opposition parties, one Zulu-speaking man encapsulated these responses when he said,

Why do we have so many political parties? Why do we have opposition parties? Who are you all opposing? We are all South Africans. We have to rally together. If you are loyal, should you not work together for the best for all? You can't work against a system that you are a part of . . . The party I belong to is nonracial and nonsexist. I joined at the age of fourteen. I was almost pushed into it. The treatment of my people, the oppressions we suffered . . . you could not help but be politically active. Mostly, it was just to survive. I did not volunteer for service. I was just born into it. Membership in the party means unity. (108)

A Zulu-speaking woman, when asked what the major political challenges facing the country were, responded by saying that opposition parties themselves were the challenge. She said,

There is a gap between the intellectuals, the academics, the opposition and the ruling party. The critics are criticizing only, rather than contributing. They are criticizing only, rather than being constructive. . . . If you pinpoint the mishaps, rather than trying to come up with an opinion, then how are you helping? Those people only capitalize on mistakes, rather than trying to find constructive solutions. (093)

A Zulu-speaking man in his sixties, a strong ANC partisan, said of the parties of the opposition, "We have a very weak opposition. They are not doing anything proactive. They only look at what the party in government does and react to it. They are not proactive, only reactive. The coalitions show how weak they are. They have to gang up" (089).

One Afrikaans-speaking woman in her mid-eighties, when asked about what she thought of the present government, said "I am not a fan of the ANC. They are not running the country properly. They are antagonizing white people, Afrikaners in particular. . . . Every day you see something that makes your blood boil. . . . I have nothing, in principle, against the ANC. If the blacks want their party, they must have it. But now they are drumming out the opposition. Zuma's definition of democracy is different from other peoples'" (044).

And indeed, this may be the case. In a mid-2012 parliamentary debate about mining and unionization, then-President Zuma said that those who were not members of the majority union could not expect to be treated in the same way as those who were. He stated, "You have more rights because you're a majority; you have less rights because you're a minority. That's how democracy works," which "provoke[ed] a huge outcry from opposition benches" (*News24* 2012a). Such statements, seemingly indicating Zuma's tenuous commitment to procedural democracy, worried both domestic and international observers.

In an interview shortly after that statement, a young Afrikaans-speaking man who had studied politics brought up that debate, and even had copies of several news articles printed about the subject. He gave these sheets to me during our conversation because, he said, I "needed to understand." When I asked what he thought of the president, he replied, pointing to the papers he had given me, "Look at the way that things are phrased . . . with Jacob Zuma's speech. Minorities do not have rights. Democracy is only the rule of the majority. He said those things on 16 September. All South Africans are equal, but the people in the majority have rights because they are ruling. It is things like that that make you feel unwelcome" (039). This speech, which also came up in other interviews, seemed to many interview participants to signal a deeper kind of rejection, not just of political partisan opponents but also of groups of people.

The conduct of political parties and elections, in many cases, seems to re-inscribe the identity politics of race and ethnolinguistic groups, rather than allowing the emergence of new, preference- or policy-driven coalitions that may bridge or obscure the divides of the past. Voter affiliation with politi-cal parties, although not a direct racial census, is based on notions of racial exclusivity. Yet it is also the case that political parties themselves seek to shore up their voter bases by using racial rhetoric and selective images of past and future that reinforce such exclusivist images. As such, the conduct of elections, and the strategies parties employ in them, reminds citizens on a national scale, and on a predictable schedule, of how their national com-munity is divided, and reinforces those divides through framing of political problems and their solutions.[9]

The effects of these strategies seem to be evident in the results of the 2019 general elections, where the major parties, the ANC and the DA, lost vote share and often failed to attract multiracial constituencies. The parties most engaged in racial outbidding, the Economic Freedom Fighters (EFF) and the Freedom Front Plus, experienced substantial gains, taking voters from the ANC and the DA respectively (Campbell 2019). These gains are in part due to a steep decline in both voter registration and voter turnout (Scholtz 2019). The resignation of Jacob Zuma, an overtly Zulu politician, from the presi-dency of the ANC, and the rise of Cyril Ramaphosa, a politician not bound by "narrow regionalism"[10] (Mkhabela 2017), led to a seismic shift in voting patterns in KwaZulu-Natal. The ANC lost more than 11 percent of its vote share overall, and more than 13 percent of its black electorate, with rural black voters opting instead for the Inkatha Freedom Party, a traditional Zulu party, and urban black voters supporting the EFF (Scholtz 2019).

EXIT AS IDENTITY POLITICS

In political theory and empirical studies, from John Locke through Albert Hirschman, the option of exit has been an important mode of dissent or opposition in legitimate and thriving firms and governments. But the exit from participatory politics, when undertaken by concentrated constituencies based on their identity or other defining characteristics, is often seen as a threat to democratic functioning. Exit from politics—in the form of not participating, expressing alienation, or emigration—means that certain voices are not, or cannot, be accommodated. In the case of nonvoting, it means that concentrated groups of citizens do not see their participation as effective or worthwhile.

As indicated in later chapters, it is not merely that signals of communal identity lead to disengagement. The opposite is often true, as evidenced by the growth of language and cultural festivals, for example. However, in the case of exit from political participation, signals of group identity lead to alienation. This outcome could be the result of simplistic demographic realities. If political constituencies are defined only in terms of race, then numerical racial minorities cannot win elections. Alternatively, exit could be driven by perceived inefficacy, wherein problems exist but participation does not seem to help to solve them. The result is the same: exit from political participation by concentrated constituencies is troubling for the growth of both democracy and the nation-building project. It signals a disengagement from both endeavors.

Exit means that voters have foreclosed the possibilities of their effectiveness, and have chosen to remove their voices or themselves from the process, through nonparticipation or emigration. In a new democracy, one that started with such high degrees of engagement and optimism, the widespread nonparticipation of the poor, the young, and certain ethnolinguistically defined communities means that within twenty years, large swathes of South Africans have chosen exit, with the attendant consequences.

Politics of Nonvoting

South Africa's five multiracial elections have seen remarkable and sustained voter turnout. In the April 2014 election, the Independent Electoral Commission reported that 73.48 percent of registered voters cast a ballot (Independent Electoral Commission of South Africa 2014). The 2019 election saw a decline in voter turnout, with only 66.05 percent of registered voters participating (Independent Electoral Commission of South Africa 2019). The steepest declines have come from the youngest eligible cohorts, as well as the poorest income deciles.

The "born free" generation, the South Africans who came of age after the demise of apartheid, are the generation of South Africans least likely to participate regularly in elections. The under-thirty cohort of voters participates at far lower rates than older voters (Scott et al. 2012). As a proportion of the total voting-age population aged eighteen to twenty-nine in the 2014 election, the voter registration rate was 59 percent, about 10 percent lower than the national average (Schulz-Herzenberg 2014). This lower level of participation has been found to be related to both alienation from politics (Oyedemi and Mahlatji 2016) and lower levels of commitment to democracy as a form of government (Mattes 2012).

However, South African participation in elections has declined across the age spectrum as well. According to Schulz-Herzenberg, "When turnout is examined as a proportion of the eligible voting-age population turnout over twenty years, the figures confirm a decline in participation from 86 percent in 1994 to 72 percent in 1999 and 58 percent in 2004" (2014, 2). Much of the overall decline in voting participation has come from among the poorest income deciles, in which South Africans are both less likely to register to vote and less likely to participate if registered (Everatt 2016).

The young people with whom I spoke did note that they voted less frequently than their elders, but for a variety of different reasons. Because of the notion of the racial census as dominating voting, some Afrikaans-speaking interview participants felt that their votes were ineffective. In a racial census, they argued, they would be perennially on the losing side, and hence they abstain from participation. One self-described "progressive" young woman, when asked about voting, said

> I have never voted. I think it is due to my parents, actually. . . . I grew up in a house where, after the 1994 elections, my Dad said "There is no use to go and vote. The black people will always win. They are more than us, and they will always stick with the ANC, so, there is no use for you to go and vote because we will always lose." So again, I sort of listened to my parents and not really did my own thing. . . . [*So your parents also do not vote?*] [*She nods*] Still not. (008)

This mathematical certainty is the logical extension of the idea of "racial census" elections.

Other young people agreed. One young woman involved in "campus activism" said of voting, "No, I do not vote. I am not into politics. It really does not matter if you vote. The time for politics is over. You cannot fight against things like BEE with voting. Rather, organizations outside of government are fighting. I do not vote. I would rather do something" (020).

When I asked him why he chose not to vote, another young man, agreeing with the sentiments above regarding demographics as party destiny, explained,

> We are a minority group. There is a lot of pressure. The truth is that 11 percent of the population does not matter. Voting is really a losing battle. We will never win. In politics, the DA seems to be doing well in the Western Cape. Look at Helen Zille. I would vote for her, if I voted. But it really is not worth it. My family does not vote. Afrikaner people just do not vote. We know that we cannot win anymore. (034)

Zulu-speaking young people, however, had very different reasons for choosing not to vote. One young woman pointed to the corruption in the ruling party and the scandals around then-president Zuma's private residence in Nkandla, remarking "No one talks about the poor until it is time for elections" (105). Despite having been involved in politics, she believed it was no longer something for which she was suited. A thirty-five-year-old man also pointed to corruption, but this time as a distinctly undemocratic driver of his decision to vote before 2009. He said,

> With voting, the goal was always to make sure your book was stamped. Unless you had a stamp in your passbook, you would not get a house. You would not get a job. . . . Without the sticker saying you voted, there would be no RDP houses. That stamp dominated everything, pensions, housing, social grants, nothing. There was no bursary or any government things. . . . Voting was not something we practiced before 1994. . . . It worked for them then. But now we know, it is not effective. We can see. (094)

He demurred, however, in answer to a question about whether he had voted more recently.

This exit from political participation, most easily observable through declines in voter participation, is not happening through random selection. The exit of particular age and income cohorts from political participation in elections poses a serious threat to the quality of representation in South African democracy. The choice to exit based on income and age means that there is a systematic lack of voices from concentrated populations with specific interests (Schulz-Herzenberg 2014).

Rejection of Politics as a Category

In addition to not participating in elections through voting, many people with whom I spoke actually shied away from the notion of discussing politics, because the word itself had such negative connotations. This rejection of politics, like nonvoting, was most concentrated among younger South Africans. In concert with the statistical evidence of lower voter participation, the sentiment of rejection of democratic politics indicates a sense of alienation from democratic politics both emotionally and practically.

The most important thing I learned early in the process of setting up interviews was to avoid the word "politics" as much as possible in describing my research. One early interview participant, an Afrikaans-speaking woman in her late twenties, on completing our interview, said "Oh, that was actually kind of fun. I am sorry I have to go now. When you said you wanted to talk about politics, I figured this would be awful." Across the spectrum of ethnolinguistic group, gender, and location, the majority of people who participated in interviews reacted negatively to the idea of "politics" as a category of activity, linking it with corruption, selfishness, dirtiness, and fighting.

For some Zulu-speaking South Africans, the dissatisfaction with "politics" is linked to the fact that the post-apartheid government for which many of them fought, has not materially or experientially changed their lives. One Zulu-speaking man in his mid-thirties, who had grown up in the rural areas in northern KwaZulu-Natal, spoke about what it was like to go to the places where he had grown up, and the view of politics from there.

> If you go to the rural areas, things may not have changed as much. In the city and the township, that is where we are modern. In the rural areas, it is the same as it was in the 1980s, the 1970s. Politics is for the city life. They see no change, no real difference. The school I went to is really the same as it was before. People in the village will say that nothing has changed. So why should they do politics? (094)

This sense of disappointment is linked to the sense of optimism associated with the transition and the underperformance of the government since then.

In another interview with a whole family in a township south of Durban, a similar set of topics came up. Four women of three different generations were sitting around the table with me. When I introduced myself and told them what I was hoping to talk to them about while going through the pre-interview consent protocols, the matriarch of the family, who was in her seventies, said that she did not want to talk about politics. I agreed, and started along a different line of questioning, hoping to ease into the topic. We had a conversation after that regarding *ubuZulu* (Zuluness, or the essence of being Zulu), what it means to be South African, and some memories the women had of the transition to democracy. Then came the question of what the women of the family saw as the most important problems in South Africa at the time. The matriarch responded by saying

> We have economic problems. We are supposed to be wealthy. But we are waiting to see ourselves becoming rich. The politics are blocking it. People are blocking it.
>
> Politics causes rifts. There are groups. We must belong to a group, but we do not want to be the opposition. If you look at black people with white people, the white people do not seem to fight as much. But, you see, the groups start to only belong to themselves. We become enemies, rather than being friends. Politics keeps people apart. If it were me, I would wish for no politics. They only make hatred. (082–085)

After that, with some subtlety, I was told that the interview was over. Instead, we had tea and discussed other things. This reticence about politics could be related to the party-associated violence that took place between supporters of the ANC and the IFP during the early 1990s through to the mid-2000s, both in KwaZulu-Natal and Gauteng. Indeed, party-based violence has recently flared up again, with politically motivated killings occurring more frequently in 2012–2014 (the period in which interviews were being conducted) in the rural areas of the province because of fighting between the ANC, IFP, and New Freedom Party (NFP). While the NFP was largely unsuccessful in subsequent elections, failing to qualify in 2016, and gaining only 1.57 percent in the 2019 elections, violence between the ANC and the IFP in KwaZulu-Natal has flared up intermittently around elections since 2009 (Karim and Shoba 2019).

Perhaps the most damning condemnation came from a young Zulu-speaking woman who, rather than referencing the lack of socioeconomic change, instead talked about how politics failed to solve such problems. She did reference political violence as a problem, but as an issue with which her parents dealt, not one that she currently faced. This young woman, who had until the previous year been involved in student politics, gave a set of reasons for why she had resigned:

> People think that politics is for people like Malema. That politics is what Malema does, rather than the solving of actual problems. . . . I am sure it does not help the struggle for people to step out, but I did. . . . I did not want to be associated with black people who are just fighting. . . . We would spend three hours debating one single point. But no one is listening. These problems are also there in the government. People leave [the University] to go to work with the government. They have the same mentality. . . . I do not like things being decided, and then we have to fall in line. But that is what they would expect. I need to know why decisions are being made. We need to have information, not just party discipline. (105)

She condemned politics as the kind of activities that sensationalists engage in, or as fundamentally about discipline rather than a greater good. The young woman who participated in this interview was not disengaged because of disinterest or even because she thought that politics were unimportant. She spoke about her disengagement as a kind of self-preservation. She had been deeply jaded by the student political process, and that had informed her evaluations of the democratic process. She had, by her own account, stopped being angry about the frustrations of politics, and instead had simply become resigned to the fact that politics was "just like that."

Afrikaans speakers also had a negative view of politics, but for a different set of reasons. Many Afrikaans-speakers, as discussed above, saw electoral politics as a racial census in which they would perpetually lose. In addition to this negative view of electoral politics, many Afrikaans speakers discussed politics as something that causes disorder and violent conflict, among other things. One man in his late thirties from Bloemfontein, when asked what the biggest political challenges in the country were, said, "Politics are just a waste of time and money. It makes people angry" (073). Another young man, one who was more predisposed to explain his answers, echoed many of the same sentiments when he said

Politics itself is a challenge. Politics destroys everything that has a chance to work. Look at Marikana; that is politics. People are saying, "white men own all the mines" as a way to score political points. Afrikaners use the poor performance of small farms as a political issue. Everyone sees politics that way. Service delivery ends up being about apartheid. Politics are the root of all evil in South Africa. I just do not mix with politics. (076)

Other interview participants were not so balanced in their condemnation of politics. One young man, who lived and worked on a farm outside of the city, when asked what his impressions of the government were, said "Blacks are prepared to mess it up for everyone here. They have nothing to lose. That is what makes politics here. It determines politics" (038). Although obviously prejudiced, this man's sentiments are mirrored in the more balanced quotes listed above. For many Afrikaans speakers (in addition to the Zulu speakers discussed above), there seemed to be a consensus that politics itself caused problems and destroyed what could, in a somehow apolitical counterfactual, have been a better situation.

One Afrikaans-speaking woman explained it concisely. When asked if she believed that anyone spoke for her in the realm of politics, she responded,

Solidariteit and AfriForum go overboard. The Woolworth's campaign was ridiculous.[11] Their take on government is extreme. But what they are saying should not be taken lightly. There are a lot of people listening to them. There are so few voices speaking on behalf of people like me. There is not really a wide range of voices. We are so desperate for a savior that we will take up anyone at this point. . . . People have no passion for politics. There is no pride in politics. (028)

Where the distaste for politics was possibly the most pronounced was among those Afrikaans speakers with whom I spoke, who work directly in lobbying the government or advancing certain causes; in other words, those who work in politics. One man with whom I spoke at his office in Pretoria, whose organization directly lobbies the government to shape policy and advocate for the interests of their dues-paying membership, when asked whether he would consider his work political, said "Politics, no, no. We are afraid of being labeled as political. We are not into politics or parties" (033). When asked about the Afrikaans cultural festivals (discussed in greater detail in chapter 6), a man involved in fundraising for a local monument committee, who said he often spoke to the city council and was a leader of what he termed a "civic organization," and whose son was involved in local electoral politics, said, "[The festivals are] also important because Afrikaans singers there, they are the mouthpiece of the Afrikaner nowadays, more so than say, political leaders. Political leaders have had their time. They are in the backseat in the new dispensation" (003).

Another young man, who described himself as a "field organizer" for AfriForum, a group that describes itself as a "civil rights watchdog" and has engaged in legal action against members of the ruling party in free-speech/ hate-speech cases (Modiri 2013), when asked about the organization's politics, said, "We are apolitical. We do not care who governs. We just want them to govern properly. We want to stay out of politics. In democracy, the needs of the many outweigh the needs of the few. We need someone who will speak on behalf of the few" (018). A young woman from the same organization, who described herself as a "campus organizer," said of the organization

No, we are avoiding doing the whole politics thing . . . we are *apolitis* (apolitical). We are not going to do things through politics, but sometimes do get involved in politics because rights and politics go hand in hand, basically. Then you get involved in a bit of politics, but we are not a political party or anything. We are a civil rights movement, and that is it. Everything with rights, that is what we do. When it comes to elections and stuff, we stand back . . . the politics of today are messy. I do not want to get involved in something that is so messy. So, this entire rights thing is the answer to us . . . and not politics. (010)

Indeed, the organization in 2013–2014 put up recruitment posters on a number of campuses around South Africa with Facebook-style text that said "Afri-Forum: Jislaaik [Thumbs up/Wow/Great], Politiek: Dislaaik [Dislike/Thumbs Down]."

This overall rejection of "politics" as a category of activity is a strategy adopted by groups representing many likely nonvoters, especially Afrikaans speakers (Afriforum), the poor (Abahlali baseMjondolo), and young people (the #RhodesMustFall and #FeesMustFall movements). In each case, these groups eschew "politics" as a label because of the associated contamination or lack of efficacy associated with direct engagement with partisan politics. However, by taking their activities from institutional contestation to non-institutionalized forms of dissent such as protests, such groups have also avoided any institutional incentives for cooperation (Holmes 2019). What seems to be clear is that, in many ways, "politics," whether understood as economics- or party-based, is a category of activity for which many South Africans hold a distinct distain. Given that twenty years ago, there was what many scholars have called election "euphoria," the pessimism about politics and the ability of political leaders to create positive change, and the rejection of politics as a potentially positive force, are noteworthy. This rejection of politics, paired with decreasing voter registration and voter turnout, signal a disillusionment with democratic mechanisms that could potentially be detrimental to the overall quality and character of South African democracy.

Emigration

Another, and more literal, kind of exit from politics that came up quite often during interviews with Afrikaans speakers was the question of emigration. In the first twenty years of multiracial democracy in South Africa, a significant percentage of white South Africans have left the country to live (mostly) in the United States, Australia, New Zealand, and to a lesser extent, the Netherlands. According to statistics compiled by the South African Institute of Race Relations, the white population of South Africa shrunk by more than 16 percent between 1995 and 2005 (Andrucki 2010, 359). A number of different scholars have offered reasons for the large number of émigrés, including alienation (Griffiths and Prozesky 2010; DeGelder 2004) and as a reaction to crime (De Klerk and Barkhuizen 2004). Melissa Steyn claims that, in fact, white South African identity is in many ways defined as a diaspora, insofar as "White South Africans draw toward white people elsewhere: 'home' is where other whites are" (Steyn 2012, 126–27). Yet, Steyn cautions, many White South Africans feel alien when traveling to Europe because of cultural differences, and fail to find the kind of racialized home community that they had believed would exist to welcome them.

What, then, is the reaction both to the individuals leaving, and to their role in defining South Africa, among South Africans who chose to stay in the country? Emigration, it turned out, was one of the most fruitful and engaging topics in the course of my interviews. Unlike "politics," for which so many felt distain or indifference, emigration as a topic among Afrikaans-speaking interview participants never failed to elicit a reaction, and often a strong one. But the decision to leave, or indeed, to stay, has taken on a political cast because of how many people have left from such a relatively small population. Almost all of the Afrikaans speakers with whom I spoke had a close acquaintance, family member, or friend who had emigrated. As such, there were many opinions about the causes and effects of emigration.

For some Afrikaans-speakers, emigration was a kind of betrayal that they adamantly opposed. To justify this position, many referenced the fact that their ancestors had lived in South Africa for generations. The betrayal of emigration, then, was of the Afrikaner *volk* as an ethnic group. For the people who tended to be more conservative in their political leanings, and more pessimistic about the future of the country, the tone of their rejection of emigration as a path bordered on the defensive. One young woman, who belonged to a political party identified by other interview participants as "far right," said, "I have considered leaving, but I know I would come back. People died so I could be here. Look at the concentration camps. Look at the wars. It would be like a slap in the face to them to leave this country" (020). A man in his mid-seventies who belonged to a similar political party had quite an angry reaction to my question regarding emigration. He said "Emigration is not an option or a solution. We are not just settlers, but '*n volk*. There are two streams of development for the Afrikaner. There are those that choose materialism, and those that choose *volksidentiteit* [people's or ethnic identity]. The *volksidentiteit* is here" (012).

There were also those who held more centrist views who talked about emigration as a kind of betrayal, not of the *volk*, but of the new South African project. One woman in her early sixties, who described her line of work as "transformation and reconciliation," when asked her opinions on emigration, said "I have a future here. I was born here. My culture and my traditions are here. This is my country. I am proud to be South African, regardless of the circumstances. I will never emigrate. I will not run away or leave" (068). In another focus group with three people outside of Bloemfontein, a man in his mid-fifties said that the only important word to describe him, besides being a Christian, was to call himself South African, and that he sought to overcome the sins of his ancestors. When asked about the issue of emigration, he said,

> It is a chicken run. . . . They are welcome to go. If they do not believe in this country, then good riddance. This country is rebuilding. There is this idea that some people say: "We work for monopoly money. We could make more overseas." But it is only really true for a minority. But when they leave, they can still vote. [*What do you think about the foreign vote?*] If you do not stay, why should you have a say? It should not even be considered. We have family overseas. We agree to disagree on most things. We will not ever share one

another's viewpoints. If you want to go, then go. But then, you do not have anything to say about us. (061–063)

This approach, of seeing emigration as a kind of betrayal, was, as discussed above, not directly connected to the political viewpoints of the speaker, except that it tended to appear largely at opposite ends of the political spectrum.

By contrast, people who held somewhat more moderate political opinions tended to hedge their bets more when it came to the question of emigration. In general, these individuals tended to offer both positive and negative evaluations of the present political situation. One small business owner in Bloemfontein, when asked what he thought about emigration, responded

> Emigration is fear driven. There is a fear of everything. Fear for safety, fear of economic instability. My daughters will not stay here. There is no place for them. . . . Emigration is always a talking point. It is always in the back of your mind. You are always thinking: How can you get your money out? How would you afford the move? How would you support yourself? There is always a Plan B. It is always in the back of your mind. (049–050)

Another woman in her early forties was very conflicted about the phenomenon of emigration and how to respond to it. When asked if she knew people who had emigrated, she responded that yes, she knew people who had left, and that when she came back from living abroad briefly she had been unsure about whether she would stay. She took quite a bit of time, but then said, "I am struggling with the idea of loyalty as a civic virtue. There is a responsibility to contribute [*trails off*] . . ." (080). When I asked the follow-up question of whether she had ever considered emigrating, she responded, "I would be dishonest if I said I did not think it would be nice. Of course, I have thought of it. Everyone has" (080).

Perhaps the most conflicted answer came from a young man I spoke with in Bloemfontein who was a student at the University of the Free State but who had grown up in the rural areas outside of the city on a family farm. When asked if he knew anyone who had left, he said that yes, he had two family members who had moved abroad. After a brief pause, he added "I do blame them. We have to stand together. . . . But if I get a chance, I am leaving. Right now, the farm is keeping me here. It will not get better here, maybe for fifty years. . . . If, by the end of [my education], there are no jobs for me, then I would think about leaving. But I am angry about leaving" (047). In the room, at the time, there was a significant feeling of awkwardness when this exchange ended, in large part because of the emotion behind the words in an otherwise fairly calm interview.

So why, then, do people leave? This was a central question I wanted interview participants to answer in the section on emigration. As alluded to above, a number of interview participants referenced specific, concrete reasons for emigration. The most commonly cited issues were crime and affirmative-action policies, which many Afrikaans-speaking participants saw as insurmountable obstacles to employment. These evaluations were present, regardless of the political affiliation or attitude toward emigration of the person giving them. Those who referenced crime often spoke of it in terms of the immediate issue of feeling safe themselves, rather than in terms of widespread social problems. According to one older Afrikaans-speaking woman, when asked why she thought people were emigrating, said,

> Personally, I have never considered leaving. I thought of it, but I do not see myself going anywhere. . . . If you are born here and you love the country, you still feel like you belong here, even with the crime. Crime is part of our lives. If we all sit down and cry about everything, you will just lose it. We have become hard people. You do not always see it, but we all know someone who has been a victim. (075)

Another woman, in her early twenties, when asked the same question, responded,

> I guess some people just decide they do not want this life anymore. . . . I would really consider it also. Not right now because my family is here, but if I would have my own children, I would really consider it. Do you want your kids to grow up in this culture of violence? Being scared all the time? Maybe not scared all the time, but having in the back of your head that you can be attacked. I think people are almost fleeing the country in a way. I do not think it is because they want to. . . . It is not because they think "South Africa is below me," or anything like that. It is about jobs and then it is about fleeing, literally running away from it because you just cannot deal with it. I think that is it. (013)

The theme of thinking of children and the future came up repeatedly, along with concerns about crime and employment issues. One woman in her early forties, who had talked about her anti-apartheid activism and the incredible feeling of voting for the first time in 1994, when asked why she thought people emigrated, said

> A lot of things we do are dependent on our ideas of the future for our children. People leave because of crime. Under apartheid, white society was safe . . . more than half of my school colleagues have left. It is a major loss, of skills and people. I have left the position where I thought that emigration was unpatriotic. I see that there is a major loss of money, skills, training. But also, now I see my nephews. I am quite frustrated that my sisters with children are not leaving. They did not leave when their children were very young, so the children are very South African. Now, leaving would be a loss. They should have left earlier. (032)

This response was surprising. In the course of the interview, this participant had said repeatedly that she hoped for better things in South Africa, that she was committed to working for future betterment, and that she was personally involved with programs aimed at bringing about transformation or reconciliation. She was also actively involved in politics. Yet when it came to the future, to the children, she wished that they had left. Since, she added, she had no children of her own, she did not feel the same way about her own situation.

Perhaps, however, the most subtle answers to the questions about emigration were the ones from people who believed that emigration stemmed, as theorized by Griffiths and Prozesky (2010), De Gelder (2004), and Van Rooyen (2000), from a larger sense of alienation among white Afrikaans speakers. The issue of alienation did come up with some frequency among Afrikaans-speaking interview participants, when asked about emigration. When asked why people leave, one pair of Afrikaans speakers, a man and a woman in their early forties, agreed, "Lots of people believe they have no future here," but the man added, "I personally could not leave. I am too much of a South African" (024–025). Another man in his mid-twenties said on the issue, "People leave because of crime, because of corruption. But also, people do not see a future here. . . . It is good and bad. We lose skills. The fact is that people are leaving because they must. . . . People leaving because they do not see a future should just leave. You cannot build a future on negativity. It is easier to build a country with positivity" (054).

Other interview participants framed the alienation more in terms of their own experience. One woman in her mid-fifties, when asked why she thought people emigrated, responded by saying, "It feels like the Afrikaner people are getting suppressed and we do not count anymore. Look at Malema and what he says. People are leaving because they are getting cold feet. Malema makes me nervous. The songs that he sings scare us.[12] It is sort of shocking. Farmers are murdered because of those songs" (064).

Another Afrikaans-speaking man in his mid-sixties gave a deep sigh when asked the question about emigration. He paused, and then elaborated:

> There really is a feeling that we are not welcome here. Just look at the farm murders.[13] The majority of the people that are killed are white. What effects does that have? How can we feel about that? Trauma is the leitmotif of South Africa. You cannot understand South Africa without trauma or fear. Fear of the police, fear of crime and the criminality in the place . . . We are not welcome. Unfortunately, it is probably true that many people do feel that way. There is a lack of belonging, a lack of ownership. A certain thread is broken. Then it is easier to leave. A certain percentage of Afrikaans-speaking people really feel that they do not belong. When icons, like that boxer, are murdered,[14] it is terrible. There is a loss on a personal level, but there are also wider psychological implications. (035)

Emigration, then, is a deeply political topic. Whether it is understood as a betrayal of an ethnic or national project, a response to policies, or disengagement because of disillusionment with the new democracy, the issue of emigration touches on a large variety of deeply political undercurrents in Afrikaans-speaking society. The loss of skills and training that go with this exit from South Africa are enormous, especially since those who leave tend to be from high-skills professions.[15]

Emigration, like the alienation from politics and the decline in voter participation discussed above, is an exit by a non–randomly selected group of individuals from the political process. In their exit, the cohort of émigrés, being concentrated among white Afrikaans speakers, changes the dynamic of South African democracy and opens the possibilities for larger-scale exit. Perhaps more urgently, however, it is a statement about the imagined possibilities for Afrikaans speakers within the context of both the democratic and nation-building projects in South Africa.

CONCLUSION

The aspiration toward democracy and the practice of regular elections have long histories in South Africa. Although largely noncompetitive, post-apartheid national elections have been regular, free, and fair, defying the expectations of many scholars of the struggle years. But what is the effect of such political processes on building a national community?

In both large-N and qualitative work, there is some reason to doubt the community-building potential of South African elections, especially when it comes to ameliorating the effects of racial divides. Both individual voter choice and the strategies of political parties writ large tend to reinforce racial cleavages. Although it is not a simplistic racial census, individual vote choice does rely largely on perceived racial exclusivity and racialized party labels. Parties themselves draw on these divides to shore up their voter bases and undermine opposition. Large-scale political support for opposition and tolerance of democratic contestation is, in many ways, thin.

Perhaps more troubling, however, are the ways in which such political functioning has led to the exit from politics of key and concentrated constituencies, such as the poor and the relatively young, who tend to vote less frequently and express greater alienation from democratic processes. The exit of a significant proportion of Afrikaans speakers, and the contemplation of exit by many more, also poses a real challenge to the notion of large-scale nation-building for all citizens. All of these modes of exit carry attendant costs and consequences for representative democracy, but also demonstrate a level of frustration or perceived inefficacy on the part of large groups of citizens.

By reaffirming such social divisions, then, the processes of democracy foreclose the possibility of forgetting them, and provide a regular, national arena in which such cleavages can be exploited and made salient based on issues of the moment. Politics becomes inherently racialized, and the practice of democracy, both in the voting booth and in citizens' other daily political choices, becomes inseparable from their racial perspective. Citizens' sense of disaffection from politics, manifested in some form of exit, limits the possibilities for democratic representation and community-building. Far from exemplifying the collective forgetting prescribed by Renan and Billig, national elections in South Africa have been an occasion to remember, and to re-inscribe, difference.

CHAPTER 5

The Social Logic of Nation-Building
Navigating Race and Gender

The strange truth that seems to be elided in much mainstream scholarship on nation-building and postconflict transitions is just how intimate the prospect of nation-building is. The cessation of hostilities involves disengagement. To work with and live alongside the people with whom you have fought, or the people you formerly believed were enemies, is not easy, even if the legal-institutional change from enemy to coequal citizen happens quickly. It requires a new way of engaging, of both remembering and forgetting. The point of nation-building projects is deeply personal, contingent on both how people conduct their private lives and the social imagination they use to define their own communities. This sense of community is foundational to binding a nation together. Democracies likewise depend on trust, both among citizens and between citizens and their government. Trust undergirds losers' consent, and the restraints on majority rule underlie central democratic values. For peaceful elections to be possible, even when they are contentious, a community must have a basic sense of being bound together.

Nation-building and democratization projects, therefore, ask former enemies to forget or overcome not only histories of violence, but perceptions of threat and senses of fear associated with others, and not only to coexist, but to engage. The nation is dependent on both the fact of actual socialization and the imagined communion of people across distance and time, and also across social cleavages. Democracy depends on a fundamental trust of people with whom you disagree. Therefore, the processes of nation- and democracy-building involve the personal choices that individuals make about the people with whom they socialize, the spaces in which they live, and the ways in which they participate in communal life.

The apartheid state apparatus was intensely concerned with policing race and gender roles, and committed to a level of brutality in maintaining the "purity" of both the white race and white women's bodies. Total segregation was the central goal, maintained through state-sponsored brutality. While the segregation and brutality of apartheid were driven by state policy, there were also ways in which individuals created and maintained the social order associated with these governmental priorities. As such, the transition from apartheid to multiracial democracy was one in which legal prohibitions against interracial conflict were overturned, but overcoming the social dimensions of divisions created and sustained by prior regimes presents a major challenge to nation-building in South Africa. The divisions are being erased, but also remembered and recreated, in micro-level social processes of association and disassociation.

Given the continuity of people's lives throughout the period of the transition, it is no wonder that reversal of social imperatives at the end of apartheid and the beginning of multiracial democracy came as something of a shock. One Afrikaans-speaking interview participant referenced the way her mother had spoken about the transition to explain how that personal discomfort affected the process of nation-building during the transition:

> My mother made the comparison between the transition from apartheid and a wedding night. Before the wedding, you are told that sex is dirty and bad and all of that. Now, with a wedding night, that is all supposed to disappear. Now you are not just okay having sex, you are supposed to have it. It was the same with the transition from apartheid. Overnight, all these prohibitions were reversed, but people were still scared, and still held on to some of the same beliefs. (016)

The process of transition was understood as intimate, in all senses of the word. In invoking the image of a bride on her wedding night, the speaker's mother signaled the new moral landscape of multiracial democracy. No one had forgotten their prior lives, but the imperatives had shifted. What had been forbidden was now expected, but that shift had not erased the memories of the prohibition, and the fears and threats associated with it.

The animating question, then, is how do South Africans primarily think of their social relationships after twenty years? Do the racial and gendered orders of the colonial and apartheid eras eclipse the integrative ambitions of the transition? Or have the institutional changes of the new democratic order also shaped the private lives of citizens in ways that are consonant with the aspirations of nation-building? After a short discussion of the ontology of separation under the colonial and apartheid regimes, the chapter will address the possibilities and challenges of interpersonal nation-building by considering how interview participants reflected on their gendered and racialized experiences of engagement with one another. These studies show how individuals' perceptions of communal threat and communal boundaries supersede the empirical realities of vulnerability to unemployment or violent crime, and as such, shore up boundaries between communities that are consonant with the gendered and racial divisions of the past.

GENDER AND RACE FROM APARTHEID TO POST-APARTHEID

The long history of combined gendered and racial domination through the system of apartheid manifested itself in a variety of ways, but all were aimed at shoring up a white, masculine state to protect a threatened sphere of white, feminine domesticity. The fact that the apartheid state had a vested interest in policing racial boundaries and hierarchies is clear in the state's pursuit of pass laws,[1] the creation of nominally autonomous Bantustans, and the laws demarcating public goods for one group or another. Yet contained within the structures of both the apartheid government and the colonial administrations was also a deep anxiety about protecting women and maintaining gender roles, both archetypal and actual.

Despite the metalogic of apartheid's separateness, the domestic sphere of white, middle-class South Africans under National Party rule was rife with interracial contact, albeit one imbued with hierarchy and dependence. The violence of apartheid was manifested not only in the soul-cramping categorizations and reservations of race categories, or in the physical brutality of security forces, but in the intimate and quotidian racism of the household arrangements of white madams and black maids (Cock 1980; du Plessis 2011). This racialized system of domestic labor continues, and is in many ways "the last bastion of apartheid" in contemporary South African life (Fish 2006).

One interview participant in Bloemfontein meaningfully noted that the first time she had spoken to a black person was in 1991. No, she quickly corrected herself, the first black person who was not a "domestic servant" with whom she had a conversation was in 1991 (080). The differences, then, were in her ability to identify the fact that she had spoken to people of color prior to liberalization, but that it was never actually a "conversation."

This, then, was the central point of apartheid. In his book *Waiting: The Whites of South Africa*, Vincent Crapanzano summarizes the effects of the apartheid system by saying

> [Apartheid] is more than a political stance. It is more than a response to a particular economic arrangement. It is an ontology that affects the very being of its adherents. Apartheid is the product of an essentialist racism in which people of color are considered to be *quintessentially* different from whites . . . this difference is preserved through distance. Apartheid precludes any contact with people of different races that might undermine the assumption of essential difference. Interracial residence, marriage, sexual relations, political gatherings, sports, entertainment (in the dark of the cinema, at bars and nightclubs, at the beach), toilets, elevators, waiting in line . . . traveling on buses and trains, eating—in short, any situation in which bodily contact between members of difference races is possible—have been precluded. Bodily contact is considered polluting. . . . It is considered very dangerous. Fear of assault, rape, and murder is widespread. . . . The body of the other simply cannot be acknowledged. (Crapanzano 1985, 39–40)

The very personal and physical goals of complete separation of race groups, in the name of protecting a heteronormative racio-social order, involved an erasure of black bodies from the places occupied by whites. It involved, in the words of Nadine Gordimer, the development of a "habit" of "*not seeing*," an un-recognition of the entirety of the black population, in the name of preserving the whites (Gordimer 1983). Leaders of the anti-apartheid struggle, in calling for a unified South Africa, then, were demanding much more than simple suffrage or freedom of movement. Fundamentally, the campaign aimed at rejecting the nominal independence of the Bantustans and uniting South Africa was a demand for equal recognition and cohumanity.

INTERPERSONAL NATION-BUILDING: GENDERED RELATIONSHIPS AND RACIALIZED SOCIAL LIVES

Given the ways that apartheid, and the preceding colonial regime, focused on physical segregation to achieve a more ambient and pervasive separation of

sification, which mapped neatly onto and reinforced existing hierarchies of class, language, and place (Posel 2001). The lived experience of racial categorization, then, has reproduced itself out of this "natural" logic in the post-apartheid era, so much so that Gerhard Maré observed, "People carry South African identity documents and passports, pay taxes, accept the powers of the police and courts, argue over the independence of the judiciary. And all the time 'race' remains, confirmed as the common sense of the essence of social identity" (Maré 2005, 509). Put another way by a Zulu-speaking interview participant from Durban, "We can hardly do something in this country without it being about race" (107). The persistence of race as a determinant of social life, as a fundamental societal division, was for many interview participants, the central point of continuity with the apartheid era.

This sense, that the logic of race permeated the daily lives of South Africans, was acknowledged in the context of interviews. One Afrikaans-speaking participant said frankly, "It is not possible to imagine a time when race will not matter" (032). Race, with its history as a basis of social mobilization, privilege, and requirements, remains a difficult boundary to cross in South Africa. But beyond simply being a relic of the past, the importance of racial divisions according to some interview participants is recreated and reemphasized in the post-apartheid era. According to one Zulu-speaking young man, "After 1994, white people became the enemy. . . . If you were white and supported the struggle [against apartheid], you are still the enemy now. That is just the truth" (055).

Although race came up often during the interviews, statements of blatant racial chauvinism were rare in the interview space. Occasionally, people expressed clearly unreformed racist statements, such as "The Afrikaners now are afraid of being labeled as racist. But race is a reality. What they mean by racism is looking down on other races . . . looking down on them because we think we are better or more clever, which we are. But we must not say that anymore in public" (009), or "If I think about blacks as a group, I tend not to like them. But I treat individuals as I would treat anyone. The vast majority of whites are the same way" (026). These expressions were the outliers. Often, race talk came in the form of comparisons, either with the United States or with the prior government. One example, which came in the midst of a very contentious interview with a young man in Bloemfontein, is particularly illustrative. After a series of questions about how he defined himself and what his opinions were of the ANC-led government, he interjected,

Well, what about you, eh? What about apartheid stuff in other countries? What about in the US? I met with students from Minnesota in the US. They blamed a lot of things on apartheid. There are lots of countries where blacks and whites were separated. What were the mistakes we made? The name and the laws. The rest of the world accepts separation as a given. I am not saying it was right, but I did not have anything to do with it. What is the difference between saying *n****r* and saying *kaffir*? Only that ours lasted longer. (054)

The accusations here are complex, regarding my hypocrisy as a researcher coming from a country with a difficult history of race relations, and the view that the apartheid state is only culpable of lasting too long with white minority government, rather than more substantial wrongdoings. I had no real rejoinder, and merely said that yes, the US had a long history of racial injustice and racism. Shortly after the above statement, the interview concluded.

As often as the issue of personal anger over racial issues came up, a more common response among young Afrikaans speakers in Bloemfontein was sense of deep ambivalence. Generational differences with regard to race relations were often referenced as a source of difficulty within families, similar to the issues referenced above with families feeling dishonored by the TRC. One young woman talked through the complexities in her relationship with her father, an Afrikaans-speaking farmer, during the course of one particularly memorable interview. She said,

If I have to tell my dad that I have black friends, he will get uncomfortable. For him, that is wrong, in a way. But they accept it because they realize that we are in a different era. But, it is difficult for them to take that in. . . . You know, we grew up like that. On the farm, with my Dad and the black people and the way they treated them . . . they never hurt them, physically, but they mistreated them. . . . For me, that was normal, because I did not know anything else. . . . That is the way you are taught, from the beginning, that black people are inferior . . . it is just the way it is. No one, when you are three, four, or five years old is going to tell you, "Listen, this is wrong," because that is where you are. That is where you were brought up. So, it is only when you grow older and you reach a stage where you think "Okay, this cannot be right," that you have to reconcile that with who your parents are, who they still are, in a way. . . . You know, I love my dad, but you have to reconcile that . . . it is a very difficult thing. . . . But, I think because I grew up with it and because it was so normal for me, it does not make me love my father and grandfather any less. It is not like they are lowered in my estimation. Maybe they should be. [long pause] I do not know. But, they are not, because that is just the way it is. (013)

For this young woman, it was difficult to parse out the different aspects of her father. He had racial prejudices. He was not comfortable with her black friends. Yet, he was still her family. At the interview, she asked me what I thought she should do. I responded, honestly, that I did not know.

In the course of another interview, a teacher in Bloemfontein recounted the story of a student taking care of her house being attacked because it was assumed he was breaking into her house. She said, "I had a student come to take care of my dog here in Bloem. I was away on holiday, and he needed some pocket money. He is Basotho. My neighbors set their dogs on him. They said his blood was the wrong color. That he must be breaking in. They eventually made peace once they spoke with me. But I was really furious" (042). The differences in age between this teacher and her neighbors were referenced as one reason why they had such different opinions on race. Yet generational differences were not the only vector through which people in the Free State discussed racism, or racial issues.

During another interview, a young woman shared a story of two of her friends, and how their racial prejudices and self-identifications shaped the ways that they built their family. She recounted the following story relatively dispassionately:

I had white friends in Pretoria who got married, and had a baby who was born black. The father demanded a paternity test, and it was determined that he was the child's father. Way back in their past, his great-grandfather had slept with the domestic help, or something.[2] Turns out, he is actually coloured. The baby looked very black. They eventually gave up the child. They gave it to the domestic worker to raise, and sent her back to her people with some money. It was sad. [*Long pause*] Ja, very sad. (016)

This story, which came at the very end of the interview, was not as a response to a question and was told without embarrassment. It was a shame, she seemed to say, that such things would have to happen. So deep, then, is the racial logic of self-identification, as evidenced by the phrase "he is *actually* coloured," in the minds of this young woman's friends that they could not accept their own child, since he or she appeared to be from a different racial background.

Whether an artifact of the past, or a division continually recreated, these interview participants' discussions of race seem to indicate the centrality of the logic of apartheid in the ways that people define their social and private lives. If indeed a nation is an imagined community, the centrality of race as the logic governing people's lives indicates that the social imagination in the post-apartheid state has fallen short of the ambitions of integration. Divides are remembered, and recreated, in quotidian and dramatic ways, and as such, are newly relevant in the democratic dispensation.

ECONOMIC THREAT AND REDRESS IN TERMS OF RACE

This persistence and reinforcement of race logic is due, in large part, to the fact that race continues to overlap with other social divisions—such as class— in ways that seem to make race a "commonsensical" way to identify self and others in the post-apartheid democracy. According to one Zulu-speaking interview participant,

> You cannot negate race. It is part of the fabric of the country. There is always a history of colonialism, apartheid, and race at the center. We need to make certain concessions. We need to not add the race dimension, but ensure that black people are on par with the previously advantaged South Africans. (081)

For many people, the socioeconomic realities of post-apartheid South Africa resemble those from the previous regime, or indeed reflect a greater degree of economic inequality between racially defined communities than before (see, for example, Özler 2007).

Embedded within populist anti-apartheid protest movements were broadly based demands for economic reform (Zuern 2011). These demands were integral to many protesters' notions of democracy, and socioeconomic redress was, for many previously disadvantaged South Africans, an essential part of the project of reconciliation and nation-building. This viewpoint was articulated in an interview with a Zulu-speaking man in Durban, when he linked the reconciliation project of Mandela with the project of employment redress under Mbeki, and credited the ANC with inspiring both. He said, "The world has made Mandela a saint. His task was to reconcile the people. It was from the instructions of the ANC, not the goodness of his heart. Mbeki also had an ANC mandate, to implement BEE [Black Economic Empowerment]. This was the next step in reconciliation" (108). Such programs were, implicitly, nation-building initiatives aimed at promoting a more equitable society.

To try to address past discrimination, the post-apartheid government has continued to rely on racial categories for a variety of programs aimed at promoting equity. Affirmative action measures such as BEE, along with other governmental functions such as taking the census and producing other statistical records, still rely on the racial categories defined under the apartheid government. The continued use of these classifications, it has been argued, is necessary because systematic injustices perpetrated along racial lines require that redress be allocated along the same lines. It is obviously difficult to dismantle the ills of a deeply racist system like apartheid without reference to the racial categories it used to impose such unequal and discriminatory conditions. As such, while nominally nonracial, the ANC-led government has pursued a number of policies in terms of the racial categorizations inherited from the apartheid regime. One Zulu-speaking interview participant characterized these continuities as "problematic," saying "We cannot build a new nation on the basis of colonial designs. The logic of the new nation must be different. . . . Now we have the same identities as before, but they exist in a better context" (092).

Yet the idea that the context changes how the categories operate was not universally accepted. For many interview participants in Bloemfontein, this continuation of the use of racial categories indicates a continuity of the social logic of apartheid. Several interview participants used the phrase "reverse apartheid" to describe redress programs, most often BEE programs.[3] One young woman said,

> It has been a long time since apartheid. Now we have BEE, which is unfair. It is apartheid in reverse. Now we will need reconciliation all over again, but in reverse. People are angry all over again. . . . Now we have black on white racism. Color and culture still have unfair advantages, but now they work against us. (016)

Another Afrikaans-speaking small-business owner alleged that such redress programs actually cut into his business, saying, "We do not get government jobs. My skin is the wrong color. Even though I am 100 percent BEE compliant, I do not get contracts" (077).

This view of BEE and redress programs was not limited to people who perceived such programs as personally economically detrimental. Indeed, many participants noted that things had changed for the better since the end of apartheid. One Afrikaans-speaking woman, when asked what had changed with the instantiation of the new government, said

> Since 1994, some things have changed for the better. Now, on paper, we have equal opportunity. But things are turning around now. It is like apartheid in reverse, with employment discrimination and all. . . . White people just do not have opportunities now. Look at the Woolworth's thing. The people listed in that advert are welcome.[4] But it is like they are saying "We do not want you." It is easy for them. They make it hard for us. (020)

Another participant referenced redistribution in an angry tone, saying

> Rather than focus all their attention on achievements, they still harp on the fact that most of the money is in white hands. They still want to make people aware of the race issue. Do they want all the white people to hand over the keys their houses, their cars? Would that help? Would that satisfy them? The power has been taken away from the white people. We are the ethnic minority in the country. What else do they want? (066)

Another Afrikaans-speaking man, the CEO of his own small business, acknowledged that although the opening up of the economy allowed him to grow his business, he still resented the implementation of BEE. He said, "BEE is the clearest form of reversed apartheid you have ever seen. . . . But even with the law in place, we make more money than we did before" (049–050). The objection, then, to the redress programs was not about the overall level of prosperity enjoyed by the white population, but rather an objection based on the idea of who the government and the programs were designed to benefit or to "welcome," rather than a realistic threat to economic well-being.[5] Objections to redress programs, like the discussion of race and social identity above, represent a meaningful faltering of the social imagination of nation-building on the part of many Afrikaans-speaking participants in Bloemfontein, rather than a reflection of material threats to well-being.

Discussion of these redistributive programs included gender dynamics as well, because the first implementation of BEE included white women as a population category in need of employment redress, along with all "black people," a category that subsumes the prior regime's categories of Black Afri-

can, Coloured, and Indian (Burger and Jafta 2010). In 2003, with the passage
of the Broad-Based Black Economic Empowerment act, white women were
excluded from these programs. Among Afrikaans speakers who participated
in interviews, these programs were a major source of resentment, particularly
along gendered lines.

South Africa's unemployment rate has hovered around 25 percent for the
last decade, and was 24.7 percent across all age and racial groups for all quar-
ters in 2013, when many of these interviews were conducted. In the prior
decade, unemployment among the black African population has decreased
slightly, from 29.2 percent in 2003 to 28.1 percent in 2013. The white unemployment rate was been substantially lower, but in that same time period
increased from 4.8 percent in 2003 to 6.6 percent in 2013 ("National and Provincial Labour Market Trends 2003–2013" 2013). Despite these disparities,
the majority of those who brought up lack of employment as a key problem
in reconciliation were Afrikaans-speakers in Bloemfontein, and those references were overwhelmingly to the problems faced by Afrikaans men. One
young woman, when asked about whether she thought reconciliation was still
important, replied in the affirmative, and added

> You must understand. We have been at war. The fact that there was not an "of-
> ficial" war does not really mean anything. . . . People were angry at the enemy.
> Now you work with the enemy, apparently. Our men have a hard time. Thirty-
> five and forty-year-old Afrikaans men have a really hard time reconciling. It
> is because they cannot find jobs. (030)

Another young woman referenced affirmative action programs as a reason
that people she knew had emigrated. Aside from violent crime, which she
said had been experienced by people in her family, many people emigrated
for employment opportunities. When asked which sorts of people these
programs affected, she responded, "White men here are having real trouble
finding work" (029). Both young women, although in different contexts, referenced employment problems as a central problem in the process of reconciliation and nation-building. These references were made despite the
fact that white men are statistically the least likely population to experience
unemployment.

But Afrikaans speakers often framed the problems with programs such
as Black Economic Empowerment as not just that people were without work,
but that people expressed a deeper, more insidious feeling of being outside of
the new South Africa. One young Afrikaans-speaking man put it this way:

There is definitely a feeling that we are not wanted, being male and Afrikaans. Black people will blame you for the sins of your father. It is only going to get worse for me. It is worse for men than for women. The ladies are more liberal. They make friends with other ladies more easily. There are less opportunities for men. We are forced into a corner. (039)

✓ plural iden. don't help him

The multifaceted nature of this young man is such that his identities as male and Afrikaans alienate him from the new South African project, and provide him with the basis for his own pessimism. His gendered identity is what may prevent him from making connections across raced lines. He suggests that women have more opportunities to forge connections among themselves. The construction of manhood, within the Afrikaner community, is what constrains this young man's actions.

Yet another Afrikaans-speaking interview participant, this one a woman, notes how gendered-racial identity constrains the actions of her and her friends.

White women will not give instructions to a black man. A friend of mine got called in to the office to make tea on a Sunday. Her boss [a black man] called her in to the office when he was having a small meeting, just to make tea for them. On a Sunday. They are just making a point. They are saying "I am in charge, and you are nothing." That is what happens now. (074)

The constraints for this interview participant, then, were also because of a combination of racial and gendered identities. Her identity as a white woman precludes certain kinds of behaviors, especially with black men.

DEFENDING OUR FAMILIES: CRIME, GENDER, AND RACIALIZED THREAT PERCEPTION

South Africa does have an obstinate problem with violent crime (see, for example, "Explaining the Official Crime Statistics for 2012/2013" 2013). Yet references to crime from Zulu-speaking interview participants differed from those of their Afrikaans-speaking counterparts. In general, the Afrikaans speakers expressed more fear, used more expressive language, and weighted the problems of crime more heavily in their evaluations of the ANC-led government than did Zulu speakers.

This is not to suggest that crime did not come up during conversations with Zulu speakers. It did, but the participants who brought up the topic often downplayed the frequency or severity of crime. One Zulu-speaking man in Durban said, "If you talk about crime, we know we have too much, but it is not as bad as people always say it is" (107). Another woman said, "You see the issue of crime. People think you cannot even sleep at night, or that we are always and constantly afraid. It is all very melodramatic" (099).

Participants who did reference crime as a serious issue or as a problem with the government did not use similarly charged language, instead choosing to look at the humanity of those committing crimes. One older Zulu-speaking man said "Yes, crime is very high. There is a lot of human destruction, but the government is too soft toward the criminals" (090). Another Zulu-speaking man suggested that if the government had focused on training and skills building or opening up the possibilities for class mobility, rather than focusing on reconciliation, "we would already have skilled people. We would not have the crime that we do. Crime here is because people are stealing bread to eat" (108). By framing crime as a problem of economic justice or a humanitarian concern, these speakers understand the criminals and the threat posed to their own health and safety in a significantly different way than their Afrikaans counterparts.

Afrikaans-speaking participants, by contrast, used words such as "slaughter" and "massacre" to describe incidents of violent crime. According to one interview participant,

> I have not been severely affected by crime. . . . My car has not been stolen yet. "Yet" is the key word. My family has not been slaughtered, yet. That is really a reality for a lot of people. You cannot stay on farms anymore, and especially in Gauteng and the bigger cities, you cannot drive around without anti-hijacking windows . . . you have a lot of people driving with bats and stuff in their cars to protect themselves, and they have pepper spray, and there are girls who walk around with Tasers. It really is a reality in our country. (001)

Another Afrikaans-speaking participant in Bloemfontein put it this way:

> At the end of last year . . . an old lady got attacked . . . right across from my friend's house. They raped her and really hurt her very badly. We are always aware. You develop an extra sense when you live here for long enough. When I come home, especially at night, and I need to get into my house, then I will always be like "Shit, I need to get in. I need to get in." And I will shake until I

get into the house. But then, when I am in, and I lock everything, then I feel fine. But you do feel vulnerable. (013)

Yet another young woman said "It is important to understand that our safety is always threatened. There is an undeclared war against whites" (020). Given the realities of violent crime in South Africa (Statistics South Africa 2017), it is not surprising that interview participants would reference crime as a conditioning factor of social life. What is interesting, however, is that the implied community of "we" and "us," most explicitly identified as "whites" in the last response but implied in the others, is invoked by this trio of unrelated Afrikaans-speaking women in response to a threat by "others."

Crime also came up when discussing the topic of why so many white South Africans have left the country. Another young woman put it this way:

People leave because they are murdered like animals. It is brutal and inhuman. You cannot do anything about it. If you say anything about it, it is racist. They kill people who speak out. It is like they want to say "This country is ours, you do not belong here." They are punishing this generation for the past. I do not know what happened in the past, and really, I do not care. (072)

Self-defense courses, offered by gyms, the University of the Free State, the local Agricultural Union, and others were advertised on campus during my stay in Bloemfontein, and were particularly targeted at young women. According to one interview participant,

Most women I know have had to go through self-defense courses. You just do not feel safe. When you are driving, you are constantly checking. You do not want to be caught unaware. As a woman, I am scared of approaching cars in carparks. They can hide underneath. You never keep anything on your seats when you are driving, in case of a smash and grab. (028)

The anxieties that this woman experienced, then, were in part a function of her gender identity, but also deeply connected to race.

The young men with whom I spoke in Bloemfontein tended to reference crime on farms and as happening to women as a primary source of anxiety about violence. One particularly enraged young man, when asked "What is important for people from outside of South Africa to understand about life here today?," went into an extended rant about crime and his family's experience with it. This conversation, with minimal interjections on my part, covered the gender and race dynamics of crime and his response to it. He said

> We had a couple of violent incidents. There were armed intruders in our house. The burglars were armed. I had to protect the women in my house. If they had gotten in, they would have raped and murdered them all. . . . I was also involved in a farm incident. We removed the attackers from the farms . . . the daughter of the farm owner had been raped. A friend of mine killed and buried a man who was attacking that farm. We did not notify the police. . . . In 2004 my sister was sent to the Eastern Cape for work. There is a lot of hostility there for whites. . . . They attempted the murder of my sister while she was there. They attacked in the hospital where she worked. The security guards hid in the office where she barricaded herself in. They were useless. I was helpless, being away from her. . . . Later, in a bar, I shoved my way through a group of young, black men. I almost got in a fight with them. I went in and punched the wall in the bathroom until my hand bled. I told my friends *"Ek haat die fokin kaffers"* [I hate the f***king kaffirs.][6] . . . I have friends and cousins that have been raped. . . . This crime is one of the main reasons I came back from the UK. I had to come back and protect my family. (026)

Palpable fear imbued conversations with many Afrikaans-speaking interview participants whenever the topic of crime came up. Many of these speakers, most of whom identified themselves as white, expressed particular anxiety over violent crime, despite experiencing such crimes at an only slightly higher rate than other groups in the country.[7]

While these differences in interpretation of threats and redress programs are not, in themselves, surprising, they signal that significant fractures exist within the national community of South Africa that accord with the cleavages of the old regime. While the policies of separation have been officially scrapped, the memory of the divisions remains strong. Such divisions, in their continuity with the past as well as their consonance with current political issues, seem to be reinforcing the lines of division between communities in ways that are not simply reducible to the empirical realities of crime or unemployment. As such, issues of threat, and particularly threat based on embodied identities, prevent both the literal coming together of South Africans within their own social lives, and the formation of a larger sense of community that transcends the divisions of the past, and the barriers of time and distance that stand in the way of nation building on a large scale.

RACE RELATIONS ON A GIVEN THURSDAY AT MIDNIGHT IN BLOEMFONTEIN

The evidence presented above largely concerns how people talk about the social phenomenon of race relations in the context of a deeply artificial setting—the interview space. That space, cluttered as it is with consent forms and recording devices, can sometimes distort how people actually live out their interracial relations. Although I saw many examples of cordial and collegial relations between people of different backgrounds while in South Africa, one particular incident of violence stands out as an exemplar of how the spaces South Africans inhabit are deeply conditioned by race in ways that are inheritances of the past and reflections of present circumstances.

One interview that I organized occurred in the home of a young man, who lived with his parents on the outskirts of Bloemfontein. The house in which they live is surrounded by a ten-foot-high metal slatted fence topped with decorative, but functional spikes. It seemed to be the predominant mode of perimeter security in the neighborhood, along with alarms and motion-sensitive high-beam lights. After the interview, we had dinner and then went outside to sit on their porch and have some casual conversation. Sitting together with the three members of this family and listening to some music, a neighbor and his son walked by on the street in front of the house, on the other side of the fence. Both men had rifles strapped to their backs, sash style, with extra clips of ammunition, and they greeted us through the metal bars of the fencing. After the beginning pleasantries that are customary for Afrikaans speakers, they were invited in to the yard and sat to have a drink with us. Almost immediately, the two new men decided to explain to me why they were walking in the street at night, and why they had rifles.

The older of the two explained that recently he had been attacked in his driveway, just down the street from where we were sitting, and was stabbed repeatedly. He patrols the neighborhood now so that he can protect his neighbors from the same kind of experience. He has set up a radio system in which he contacts the closest neighbors with code names and safe words. If the neighbors failed to respond, he would come to their assistance. The younger man then chimed in to show me the flashlight he carried, which was at least sixteen inches long and extremely heavy. He demonstrated, in slow-motion and with reduced force, how he could inflict serious harm on anyone with this blunt instrument. If all else failed, he told me, he had an extendable metal nightstick that could be used as a whip.

The men retired inside to help themselves to drinks from the refrigerator. The father of the family impressed on me while we were gone that his friend remained severely traumatized by his assault. He told me, "Please, you must understand. He does not do this because he is racist. He is just terrified, all the time. He does not know what else to do. Please report that. He is a man who suffered severe trauma." Unclear of what to do, or how to proceed, I just nodded and said "Of course."

When the two neighbors came back out, the older of the men sat next to me and immediately began to discuss, in shocking detail, the story of his assault. There were many men, he told me. They snuck in through his gate while he was driving his car in on his way home from work. He was stabbed and incapacitated. He lay in his driveway unable to move, bleeding. There were several of them, and they entered his house and attacked his wife. He impressed on me the importance of the fact that he was unable to protect his family because he had been surprised, overwhelmed, and unarmed.

Now, he told me, he wanted to leave. He had lived his whole life in South Africa. He was a game hunter, and a prize-winning biltong maker. He knew that if he went to Europe or Australia or the United States, he could not do these things anymore. He had never known anywhere else. But he needed to leave; to emigrate.

Shortly thereafter, the conversation took another route, and we discussed music and work and what was essential for a visitor to see in South Africa. The men had several more drinks, and I assisted in the washing up with the mother of the house. The neighborhood watchmen left to finish their patrols. When it was time for me to leave, instead of calling a cab, I was offered a ride home by the young man with whom I had scheduled the interview.

Backing out of the driveway, we spotted several flashlight beams and heard people yelling about four houses down. We slowly drove over and came upon the scene. The neighborhood watchmen stood over a squatting young black man. The wife of the older man was screaming at the young man, in English, "I will f**king kill you. What the f**k are you doing here?" She then demanded that her son give him the nightstick so she could "Beat the answers out of [him]."

The crouching young man, who looked to be in his mid-twenties, was casually dressed, in white pants and a green jacket. He had his back about one foot away from the ubiquitous metal fencing. With the flashlights shining in his eyes on the otherwise dark street, he squinted and did not respond to the questions or the threats. The younger neighborhood watchman started to yell people based on racial and gendered chauvinism, it can come as no surprise that the ways people talk about their social lives are still shaped by these approaches, twenty years after the first democratic elections. Although there was certainly interracial contact, including relationships of all kinds, under the apartheid regime (see for example Maharaj 1999), the ambitions of the government toward separation meant that the advent of democracy ushered in a new set of social dictates. The emergent multiracial South Africa required the renegotiation of social life and of relationships between people that government policy and consonant private choice had previously separated. So do participants in these interviews reference social relations in the frame of the old paradigm or the new? How much of the divisiveness of the old regime has been forgotten, and how much recalled and re-inscribed in the new, democratic dispensation?

Many interview participants referenced a level of personal and physical discomfort with a racialized "other" during the course of interviews, referencing both the strictures of the past regime and the realities of the present. Such a visceral sense of discomfort being reproduced in the democratic era would seem to impede the formation of both the literal and the imagined national community.

One Zulu-speaking interview participant spoke about how, yes, the idea of a rainbow nation was present in the racial diversity of the country, but qualified her statement by saying, "We are still segregated. Sitting with white people is just uncomfortable. In terms of settling in together . . . I am not sure" (095). Yet the physical discomfort that many interview participants expressed was not simply one of ambient tension across racial lines, but a much deeper sense of fear.

In large part, this can be attributed to the fact that many people in South Africa emerged with the legal prohibitions of apartheid removed, but with potentially little else changed in the ways they conducted their lives. One young woman in Bloemfontein evaluated the intergroup tensions by saying, "There is still too much going on below the surface . . . the white people would never, in the open, go on about "we do not like black people," but if you go sit in their living rooms and chat with them, especially the older people, then you realize how much hate there still is, and . . . how they miss the old South Africa" (013). The logic of a racialized other posing an imminent physical threat emerged in many ways unchanged from the apartheid discourse during the course of many interviews.

The insidiousness of racial categories defined and implemented by the apartheid regime was their reliance on a "common-sense" approach to clasat the young man, in English and Afrikaans, that he needed to "Sit down, sit the f**k down," ostensibly as opposed to crouching or squatting. When the young man failed to comply, the younger of the two watchmen shoved him, and he went sprawling.

Throughout the interaction, my host was trying, from the car, to mollify the watchmen. He said things like "Calm down," which elicited no response, or even acknowledgment. At this point, the older watchman's wife became hysterical. She turned to address me and my host in the car. "He has no reason to be here," she explained. "He was peeping at people's gates. He is an illegal. His papers do not check out. It is not right for him to be here. Why is he here?" Throughout the confrontation, the only person who remained quiet was the elder of the two watchmen, whose gun had been unslung from his back and held at the ready. The young man did nothing to provoke the watchmen or arouse suspicion, other than simply being in the neighborhood.

About ten minutes after we encountered the scene, my host looked at me and said "There is nothing we can do here. Best just get you home safely," and drove away. The ride back to my flat was largely quiet.

It is an oddity of South Africa that even in the quietest suburbs, there is little or no foot traffic after dark. The neighborhood in which the confrontation took place is not within walking distance of the city center, the university, or any shopping centers, even if such shops might be open at midnight on a Thursday. Aside from the watchmen, this young man was the only person walking that I saw in any neighborhood on the twenty-minute drive back to where I was living. Indeed, he may have been the only person I saw for weeks out at night outside of a secure perimeter. Even on the university campus, on a separate occasion, I was barred by colleagues when leaving a reception from walking the 500 meters to my flat, because of their concerns for my security.

The following day, I happened to run into my host during the course of my travels around the city. He informed me that the police had been called to the scene, and that they had escorted the young man away—unharmed, as he was at pains to emphasize—from the scene. After a brief pause, he added, "I am sorry that you had to see that." Unsure of how to respond, I made a throwaway comment about how Americans abroad always feel the need to apologize since we have such a bad reputation as rude and arrogant people. My host immediately brightened. "See!" he said. "I feel the same way! I will not apologize either. Those people were scared. I will not apologize for them. I will not apologize for the fact that they had to protect their home from black criminals either!"

This episode presents a number of inarguable points—that violent assault in a person's home almost certainly causes extreme trauma, and that the actions of the vigilantes were almost certainly traumatizing in their turn. It also presents many questions about the intentions and justifications of all involved. Like the interview evidence presented above, the empirical realities of the circumstances are a function of how individuals within them experience the subjective environment of threat and trust. What is certainly true, in the interpretation of the events offered by my host post facto, is that he thought of his neighbors as part of a community to which he belonged, with the young black man as an outsider, not just because of familiarity, but because of the assumptions and threats he associated with people from different racial backgrounds.

CONCLUSION

Colonialism, apartheid, and the transition to democracy have left South Africa with enormous burdens. The racialization of the public sphere and the accompanying economic and social privileges accorded by the old regime based on race have an enduring economic and social legacy that should not be underestimated. As with the young woman quoted at the beginning of this chapter, it remains important to realize that the transition to democracy was a fundamental but somewhat sudden change in the morality and intimacy of social relations. Many interview participants fundamentally understood the process of transition through race and gender roles. The physical brutality of the old regime was in some cases translated into imminent physical threat from or latent discomfort with people from other race groups. Indeed, race and gender not only conditioned interview participants' threat perceptions and comfort levels, but were topics of conversation that came up in a variety of interviews in relation to employment, living space, and crime. Race is constantly re-signaled as the fundamental basis of identification and community, and as such cannot be forgotten or even deemphasized. Now people remember the divides of race not because of apartheid, fundamentally, but because of the ways the apartheid legacy plays out in the democratic era.

All communities have social divisions, and it is certainly not surprising that race and gender continue to be powerful forces in South Africa (as everywhere else), even twenty years after the end of the apartheid regime. But the personal racialized and gendered friction noted by the interview participants, and the ways in which such divisions are reported as being continually re-signaled in the course of daily life, present potential problems for the creation of a unified South African political community. The nation, as a community of sentiment, whether created before or after the genesis of a state, fundamentally relies on the ability of fellow citizens to imagine their fates as tied to or at least in concordance with one another. Democracy, especially through the contentious conduct of elections, fundamentally depends on interpersonal and institutional trust. In postconflict settings, both nation- and democracy-building involve the diminution of identities associated with past conflict, and the emergence of new forms of solidarity that cut across those trenchant social divides (Verdeja 2009). The definition of community in the interviews above—including the use of words signaling collective sentiments, such as "we," "us," and "our"—is one that is still fundamentally predicated on racialized and gendered subnational groups. The divisions of the past are not only from the past: they are re-signaled and remembered in everyday life post-apartheid. The quotidian ways in which South Africans report, and also enact, their raced and gendered identities mean that the intimate aspects of nation-building, those that rely on both literal socialization and imagined communion over time and distance, stand in the way of the creation of a broader community.

CHAPTER 6

Community Theater

Ceremony and Performance of Nationhood and Identity

In 2006, popular Afrikaans rock-pop singer Bok van Blerk caused a stir when he released a single off his album originally called *Jy praat nog steeds my taal* (You Still Speak My Language). The single, entitled "De la Rey," has a chorus that calls on Anglo-Boer War general Jacobus Herculaas (Koos) de la Rey, asking "*Sal jy die Boere kom lei?*" (Will you come lead the Boers?) This song, voiced by van Blerk in the persona of an exhausted Boer commando, includes evocative verses:

> [T]he Khakis [British Soldiers] are laughing / a handful of us against all of their great might / with the cliffs at our backs / they think it is all over. / But the heart of a Boer is deeper and wider / And that they will see / On his horse at a gallop he comes / the Lion of the West Transvaal [de la Rey] . . . / Because my wife and my child languish and die in the camp / and the Khaki's vengeance pours over a nation that will rise up again. (Translation by author)

This anthem was enthusiastically received by a white, Afrikaans-speaking audience, and it propelled van Blerk to stardom. The reason this song resonated so strongly with young, white Afrikaners has been debated at length in both Afrikaans and English media. Hermann Giliomee, a prominent Afrikaner historian, has claimed that the song's popularity is due to "the Afrikaner youth's desire for political incorrectness" and to "show up the Afrikaners in their middle age, who tend to live on their knees politically . . . by singing a song about a fearless leader in the past who was driven by his convictions and prepared to pay the price for unpopularity" (Giliomee 2007). The editor of the Afrikaans-language Sunday newspaper *Rapport*, Tim du Plessis, and Koos Kombuis, prominent member of the Afrikaans protest-music movement of the 1980s, saw the song as signaling a new era of Afrikaner identity and unity, divorced from the history of apartheid, party politics, and the *verkrampte* (literally, cramped; read figuratively, hardline) mindset of the older generations. The song, in this interpretation, was an anthem for youth choosing a new path, and having something to say. In the words of du Plessis, "[Afrikaners] had no choice but to become new South Africans. Now they want to be new Afrikaners" (Du Plessis, quoted in Bezuidenhout 2007, 2).

Other observers were not so optimistic. Max du Preez, a leading figure in the alternative Afrikaans press in the late 1980s, said of the song on popular South African television show *Carte Blanche*, "While the song is in no way racist . . . when young people stand there when they sing about how nasty the British were to the Boer women in the concentration camps, and how general come and lead us, we will fall around you, they are not thinking about the British, they are thinking about blacks. The enemy is now black" (Du Preez 2007). By defining an enemy, and demonstrating the resonance of such a threat through use of war-time imagery, this song is a powerful signal of how and where young Afrikaans-speakers see their place in the post-apartheid social order.

In practice, how fans responded to the song is certainly connected to apartheid symbols. On multiple occasions, fans of van Blerk spontaneously broke into their own rendition of the apartheid-era South African national anthem, *Die Stem*, to call van Blerk to the stage. They flew apartheid-era flags at his concerts, or stood at attention with hands on their hearts in response to the singing of the song (van der Waal and Robins 2011). Van Blerk himself has been somewhat ambivalent about these connections. In one particularly public interaction, he removed an apartheid-era flag from his guitar when it was placed there by fans, though he also agreed that he would play for a far-right militant organization if they paid him to do so (Bezuidenhout 2007).

Although six years had passed between the song's peak popularity when I went to South Africa to conduct interviews, it came up regularly and entirely unprompted during interviews with Afrikaans-speaking people from all self-expressed partisan positions. The conversation was often about the search for a way to be Afrikaans in the new South Africa. In response to a generic interview-ending question about what was important for outsiders to understand about South Africa today, one young woman said,

Maybe [the important thing to understand is] the need of the Afrikaans culture to still be recognized as a culture. I do not know if you have ever heard
of the De la Rey song? That song was such a hit. It was a *huge* hit. I think the
main thing was that, after apartheid, because Afrikaans people were the insti-
gators of apartheid, our whole culture was not allowed in a way. You are not
allowed to be an Afrikaner, because that is a bad thing. . . . We love our culture
and that is the way we live. . . . [You must] understand that we still need to be
us, without the guilt. We will probably never get rid of the guilt . . . my biggest
wish would be to not be *the culture* that is evil. (103)

This rather run-of-the-mill pop-rock song, for some people, not only miti-
gated the feeling of collective guilt associated with apartheid, but acted as a
kind of cultural redemption. Afrikaans/Afrikaner history, in this interpretation, could be celebrated, and more fundamentally, be permissible because
of its association with the heroic narrative, centered on resistance to British
imperialism, presented in the song.

Popular music is often connected to expressions of identity and politics,
and identity itself is often described in terms of performance and enactment.
This is true especially in South Africa, where music "has been actively mobilized as a tool for the production of a national populace . . . because it is
perceived as both a marker and a shaper of identity . . . performing and listening to South African music becomes a fairly low-stakes way of identifying
as South African" (Hammond 2010, 2–3). Additionally, the role of Afrikaners
in South Africa, especially given the relationship of the Afrikaans community
to the National Party and to apartheid, has been a theme that runs through
Afrikaans music that has become popular in the first two decades of multiracial democracy (Senekal and van den Berg 2010).

But what is the role of performance, ritual, and ceremony in the landscape
of identity politics and the building of a national community in South Africa?
In what ways do ceremonies and performances serve to remind people of the
boundaries of class, race, language, and location, and in what ways are they
forces that bridge or obscure these divides? This chapter considers the temporary spaces created by festivals, sporting events, and national holidays. These
are events that emerge and proceed according to rules of "social sacrament,"
which "make and remake social facts and collective identities" (Comaroff and
Comaroff 1993, xv–xvi); they are connected to both national and subnational
identity communities. Such social sacraments contain "processes of both
social cohesion and conflict" and have the ability to reward group identifi-

cation (Hermanowicz and Morgan 1999, 199). As such, these temporary performative spaces help to signal communal values, history, and identity, while also defining the boundaries of a given community. As discussed below, there has been a growth in the popularity of explicitly segregating ceremonies, as well as in performances of identity that are nominally integrating but segregating in practice.

Cultural rituals, such as arts festivals or religious holidays, involve creating temporary spaces in which structured observances are linked with the creation of identity and maintenance of community. This chapter looks at three classes of events aimed at celebrating heritage and culture in South Africa, for largely domestic audiences. The first class of events, labeled as "strictly defined ethnocultural rituals," are those that employ largely descent-based forms of identity to define their target audience and set of participants. The two ceremonies considered here are the observances associated with the Day of the Vow at the Voortrekker Monument in Pretoria and the Reed Dance at the Enyokeni Royal Palace in Nongoma. These ceremonies are performed primarily by people who consider themselves moral gatekeepers for their communities, and there are generally relatively few observers from outside of the ethnoracial constituency as defined by the gatekeepers (Afrikaners at the Day of the Vow and Zulus at the Reed Dance).

The next set of events, termed "affiliative rituals," is comprised of events that seem to have a more open definition of participation, based on associational identities. This section addresses Afrikaans arts and culture festivals that have grown in the country since the advent of democracy, as well as the experience of watching sports in arenas. Outsiders—those not directly affiliated with the ethnoracial communities designated as core audiences—are somewhat more likely to attend these events, and participants employ a more associative form of identity. These associations, based on enjoyment of particular sports or language, are framed as chosen identities, rather than implicit or primordially understood connections. Indeed, they are seen by participants as a way to practice their culture in public and inclusive ways. Yet the experience of these festivals and ceremonies is one that is lived in largely segregated spaces, or in integrated spaces (like the 2010 World Cup games) that interview participants did not say had long-term effects on their social relationships.

Celebrations aimed at being inclusive and "bridging" in the context of South Africa are considered in the final section, "Open Rituals." Despite their unifying intentions, the effects of such interventions are often shallow. All of the ceremonial spaces discussed imply notions of community and the boundaries of belonging in those communities. The fact that the majority of these performances are created by and for de facto segregated communities, however, limits their contributions to nation-building, even if the stated intention of the performance is integrative.

STRICTLY DEFINED ETHNOCULTURAL RITUALS

Within the framework of the new South Africa, certain rituals are being enacted that create and sustain identities developed or codified under the old regime, such as the Day of the Vow and the Reed Dance. These kinds of activities bind together people on the basis of relatively static conceptions of identity, either as Afrikaner or Zulu. Although stemming from different religious traditions, both of the ceremonies considered here involve codes of morality, with participants framed as guardians of virtue for the larger community.

A unifying element of such ceremonies is that their pools of participants and their intended audience are from strictly defined ethnocultural communities contained in South Africa. Inherent in the celebrations of the Day of the Vow is a descent-based notion of Afrikanerdom, defined as those who are bound by the covenant made in 1838.[1] For Zulu speakers, the population of young women who are eligible for participation in *ukuhlolwa kwezintombi* (the examination of the young women) is defined as daughters born to men whose fathers belong to clans who historically have given fealty to the Zulu royal house (Marcus 2009). Passing these examinations is the central prerequisite for participation in the Reed Dance.

Such ceremonies, and their definitions of their target communities, seem to echo the apartheid government's focus on patrilineal descent to define the ethnic constituent communities of Bantustans, as well as the descent-based notion of race used for population registration, especially after the 1967 Population Registration Amendment Act.[2] As will be discussed below, there is some resistance to such definitions of community, and regarding the extent to which they continue to be meaningful in post-apartheid South Africa.

Geloftedag—The Day of the Vow

Geloftedag, Day of the Vow, is a holiday commemorating the Battle of Blood River[3] in which a group of about 500 Voortrekkers, in a defensive formation along the Ncome River, successfully defended their position against a Zulu *impi*[4] numbering approximately 10,000 (Thompson 2001, 91). The battle was named Blood River because the Ncome River allegedly ran red with the blood of the defeated Zulu *amabutho/amaqhawe*.[5] Prior to their victory in battle, the individual Voortrekker *kommandos*, according to popular legend, vowed that if they were successful, they would commemorate that day forever to God's glory. Originally celebrated as Dingaan's Day, 16 December was first made a holiday in 1910 by the newly established national parliament of the Republic of South Africa (Thompson 2001). Since 1994, although 16 December is still a public holiday, it has been renamed Reconciliation Day, which commemorates both the older version of the holiday and the founding of the ANC's armed wing, Umkhonto we Sizwe, in 1961.

The Voortrekker Monument, on a hill outside Pretoria, was opened in 1949 as a physical representation of the vow made by the Voortrekkers. The monument has become a site of yearly celebration for the Day of the Vow since the monument's opening. There are celebrations at other memorial sites associated with Afrikaner Nationalism, such as the Blood River Museum and the Vroemonument (Women's Memorial) in Bloemfontein, although the official Geloftefees organizing committee listed celebrations in every province in 2014.

The monument in Pretoria (see fig. 2) was constructed in such a way that at noon on 16 December every year, the light of the sun hits an oculus in the domed ceiling of the building and shines a beam directly down to a cenotaph below. The sunlight traces across the words "*Ons vir jou, Suid-Afrika*" or "We for Thee, South Africa" inscribed on the cenotaph in the lowest level, which itself is a symbolic burial site for Piet Retief, a Voortrekker leader, and all those who died on the Great Trek. The light of the sun shining on the cenotaph, according to the monument's architect, Gerard Moerdijk, is meant to symbolize "God's blessing on the life and work of the Voortrekkers" ("Cenotaph Hall/Voortrekker Monument" 2015).

Each year on 16 December, a church service and cultural gathering are arranged in the morning, culminating in all those present watching the light of the sun traverse the cenotaph's inscription for about fifteen minutes. When the light first hit the cenotaph's inscription in 2012, the crowd burst into a rendition of the apartheid-era national anthem "Die Stem van Suid-Afrika," which concludes with the phrase "Ons vir jou Suid Afrika" in an echo of the words on the cenotaph. When the song ended, I looked over at the young man who had accompanied me to the ceremony as an acquaintance and guide. Although normally stoic, he was visibly moved in the moment. When I asked him how he felt and what he thought of the day's proceedings, he simply replied "*Ag, nee*.[6] I am proud, man. So proud."

Fig. 2. Voortrekker Monument, Pretoria.

The pulpit erected in the Voortrekker Monument is the centerpiece of this day on which the Afrikaner nation goes to church. The sermon delivered on this day has often been concerned with the role and identity of the Afrikaner people in South Africa, and on the continent more generally. The messages delivered from this pulpit have remained quite stable, given the change in Afrikaner circumstances, from a militarily defeated marginal group in the wake of the Anglo-Boer war, to a group powerful enough to sustain the National Party–led apartheid regime for forty-six years, to a group who comprise a distinct minority in a majoritarian democracy yet still hold far greater wealth per capita than the national average. Throughout this evolution the sermon has consistently been on the subject of the justification for and defense of the place of the Afrikaner in South Africa. The durability of this message can be seen in three selected quotations from sermons delivered at the Voortrekker Monument in 1939, 1965, and 2012, and at the Blood River Monument in 2014. At the centennial celebrations of the Day of the Vow in 1939, D. F. Malan, then leader of the National Party, declared from the Geloftedag lectern, "On the Blood River site we stand on holy ground. This is where the future of South Africa, as a civilized Christian Country, and where the future of the white race are determined. We stand today in our own white army, at our own Blood River, while black masses gather around us" (Van Jaarsveld 1979, 71, cited in Van der Merwe 2012, 5, translation by author). In 1965, leading Afrikaner theologian and academic H. B. Thom delivered a similar message to the crowd gathered at the monument in Pretoria:

> South Africa is at war. . . . At this time, the Afrikaner therefore must be strong. It is his own past, his own spiritual/intellectual[7] inheritance, which are things like the Covenant, which helps one to give him life force. He should know that he, like the Voortrekkers in 1838, stands for Christianity and civilization. He must know he is still today as a beacon of light in a darkest Africa. . . . Born from our own soil and our own people, the Covenant and the Day of the Vow is for us a source of power. Let us accept and understand this. Let us be unambiguous and determined to take a stand against the approaching masses. Let us—as Dr. Donges has recently said—entirely refuse to be afraid. If we do that, as the men of the Covenant have done, we can win an even greater and more glorious victory than the one they had in 1838. (Thom 1965, translation by author)

From the same pulpit in 2012, Afrikaner theologian and minister Dr. Danie Langner gave a sermon on the biblical figures of Rebekah and Isaac, as parents of the nation. He repeated throughout, "You belong in South Africa. Your children have a future in their fatherland. This is the land of the Voortrekkers. This is our land, and this is our future." Two years later, Langner delivered another Geloftedag sermon in which he listed several reasons for Afrikaners to be proud in the twenty years since 1994, including "Pride that Afrikaners in a time of many crises still roll up their sleeves and work hard so that our children can have a future in South Africa" (Langner 2014, translation by author). The sermon concluded with Langer quoting a song from the Voortrekker scouting[8] songbook:

> As campfire logs through the night with bright flames burning, / So burns in us the love for the youth of this land. / To the children of our Fatherland, oh yes, homeland still remains the most precious land. / And if we as sons and daughters of the Trekkers work, / Then faith and love will make our hearts and hands strong. / And together we will in this country, oh yes, in this country build a bright future. (Langner 2014, translation by author)

This theme, justifying the presence and future of Afrikaners in South Africa, presents a definition of community rooted in claims to land and belonging, based on descent. Such themes are resonant of apartheid-era understandings of the monuments and the community they represented. An early guide to the monument suggests that, in fact, the tableau of friezes depicting the history of the Voortrekkers was constructed as "not only a representation of historical events. It also serves as a symbolic document showing the Afrikaner's proprietary right to South Africa. . . . A people that have sacrificed so much blood and tears, have left their mark on such a country, and therefore spiritually and physically that country belongs to them and their descendants" (cited in Coombes 2005, 178–79).

Visits to the monument on nonholidays, however, are markedly different. A free pamphlet distributed at the monument discusses not the nationalist political motivations behind the construction of the monument, but the importance of "freedom, even until today," and the anti-imperial sentiment of the Afrikaners' war with the British, rather than focusing on the battle with the Zulu *izimpi*. In the pamphlet entitled "Hall of Heroes and Friezes," the description of the main hall of the monument, the central point of the Day of the Vow celebration, includes the passage, "The marble on the floor is laid according to a specific pattern. It takes on the form of water rippling further and wider apart, with the Cenotaph as its focal point symbolic of a move to freedom which started on a small scale but eventually culminated in a huge historical wave that still reverberates to this day." In the context of a monument that includes graphic friezes of Boer kommandos slaying Zulu warriors, and includes plaques describing the "betrayal" of Piet Retief and the violence of Zulu warriors against defenseless women and children, the fact that the one symbolic space containing no human depictions or words has been reinterpreted to talk about freedom for a larger national community is an interesting rhetorical shift.

Yet such reinterpretations are lost in the actual commemoration of the Day of the Vow. When asked about the symbols of the monument on that day, most attendees with whom I spoke referenced the depictions of the friezes, the light on the cenotaph, and the importance of the Afrikaner nation standing on its own, and growing. The same was true for people who expressed support for the Day of the Vow celebrations during the course of interviews. One older man, who identified himself as being on the organizing committee for the local celebration, said of the events, "I can say that I think the number of people that are coming to it is increasing. You know the Afrikaner nowadays is under threat, is under pressure, and we are serious" (003). Another man, in his mid-thirties, when asked about the celebration, said "The numbers of attendees are improving. There is a new sense of association. The day was misused pre-1994. Now people do want to come together. . . . We are celebrating our heritage more and more. Post 1994, people were very sensitive. Now we can celebrate our culture more openly. The young people are more freely associating with our culture" (051–052).

This assertion that the celebrations are growing is difficult to corroborate. However, observers at the celebration in 2000 estimated the crowd at the monument to be 1,500 (Team Report 2000). A 2008 statement by the organizing committee published in *Rapport*, a weekly Afrikaans newspaper with a national circulation, states that although there will only be 2,000 chairs available, they have made provisions to broadcast the service over loudspeakers so that all who attend can hear (*Rapport* 2008), which suggests that they expected crowds in excess of 2,000 visitors. In 2010, *Die Beeld* described the crowd on a particularly inclement day as being comprised of "a few thousand people" (*Het 'n paar duisend mense*) (van Rooyen 2010), and in 2012 the same newspaper estimated attendance at "several thousand visitors" (*etlike duisense besoekers*) (Rademeyer 2012). Although vague, the two words of "a few" compared to "several" suggest larger crowds in 2012. The Naspers Afrikaans news service estimated that despite inclement weather, the 2014 Day of the Vow service at the Voortrekker Monument attracted between 5,000 and 7,000 visitors (George 2014). Although unofficial, this set of data suggests significant growth over time of the crowds attending the ceremony.[9]

Despite this growth, the majority of people with whom I spoke—especially those under age thirty-five—felt decidedly ambivalent about Geloftedag. One young woman, although she said she did not regularly attend the celebrations, said,

[Geloftedag] is a public holiday now, which is nice. At the Vroemonument they have a church service. It is a very Afrikaner celebration. It is about the war. It is a way to keep values alive . . . but it makes me very uncomfortable. I love the Voortrekker Monument. It is an amazing structure in Pretoria. . . . There are hundreds of people that gather there for the holiday. It is packed every year. If you look at those carvings inside the monument, those make me *trots* [proud] to be a Boer. (023)

Another young man, aged twenty-six, when asked whether he celebrated the holiday in any particular way, said "No, I do not really celebrate Geloftedag. I am not going to either. . . . It is almost like the AWB[10] people who celebrate it . . . the khaki-wearing folks.[11] It still has some meaning. If it was not for that day, white people might not live here" (054). The connection between Day of the Vow celebrations and right-wing politics was echoed in several interviews, including one with a man in his mid-thirties, who said "I am not going to services at our church, but we also do not go to the celebrations at the monuments. Typically, the people who call themselves Afrikaners and Boers[12] are the ones who celebrate at the monuments" (076).

For others, the difference in celebrating Geloftedag was not political, but generational. Two women, aged twenty-eight and fifty-six, spoke about their parents having celebrated the day, but not observing it themselves. The younger woman said, "My parents do value that day. Now, it is hard to celebrate when you know the history. People were killed. One person believed that he was doing the right thing, but I just do not know . . ." (029). The older woman, in a separate interview, said that no, she did not celebrate Geloftedag, "but my parents did. It was part of their history. Now I have no real connections to it. It is not relevant to me. It is not part of South Africa now" (015).

This ambivalence about festivals based on strict ethnocultural notions of descent-based identity, or associated with Afrikaner nationalism inherited from the apartheid days, was evident even during the apartheid regime. A 1989 article characterized the Day of the Vow celebrations of 1988 by saying "the Great Trek has lost much of its emotional appeal for mainstream Afrikaner adherents of the National Party. . . . The celebrations of December 1988 were indeed a far cry from the euphoria and triumphalism of the 1938 celebrations and did not contribute to any degree of unity between different sections of Afrikanerdom" (Grundlingh and Sapire 1989, 37). The decline in expressed affiliation in the ceremonies associated with the National Party does show a distancing among mainstream Afrikaans speakers from what Grundlingh and Sapire call the "sacred history" of Afrikaner nationalism. The idea that such celebrations are extreme, or even retrograde, means that they do not draw in the huge crowds that they did at the height of the apartheid era. Yet the data presented above do suggest that there is a durable appeal of such ceremonial observances, and that they are growing in the post-apartheid era, even if interview participants did not express widespread support for them.

Umkhosi womHlanga—The Royal Reed Dance

Annually, since at least the mid-1990s,[13] virginity testing (*ukuhlolwa*) has been practiced in communities around South Africa to certify young women as virgins before their annual presentation to the Zulu monarch. To date, hundreds of thousands of young women have been tested. The testing season culminates in the celebration of Umkhosi womHlanga (Presentation to/ Greeting of the King), wherein the "certified virgins" present a reed, symbolizing their purity, to the Zulu monarch in a weekend-long celebration. Because of the centrality of the reed presentation to the ceremony, the festival is often called the Reed Dance in English.

Virginity testing has become controversial because the ANC-led government classified the practice as a violation of young women's human rights, in part because of the physical examinations involved in the certification process. The issue of virginity testing came to a head during debate over the 2006 Children's Rights Bill, in which the practice was officially recognized, but participation was restricted to those over age sixteen (Vincent 2006). In 2011, then-president Jacob Zuma, although he didn't officially change the government's policy regarding the Reed Dance or the practice of virginity testing, attended the festival in Nongoma and planted a commemorative tree to mark the occasion. But a 2015 press release by the ANC Women's League classifies the practice as "gender-based violence" and calls for its abolition, claiming that "the custom of virginity testing of young girls exposes the girl-child to rape, incest, abuse and sexual violence" (ANC Women's League 2015).

Despite these controversies, in September, from all over South Africa, Umkhosi womHlanga draws tens of thousands of young women who consider themselves the subjects of the Zulu king. Their chaperones, mentors, observers, and local dignitaries accompany them to the Enyokeni Royal Palace in Nongoma. The 2005 Reed Dance drew the participation of more than 20,000 "certified" virgins (Vincent 2006). Estimates from 2010 put the number at 26,000 (Keepile 2010), while participation in 2014 was projected to be 30,000 in advance of the celebration (SAPA 2014), with some newspapers estimating participation to be as high as 40,000 the year before (Ngwenya 2013). During the Reed Dance at Nongoma, regiments of forty-five to sixty young women present themselves to the king with their reeds in quick succession in a parade lasting upwards of eight hours. Each maiden holds one reed, as seen in figure 3; the reeds extend down the road and out of the right

Fig. 3. Maidens awaiting the opening of the Enyokeni Palace Gates, September 2012.

side of the frame, because so many young women were standing awaiting their presentation to the king.

The Reed Dance and the virginity-testing festivals held in the lead-up to the celebration are not public events. On the two occasions I attended such gatherings, it was because of local connections and local invitations to the events. Like the Day of the Vow celebrations in Pretoria, the Reed Dance is not a performance aimed at an outside audience. The observance of the rituals is directed at an audience that is situated similarly to those participating, people who define themselves, and are defined by the monarchy, as subjects of the Zulu royal house.

By and large, the Zulu-speaking interview participants, especially men, approved of the practice of virginity testing and the celebrations of it. One man in his mid fifties, when asked about the ceremony, said "It works well, and it instills discipline. It helps girls to know who they are, and being able to respect them is easier. If I had girl children, I would love for them to attend. . . . Globalization is eroding the traditions of the Zulu people, but we stand strong" (089). Another man, age forty, said, "This is something that is being done for culture and to encourage the culture with young Zulu girls.

It is about how they should behave. . . . There is nothing else without being a Zulu cultural person. This is who we are" (100). Another middle-aged man agreed, saying, "I like it on its own. It is a good way to instill culture. Good to make sure that the girls are brought up right. It is a custom that must happen. Without it, what kind of a world would we have? . . . That gathering is where the girls learn how to be. Social cohesion is taught. They are also taught how to treat their family, their elders" (094).

The young Zulu-speaking women with whom I spoke mostly supported the practices of virginity testing and the celebration of Umkhosi womHlanga, and most knew others who had participated. Of the women I spoke to, however, many expressed some doubt about their own participation. One young woman in Pretoria in her mid-twenties, who identified herself as a "Zulu maiden," said of the ceremony, "I have cousins who attend. For them, it was a proud thing. . . . I do not know. I get it is about being proud in the modern world. . . . But for me, I am not a showy person. My life is mine. It might be that I do not like to walk around bare-chested. . . . The whole idea of people looking at me is uncomfortable" (105).

Unlike the Day of the Vow celebrations, which were largely populated by older Afrikaans speakers, the Reed Dance drew enthusiastic participation from many young women. The enthusiasm at the Reed Dance in 2012 was infectious. The young women participants with whom I spoke were optimistic about the future and about their country. Whereas the Day of the Vow celebrations seemed to be looking backward, with reference to the past, many of the young women attending the Reed Dance referenced future promise when asked about their motivations for attending. Although both celebrations are, at their core, deeply conservative in orientation, they had vastly different points of reference. What was similar in both ceremonies was the defensive posture of cultures under threat from outside forces and the descent-based notions of belonging to their constituent groups.

Growth of Strictly Defined Rituals

Both the celebration of the Reed Dance and the Day of the Vow present identities that are in some ways out of step with the project of "New South Africa." The Day of the Vow has been officially renamed as a public holiday, and is now called "Reconciliation Day." The government's proposed ban on virginity testing demonstrates the presence of official opposition to the ceremony in at least some factions of the ANC, and in some activist groups.

There seem to be dedicated and growing cores of people invested in both rituals. But such ceremonies also met a degree of ambivalence from a larger sample of my interview participants, who are largely urban, educated people. The majority of people who would fit the descent-based definition of being Afrikaner or Zulu do not participate in either of these rituals. Despite these points of opposition, reports from news coverage of both events suggest that they are steadily growing in popularity and attracting more participants and audience members. This growth indicates an appetite for ceremonial spaces that are explicitly defined as commanding loyalty within strictly defined ethnic communities.

Such observances are not necessarily at odds with the creation of nationalist sentiments. As Stepan, Linz, and Yadav argue, robust subnational identities do not necessarily have to compete with or supersede national identities, but could exist within the framework of a "multiple but complementary" network of identities (2011, 15–16).[14] However, some of the signaling at the events described above indicates that the communities being invoked in these rituals are not complementary to, but rather are in competition with, national identifications. The use of apartheid-era symbols—the old national anthem and the old flag—in the Day of the Vow celebration seems to indicate an antagonism to the new dispensation. While the Reed Dance has had a more complex relationship with the ANC-led government, both the provincial and the national Departments of Arts and Culture had representatives in attendance in 2012 and 2013. Yet even so, the issue of virginity testing has been decried both by political incumbents such as the leadership of the ANC Women's League and by activists as being in contravention of the norms of human rights, in addition to undermining young women's autonomy and reinforcing patriarchal, traditional, and therefore nondemocratic authority (Chisale and Byrne 2018). As such, both of these exclusively defined rituals seem to work in ways that promote identities that are in competition with the national community that supports South Africa's multiracial democracy.

AFFILIATIVE RITUALS

The ceremonies in this section are those that employ a more flexible, associative notion of identity to describe their target audience as well as the boundaries of participation. Like the strictly defined ceremonies discussed above, these festival spaces are performed not for an external audience, but for an audience of like-minded people. The first example, of sports events, especially in stadiums, is complex. Much scholarship has been devoted to the idea of sports as vectors of nation-building and reconciliation in South Africa, yet many of these articles do not engage directly with the ways that ordinary people talk about the experience of sports, or address the experience of being a spectator at such events.

The second group of events in this category are the Afrikaans arts and culture festivals that have sprung up in cities across the country in the post-apartheid era. Billed as part of the new way to be Afrikaans in South Africa, rooted in an elective, language-based identity, these festivals are a major way that the post-apartheid Afrikaans-speaking community makes itself visible.

Although the identities in these ceremonies are being defined as elective and associative, rather than rigidly racialized, I argue that the experience of attending such performances and festivals is a deeply segregated one. Despite the bridging potential of such "national" points of identification, the integrative aspects are either nondurable or nonexistent.

Sports in Stadiums

If one looks more closely at the phenomenon of pride in sporting events as a performance of unity, it becomes a complex point of reference. South Africans have, since the transition, consistently ranked "sports" or "sports teams" as a primary component of national pride, across different racial and ethnic groups (Møller, Dickow, and Harris 1999). Sporting events, such as the World Cups in 1995 (rugby) and 2010 (soccer), have tremendous potential to be sources of national unity and pride. The presence of Nelson Mandela at the Rugby World Cup in 1995 was called "the Game that Made a Nation" by the author of a book on these events (Carlin 2008). However, sporting events have long been deeply tied to the politics and lived experience of race in South Africa. Rugby has historically been associated with the white Afrikaans community, cricket with the English-speaking community, and soccer with the black community. It is these divisions, and the ways that they were transcended, that made the symbolism of the 1995 Rugby World Cup so powerful.

These racial divides between sporting communities, in terms of both players and fans, are slowly being broken down through a process that the South African government is calling "transformation," yet they are still largely unchanged. This fractiousness in sporting culture means that sporting events, in many instances, are neither diverse nor inclusive. In the Free State, the issue of sports came up often in casual conversation.

One participant in my interviews, a twenty-seven-year-old Afrikaans-speaking man from Bloemfontein, stopped the interview questions and told me that I had missed a vital part of understanding South Africa. Rugby, he told me, was central to being a Vrystaater (Free State citizen) and a South African. When I asked him to speak more about the role of sports, he said, "Rugby! Everyone here watches that. Black people mostly watch soccer" (053). The "everyone" for this young man was his largely homogenous group of Afrikaans-speaking friends and family in Bloemfontein. He was an avid supporter the local rugby team, but his support for the team was a facet of his cultural engagement with people within his ethnolinguistic community. The matches in the local stadium are still attended mainly by Afrikaans speakers, and the publicity materials and media from the team are almost entirely in Afrikaans. The experience of going to the stadium is still conducted almost entirely in Afrikaans. Afrikaans people, despite being a numerical minority in the Free State, are the overwhelming majority in the stadium. Rugby, in the Free State, is still an Afrikaans sport, while soccer is played by and for black Africans.

I saw this dynamic at play at the University of the Free State in Bloemfontein. The large campus mall was divided roughly in half by a sidewalk that created two sports-field-sized patches of grass. On many afternoons, after classes, groups of young men would assemble to play sports on these lawns. While walking down the middle path, it was clear to see that on my right was a spirited rugby match, complete with spectators, played by white, Afrikaans-speaking men and watched by a white, Afrikaans-speaking crowd. On my left was a soccer game, with black men playing and black spectators.

Yet in 2010, South Africa hosted the FIFA World Cup, and many international observers saw it as an event with major potential for nation-building. Soccer, a sport associated largely with black African communities in South Africa, came to center stage in five geographically disbursed stadiums, which played host to thousands of domestic and international spectators. Displays of patriotism abounded and the South African flag was almost omnipresent in host cities. Many interview participants did report feeling proud of the World Cup and enjoying the sense of togetherness that it brought to the country. One young Afrikaans-speaking woman said of the World Cup, "We are very diverse, black, white, coloured . . . but we went to the soccer games together. Everybody was excited. . . . It was really like a bonding factor for us. To literally sit in a stadium and shout for South Africa, or not even in a stadium, sometimes we just went to a pub and watched it on the televisions. Everybody was hugging one another. It was just a nice spirit" (008).

But two to three years later, much of the luster of the nation-building possibilities of sports had worn off. There was deep ambivalence among interview participants about the World Cup's long-term effect on the nation and the possibilities it presented for bridging divides. According to one Zulu-speaking participant, "Yes, the 2010 World Cup brought out South African-ism. We wished it could go on. We saw it, we felt it, and then it faded" (099). Another Afrikaans-speaking participant echoed the sentiments in differ-ent words, saying, "In the World Cup in 2010, we had a very united feeling. Mostly, though, it is not that way. . . . We are going back into our race camps. That is the natural thing, but I also mingle with my black colleagues. If push comes to shove, we are on our own and so are they" (056).

Indeed, even though there was a surge in patriotic displays around the time of the World Cup, according to Adam Habib, "it should be understood that temporary national pride and celebrations are not an adequate gauge of public attitudes, and need not be incompatible with the lack of a South Afri-can identity" (Habib 1997, 20). So, although there was a surge in nationalist sentiment around the World Cup, for many South Africans that spirit has faded. Pride in sport is still largely correlated with ethno-linguistic commu-nities rather than a national community. As such, pride in sports or sporting teams is, at best, a thin source of national identity and not necessarily a per-formance or ritual that would bridge the divides of the past.

Afrikaans Arts and Culture Festivals

In 1995, in Oudtshoorn, a small town on the eastern side of the Western Cape province, two businessmen hosted the first-ever Klein Karoo Nasionale Kun-stefees (Little Karoo National Arts Festival), an Afrikaans counterpart to the increasingly English-medium Grahamstown National Arts Festival. Three years later, after a conference in Stellenbosch, an Afrikaans task group es-tablished Aardklop, an Afrikaans music and arts festival hosted in Potchefst-room in the North West province. Since then, festivals have been established in a number of different towns throughout the country.

These festivals, aimed at promoting Afrikaans language, artistic endeav-ors, and culture, have grown dramatically in the post-apartheid period. All of these festivals have roughly similar structures. They are centered on a set of performances, both musical and theatrical, as well as a book fair with discus-sions and a market area selling food, crafts, and artwork.

In the context of South Africa's art scene, which is festival- and event-centric, there are dozens of festivals each year. What differentiates the festivals listed above is the focus on Afrikaans as both the medium of the event and the organizing reason for the arts being presented. According to one festival observer, "The common denominator in Oudtshoorn [KKNK] is not culture, nor even the somewhat conservative, wordy Afrikaans theatre. It is something more pervasive. It is *Die Taal* [The Language]. . . . The festival is another kind of country—a vibrant space where English and other languages are tolerated. . . . But Afrikaans is alive—enthusiastically used, relished, and celebrated" (Hauptfleisch 2006, 190).

During my time in Bloemfontein the annual Vryfees was held on the University of the Free State campus. It was, as Hauptfleisch says, something of another country. The vast majority of those in attendance—at the free stage, the paid performances, the book festival, and the market areas—were speaking Afrikaans and were apparently white. In a town where, according to the 2011 census, more than 56 percent of people identify as black African (Statistics South Africa 2012) and in the context of a university whose population is almost 71 percent black African (University Council 2014), the festival constituted a major break from the everyday demographics of the space.

Such festivals, focusing on arts and culture in Afrikaans rather than a rigidly racial notion or a descent-based understanding of Afrikanerdom as was evident in the Day of the Vow celebration, seem to tout the ability of anyone to associate with the culture on display. The idea that Afrikaans culture can be capacious, artistic, intellectual, and modern was central to the self-presentation of Afrikaans speakers during the festival. As one interview participant said, shortly after the conclusion of the Vryfees, "It is amazing, it is so important. You get the chance to express yourself in Afrikaans. . . . The culture is alive. The language is alive. It is there for everyone to enjoy" (023).

During the course of interviews, I asked people in Bloemfontein how they felt about the festival, whether they attended, and why they thought others did. For many people, the drive to preserve language that was at the core of the founding of the festival was central. In the words of a young woman who said she regularly attended multiple Afrikaans festivals, the festivals were important because "it is hard to think that the language will not exist in the future. That it might disappear. The festivals keep it alive" (029). A man, aged thirty-eight, who also attended multiple Afrikaans festivals including the KKNK and the Vryfees, said "[Such festivals] are necessary. A group must remember where it comes from. Our language is under pressure. As a group, we go to enjoy the arts. It is getting more scarce, the opportunity to be among ourselves . . . People crave it" (073).

Other interview participants referenced a broader notion of the "culture" as the important thing that the festivals preserve. One middle-aged man, after being asked why he asserted so emphatically that the festivals were important to him personally, said "This is a breathing space for art and culture, especially Afrikaans art and culture" (024). A man in his early fifties, when asked his opinion about Afrikaans arts festivals in general, said "They are positive. . . . They are important places of association. There is a high level of skepticism about the Afrikaans community associating with itself. Why should that be? The festivals are growing now because there is a strong sense of wanting association with ourselves. . . . People just want to associate, to be together" (069). A man in his mid-sixties who I saw repeatedly attending the festivals elaborated on this idea of skepticism about the Afrikaans community seeming to rally around such festivals. He said

> I am a bit uncomfortable with the arts festivals, as such, because of the role that the arts played as a basis for Afrikaner nationalism. But I doubt that would happen again. Are they rallying? Maybe, but against what? . . . If the rise in the arts festivals is happening, it is awakening an interest in arts, not politics. There are lectures, and they can and must play a role in propagating scholarship and arts. (035)

This defensiveness over the idea that the celebration of Afrikaans culture or language is itself inherently white nationalist, or isolationist, or in some way antidemocratic was not always voiced directly, but was often evident through context and delivery in participants' answers to questions. When asked why he thought Afrikaans arts festivals, which he was not particularly enthused about but had attended, were so popular, one twenty-six-year-old interview participant said "There are lots of factors. After apartheid, the country became a lot more free. We were inviting a larger pool. There was an international arena. But we still wanted to be us" (054). He hastily added without further prompting, while I was transcribing his response, "The end of apartheid was a big push in the right direction. It gave everyone a chance for freedom" (054). The fact remained that these festivals were remarkably white, and almost entirely Afrikaans in attendance and in presentation.

Among the people working at or patronizing the craft and food tents, there was a wide range of political viewpoints. One artisan from the North West province, when I told him that I was visiting and I had heard that his part of the country was quite pretty, responded by saying "Yes, but the problem is it is very black." When I asked him to clarify, he said "It is very black, lots of black people, and they really are not civil anymore. You know about this farm violence. They kill us in our beds. Everyone I know is in danger."[15] An artisan from Cape Town, who sold coins, when asked about one minted in 1948, said, "That was an interesting year. The Nuremburg trials were going on, yet the people here voted in the same kind of system. Shame. They just called it 'class segregation,' can you believe? Shame." Another group of farm-ers from the Northern Free State, all of whom were at least seventy years old, who I met at the free music stage during a *boeremusiek*[16] concert, said it was very exciting to have foreigners listen to the "music of [their] nation." They told me, however, that my Afrikaans would need improving before they asked me to dance.

This diversity of opinion, if not demographics, may signal a more asso-ciative politics, rather than a racial or descent-based identity, or a broader range of political associations that are possible within the identity context of the Afrikaans arts festivals. Yet the inclusivity of such festivals is somewhat in doubt when placed in the larger context of the South African arts scene. Even the KKNK, which takes place in a district populated by a majority of coloured Afrikaans speakers, draws an overwhelmingly white audience, despite the emphasis on language as the animating theme (Daneel 2008).

The other major festival held in Bloemfontein annually is the Mangaung African Cultural Festival (Macufe), which was launched in 1997. Held in early October, less than two miles from the scene of the Vryfees at the Free State Stadium and Loch Logan shopping plaza, the Macufe festival feels as if it is held in yet another country, borrowing again from Hauptfleisch. The majority of festival-goers seemed to be speaking Sesotho (a language I do not speak), and seemed to be almost entirely black African. As with the Vryfees, there were tents selling food and crafts, as well as musical performances. While the Vryfees featured *boeremusiek* concerts and traditional country dancing, Macufe featured jazz music and dancing. Because the events were held so close to one another and did not overlap in their timing, they could draw from the same interested population in terms of their attendance, but the stark segregation of the two events was the strongest impression I recorded.

Yet the topic of Macufe often came up during the course of discussions of Afrikaans arts festivals. As a reason for not attending Macufe, many Afrikaans-speaking interview participants referenced time constraints, dis-organization at the festival, or general discomfort at the type of offerings at the festival. Yet one woman, aged twenty-eight, ran through both her moti-vations for attending the Afrikaans festivals and not attending Macufe in the course of one response. When asked about the festivals, she said

> Yes, I do attend the festivals. It is a cultural revival. It is very important for Afrikaner culture. . . . We want to be able to get together without bitching. We need space to develop our music and arts. . . . It is important to have a setting where you can interact with one another. There are so few opportunities to introduce other people to your culture. The festivals are a chance to get to know one another. You cannot accept one another without understanding. It is sometimes about pride. I do take pride in the arts. (028)

Without a follow-up question, while I was writing her answers down, she continued:

> But I also do not go to Macufe. I do not feel welcome there. It is very threaten-ing to be there. But these festivals have nothing to do with apartheid. Afrikan-ers constantly feel like they are being threatened. I agree with the changes to government, but they are doing things wrong. It is a problem of competence. People need running water and electricity. *Ag*, but anyway, festivals. Where do you get so many white Afrikaner people together? There are not a lot of opportunities for that. They [blacks] do have Macufe, but I do not feel wel-come there. I feel scared. I am intimidated by the masses of blacks. There is a lot of drinking. I do not understand the language. You know they are speak-ing about you, but there is no way to respond. (028)

This dichotomy of festivals, based on race as well as language, shows how spaces may have integrative intent, but may ultimately reinforce the cleav-ages associated with the prior regime. By contrast, sporting events such as the World Cup have the potential to bridge divides, but may not have long-term positive effects in terms of nation-building.

NATIONALLY ORIENTED RITUALS

There are public celebrations of identity that have the potential to be both oriented toward a national community and true to the experience of people who live within the state. The remapping of the calendar of public holidays in South Africa in 1994 added a holiday called Heritage Day. The South African government said of the day,

> its significance rests in recognising aspects of South African culture which are both tangible and difficult to pin down: creative expression, our historical inheritance, language, the food we eat, as well as the land in which we live. Within a broader social and political context, the day's events . . . are a powerful agent for promulgating a South African identity, fostering reconciliation and promoting the notion that variety is a national asset as opposed to igniting conflict. (South African Government 2015)

In 2005, an eponymous group began a campaign to remake the holiday into National Braai[17] Day, celebrating the culture of outdoor grilling as central to the South African national ethos. Archbishop Desmond Tutu became the official patron of the organization in 2007. In 2011, the group released a song celebrating Braaidag, and claiming that "we stand united at the bonfire / We raise our glasses to the clear blue sky / Tell me your story and I'll tell you mine / Things will be better and I am feeling fine." The foundation's mission states,

> *Across race, language, region and religion, we all share one common heritage.* It is called many things: Chisa Nyama, Braai and Ukosa to name a few. Although the ingredients may differ, the one thing that never changes is that *when we have something to celebrate we light fires, and prepare great feasts.* We encourage all South Africans to *unite around fires, share our heritage and wave our flag* on 24 September every year. . . . This is a noble cause, which will *contribute to strengthening South Africa as a nation* through this act of nation-building and social cohesion. ("National Braai Day Mission and Vision" 2015, emphasis in original text)

Indeed, Braaidag (Braai Day) was how the majority of my friends and acquaintances in Bloemfontein referred to the holiday on 24 September. In one dual interview, an Afrikaans-speaking young woman said "We also have Heritage Day. But we called it Braaidag, and now everyone is using that" (051–052). Another young woman, in a mid-September interview, said "Heritage Day is coming up. It is Braaidag, Braai Day. Braai, you know, that is something we all have in common" (023).

Heritage Day, or Braaidag, is often accompanied by a wave of advertising campaigns by liquor distributors, supermarkets, banks, and other industries celebrating the connections made over the braai, and the possibilities for reconciliation and forging bonds across old divides. Yet as Hermann Wasserman, a prominent South African scholar, notes in his personal blog, such depictions sit uneasily with the realities of a South African social arena that is still deeply divided along the lines of race, class, and language. According to Wasserman, Braaidag and the depictions of it in advertising have to potential to make "us [South Africans] believe we have already arrived in fantasyland. Sure, the purpose of parties, like those around braai fires, is to make us forget reality for a while. . . . But to elevate a party to national heritage status is problematic because it could get us stuck in the gap between the ideal and the reality, and even make us feel quite comfortable there" (Wasserman 2013). The reality, for Wasserman, is that he still lives in a profoundly divided society.

Despite the fact that Heritage Day is intended as a cross-cultural celebration of the history of South Africa, for many South Africans in practice, it is not a day that is inherently integrative. In the words of one young Afrikaans-speaking man, "Braai culture, yes, that is my culture. I am proud of that. . . . But you know, we will not go out to braai or party with black people. We sometimes mix with English white people, but not with blacks" (034). Shared heritage, in this case, is not the same as meaningful connection based on that commonality.

The other holiday that could be said to celebrate the heritage of South Africans as a whole is Reconciliation Day. The rebranding of the Day of the Vow in the post-apartheid era, Reconciliation Day celebrates both the battle of Blood River and the founding of the ANC's armed wing, Umkhonto weSizwe. In an effort to expand the audience for the Reconciliation Day interpretation of the day, in 2011, President Zuma opened up a road of reconciliation between the Voortrekker Monument, the epicenter of the Day of the Vow celebrations, and the newly established Freedom Park, a monument to those who died in the struggle against apartheid. According to newspaper coverage, in 2012 there was a meeting of the leaders of a reconciliation service from Freedom Park and the leaders of the Day of the Vow service on the road connecting the two monuments. Despite having been at the monument all day, I was unaware of such a meeting.

Two journalists who covered the meeting for the *City Press* newspaper, a black African reporter attending the Day of the Vow celebration and a white reporter attending the Reconciliation Day service, wrote on the event from separate sides (Mabandu 2012; Blignaut 2012). Charl Blignaut, who attended the Freedom Park services, was part of the delegation who got waylaid on the way from their service to the meeting. Both parties, apparently, were late. During the confusion, and as a conclusion to his representation of events, Blignaut said of the event, "We are lost on Reconciliation Road and the PR lady phones to find out where the meeting will be. A white SABC camera-man grumbles. 'It'll be quick,' chides the PR. 'They'll meet and say I forgive you, I forgive you and then it's over.' The cameraman jokes: 'My people don't forgive.' It's funny and it's not so funny" (Blignaut 2012). This joke, in its dark humor, points to the fact that while large gestures—such as symbolic meet-ings on roads or renaming of holidays—can and do occur in post-apartheid South Africa, their resonance is sometimes lacking.

CONCLUSION

Ritual and ceremony are closely tied to the performance of identity and com-munity in post-apartheid South Africa. In many ways, the expressions of eth-nonational chauvinism and strictly defined communities associated with the prior regime are not central to the ways that people identify themselves in the post-apartheid era. However, in a number of different more-or-less exclusive ceremonial spaces, the performance of identity is reified along divisive lines, where people are reminded of their subnational identities in ways that seem to be in direct competition with national identities.

Whether affiliative or strictly defined, much of the ceremonial and ritual space in South Africa is segregated. Such spaces serve to remind people of their communities, and the boundaries of belonging in those communities. While socially conservative people might opt to go to the Day of the Vow or to send their daughters to the Reed Dance, those who have a more progres-sive or liberal bent may prefer the affiliative spaces of sports stadiums and arts festivals. However, the outcome is largely similar: the creation of spaces that are segregated in practice. The key difference, though, is in how individuals orient themselves toward the communities created in such spaces. The idea that an affiliative community, which commands loyalty and shapes identity, is nearly as profoundly segregated as descent-defined ritual spaces, is insidi-ous. The affiliative rituals, in being consonant with the idea of an integrated South Africa but reproducing segregated spaces, ultimately signal notions of community that do not transcend the divisions of the past, but elide their rigidity by framing participation in terms of choice. Where bridging attempts have been made to create ceremonial spaces that are more broadly defined, to include a national South African community, these rituals often fail to command loyalty, or once again provide an opportunity for de facto segregation.

The upshot of this segregation is not only in the fact of who is socializing with whom, but also in the ways that such ritual spaces serve as reminders of boundaries and the consonant narratives of history and community that they reproduce. By signaling communal identities, and providing spaces for their expression that are imbued with ceremonial significance, these performances of community serve to remind South Africans who participate in them about the boundaries of their social imaginary, and the lines that continue to divide their national community.

CHAPTER 7

Homes, Farms, Parks, and Walls

Land, Space, and Ownership of Democratic South Africa

The idea of national self-determination implies connections between identity and territory. The puzzle in circumstances of postconflict nation-building, however, lies in the fact that the territory is already set, and the aim is to build a community that is coterminus with the population of that land. Rather than starting from a point of self-determination, nation-building asks formerly conflicting communities to remap their identities in the name of the territorial persistence of the state. The politics of space in building nations is about co-habitation and integration: the meaningful sharing of space in ways that help to build community. This imperative holds in both public spaces, which must be shared, and private spaces, which must coexist.

But how have changes and continuities in the management, ownership, and representativeness of both public and private space served to remap identities and buttress commonality, rather than to reinforce divisions inherited from the past? Debates over the management of public space and the ownership and securitization of private spaces are of central concern in the project of nation-building, because they fall at the intersection of belonging and exclusion. Who is welcome, who is represented, who is safe, who owns and who is only allowed to reside—these are questions not just about land and rights, but also about a sense of belonging, tied to an "emotional (or even ontological) attachment, about feeling 'at home'" as contrasted with being alienated or unmoored (Yuval-Davis 2011, 10–11).

The apartheid state policed not only where people could make their homes, but where they could work and how they could move, and it regularly and violently changed the requirements for each, in forced removals, racial reclassification, influx controls, and Bantustan policies. With the advent of multiracial democracy, then, there was an imperative to change how South Africans experienced the space of their country. The codification of rights to freedom of movement and residence in the Constitution of 1996, along with symbolic and memorial changes in public space such as the installation of statues of Nelson Mandela and other anti-apartheid fighters, were central to the creation of a more representative public sphere (Coombes 2003). These changes were a way to remind the public that while the territoriality of South Africa remained the same, the significance and availability of that space had changed.

Despite these changes, and also because of them, a series of protests began in March 2015 over the issue of monuments and statues in the public eye, under the auspices of the #RhodesMustFall movement. On 9 April 2015, a statue of Cecil John Rhodes was removed from its plinth in the middle of the University of Cape Town campus after months of sustained protest. The same week, an Afrikaans pop star chained herself to the statue of Paul Kruger in Church Square in central Pretoria. Joined by about one hundred people holding signs alleging that the removal of statues was tantamount to personal violence, the protest was in response to the vandalism of the statue the previous weekend (de Villiers 2015). The contestation over statues, and protests for their removal or their "protection," was not simply a matter of beloved objects, but of the character of public, national space and its implications for national belonging. While the integrating impulses of the transition had emphasized the need for public space to accommodate and represent all groups, the confrontational nature of the protests over memorials signaled a return to an agonistic mode of understanding public space (Holmes and Loehwing 2016).

The zero-sum contestation over statues, in which the removal of a statue is the ostracization of a community while its persistence signals a continuity of affiliation with systems of oppression, is mirrored in the conversation about ownership and land. This parallel arises, in part, because of what James has called the "property/citizenship hybrid" in South Africa (2007),[1] in which the right to access land was not merely about economic conditions, but a democratic entitlement that resulted from apartheid-era deprivations. Thus, South African debates characterize the issues of land reform and the securitization of private property as not merely about economic well-being or the threat of crime, but also about the rights of citizenship and the boundaries of the national community.

Divided into three sections, this chapter investigates the debates over land, space, and politics in three different contexts: land reform, integration of public and private space, and white-separatist communities. Each section focuses on the boundaries drawn within the national community, and how such boundaries are challenged, how space is meaningfully integrated and shared, and how space can be legally integrated but functionally exclusionary. In inhabiting space, claiming ownership of land, securitizing private property, or in the extreme, declaring a kind of newly segregated space for a rigidly defined community, space is being used and deployed as a way to demarcate group identity, in ways that signal both new integration and resilient segregation.

LAND OWNERSHIP AND LAND REFORM: WHO OWNS WHAT?

The issue of land ownership, both during apartheid and now, is one that seems to divide opinions along almost strictly racial lines. While land is partly an economic concern, it largely represents "security, identity and history, rather than being just an asset" (James 2001, 93). The debate over land reform, then, "has been a struggle over being. For the people most affected by land reform debates, much of their existence and meaning is tied directly to the land. They see in land their ancestors, their identity, their means of subsistence and profit, their relationship with others" (McCusker, Moseley, and Ramutsindela 2015, 6). Because of these identity-based conceptions of land reform, the issue of redistribution is often framed as a zero-sum game, about ownership not just of private property, but of the country. In such debates, land is owned by certain groups, legitimately or illegitimately, while others are dispossessed or threatened by expropriation. Although the government, through market-led approaches to land reform like "Willing Seller, Willing Buyer," has framed the issue as solvable through individual cooperative initiatives, these plans have met with little success (Lahiff 2007).

Despite the fact that almost two-thirds of South Africans live in urban areas, the symbolism of rural land has proven to be durably important in the post-apartheid era (Walker et al. 2010). The issue of land reform demonstrates, for many urban constituencies, the progress toward the goal of transformation and democratization by proxy. Many Zulu-speaking interview participants, referenced below, lived in the city. Despite this distance, they reported that land reform was a central issue to them in the project of transformation within South Africa. The lack of movement on the land-reform issue signaled to many that the government was unwilling to undertake programs aimed at real integration and economic transformation. Afrikaans speakers, similarly urban in Bloemfontein, also reacted strongly to the issue of land reform, but in an entirely different manner. The (to date, largely empty) threats of expropriation of land, with or without compensation by, for example, members of the ANC Youth League, were seen as an existential threat. The threats of land reform, even in the context of very little movement on the issue, were interpreted as signals of the government's direct hostility toward Afrikaans speakers. These interview participants, ensconced in city living and with little or no direct connection to agriculture or rural areas, saw the issue of land reform as one that was, in many ways, a referendum on their belonging.

The continued salience of land reform is partly a result of how ownership patterns have remained largely unchanged in the first two decades of democracy. Land reform, which was touted as central to the project of "transformation" in the mid-1990s, has largely stalled, despite continuing demands by agricultural unions, as well as "shack dwellers'" organizations such as Durban's Abahlali baseMjondolo and the Landless People's Movement. The land redistribution program, which targeted 30 percent redistribution or redress within the first five years of democracy, had only redistributed about 8 percent of land by 2010 (Atuahene 2011, 121). This shortfall, according to Walker (2005), is "perceived not simply as a failure in land policy but, more fundamentally, as a failure to transform the very nature of society—to address black claims to full citizenship, through land ownership, and to make amends for the insults to human dignity that black people have suffered as a collectivity through dispossession in the past" (806). Although framed by advocates and activists as a demand for collective reparations, land reform in actuality has been carried out on an individual basis, and been framed by policymakers as redress for individual historical dispossessions, rather than as a process of ensuring "distributive equity" (du Toit 2013). Land-reform programs, far from attempting to radically alter the patterns of land ownership in South Africa, have instead focused on the rights of individuals.

The incapacity of programs aimed at redistribution to live up to the kinds of demands made by land-reform activists has left many South Africans dissatisfied. The majority of my interviews with Zulu-speaking participants took place in 2013, which marked the centenary of the passage of the 1913 Land Act. ANC partisans used the occasion of the centenary as a way to shore up support for the party, and activist groups used it to challenge the lack of mean-ingful land reform in the post-apartheid era. As such, the Land Act loomed large for many interview participants, who referenced it often, although the interview questionnaire included no questions directly having to do with land or land reform. However, the centenary of this agenda-setting piece of segregation legislation gave many the opportunity to reflect on how the dis-tribution of land affected their perceptions of the post-apartheid era. One Zulu-speaking interview participant, who lived in the city but had grown up in rural areas, when asked what measures could be taken to further the cause of nation-building, said

> I would like to see blacks having economic freedom. We need to overcome the challenges of earlier. We have to address the 1913 Land Act. 87% of the land still belongs to 13% of the population.[2] The government knows that the willing buyer/willing seller thing is not working. Food security is connected to land and income. Having things as they are does not make South Africa a rainbow nation, with the imbalances we have. The land in the rural areas, the homelands, is not arable, so that contributes to the problem. You cannot farm on those lands. Land is what needs to change for reconciliation. (089)

Another Zulu-speaking interview participant from the city agreed, but in somewhat more reserved terms.

> The issue of land is still very important. . . . The government has dragged its feet on this issue. . . . If we can really talk about land, it will go a long way. But you cannot just give land for the sake of land. You must be trained to understand the significance, and what it takes as a landowner. . . . We have to give land in a responsible manner. Feeding families and promoting economic activity is what is important. (099)

In part, she seems to be referencing some of the anxieties that I heard on multiple occasions about the example of Zimbabwe as a cautionary tale of land reform. As South Africa's neighbor to the north, in addition to the close bonds between the ANC and the ZANU during the anti-apartheid struggle, the Mugabe-led government in Zimbabwe undertook large-scale land redis-tribution in the early 2000s. The Fast Track Land Reform Program, which involved the violent expropriation of large tracts of white-owned farmland by war veterans without compensation, has been blamed by critics for the large-scale drop in export-crop production, with accompanying international sanctions and detrimental macroeconomic effects.[3]

Both Zulu-speaking and Afrikaans-speaking participants referenced the example of Zimbabwe, although to different ends. One Zulu-speaking participant said

> What is needed is a paradigm shift. We need to become the owners of the land. Whites are still running the place. Behind the scenes, they are corrupting whom they want to corrupt. We need to make people feel like the owners of the land. . . . We need them to look to the future, not think in terms of hand to mouth. The land issue is the main [unresolved] thing. Willing buyer/willing seller is not working. We are afraid to do like Zimbabwe. The government is trying to protect the economy. But does it protect the economy? Does it protect the economy to keep our people poor? It is undermining getting black people back to the driver's seat. The majority of black people have minds working as workers. They are only thinking about what they will eat this afternoon. (088)

The paradigm shift, then, for this interview participant involved land first and foremost, but also the idea of ownership, control of economic and productive capacities. Referencing Zimbabwe, this speaker downplayed the idea of the macroeconomic consequences of the process of land reform, looking instead to Zimbabwe as a model of economic transformation and empowerment of majority communities.

Yet for many South African large-scale landowners, particularly those tied to agriculture, the examples of land reform from Zimbabwe and elsewhere in Africa tend to loom large as points of fear and threat, rather than positive transformation. In conversations with Afrikaans speakers regarding the issue of land reform, words such as "nervous" and "anxious" came up often. In the context of a question about what it is important for outsiders to understand about South Africa, one Afrikaans-speaking young man said, "You must understand that land reform makes us very nervous. . . . We do not want to leave. . . . First, there was land reform in the Congo, then in Zimbabwe. You can see what happened there, with the farmers and the countries. Will it be like that next for South Africa?" (018).

Because I did not specifically ask questions about land reform or its importance, the contexts in which it arose were different. In the context of a discussion on voting, a young Afrikaans-speaking woman said

it really feels important for me to vote, especially with stuff like the land reform policies . . . especially after what happened in Zimbabwe. . . . [Y]ou have
people in South Africa like Julius Malema saying "No, but we are going to do
that in South Africa." That makes me mad. Because you see what is happening
in Zimbabwe. People are dying from hunger. And now you want to come and
do this here. So, if they get a 2/3rds majority, they can change the Constitution, obviously, then they can bring stuff like that in. So, for that reason, it is
really important for me [to vote]. Not just for the Afrikaans people, and not
just because my parents are farmers, but because the whole country will suf-
fer. People will die of hunger. (013)

Although many Afrikaans-speaking participants saw the necessity for some
kind of change in the ownership structure of land, many expressed sentiments similar to those reflected above. This could be because, as discussed
below, "the land" has a good deal of symbolic resonance in the Afrikaans
collective psyche. Such contesting claims to land, especially symbolically resonant and important land constitutive of belonging to a place, will inevitably
cause conflict.

The discussion of land reform, then, at least in ordinary language, is so
much larger than a question of which piece of ground is tilled or tended
by whom. Belonging to the land, and the land belonging to people, are
constitutive of claims to autochthony. Claims to a kind of "new nativism"
form a central point for understanding the South African black imaginary
in the post-apartheid era, in which claims are deployed to give credence
to demands for either further land reform or additional protections from
expropriation (Ndlovu-Gatsheni 2009). Ownership of property is symbolically resonant, and the contestation over possession of property involves
the discussion of more than simply the facts of land redistribution. Owning
the territory of the nation, either literally or symbolically, becomes a zero
sum game: ownership provides a deep sense of belonging, while depriva-
tion results in profound alienation. While land ownership and redistribution debates are certainly about economic transformation, they are also
about who is at home, who belongs, in the post-apartheid era. For both
Zulu speakers and Afrikaans speakers, the issue of land ownership signals
who belongs in the nation and who does not, in the former case because of
a seeming lack of commitment to make change, and in the latter because of
threats of change.

INTEGRATING PUBLIC SPACE AND PROTECTING PRIVATE SPACE: CONTRASTING DYNAMICS

The post-apartheid emphasis on integration seems to be in direct conversation and confrontation with the spatial policies of apartheid, which focused on segregation and control of spaces and places, as well as movement. A major imperative for the post-apartheid government was not only the dismantling of the legal restrictions on movement, but the codification of rights to freedom of movement and housing in the constitution. Far from being a simple matter of allowing people to go where they want, this change represented the creation of a public sphere that was consonant with the idea of multiracial democracy.

Interview participants frequently identified changes in space and freedom of movement as major differences before and after apartheid. One young Afrikaans-speaking woman suggested that the differences between growing up during and after apartheid were largely spatial, with changes in mindset coming as a consequence of the integration of space.

> During apartheid . . . everyone was kept apart.[4] So, my parents did not go to school with black people. They did not even have black people near them. . . . They used to tell me that at 6 or 7 o'clock at night, or maybe a bit later, a bell would ring in the towns which would mean that all of the black people would have to be out of the towns. They were not allowed to be in town any longer. So, they really grew up in a completely different world than what we grew up in. When apartheid ended, everyone merged in the schools, so we grew up with them. . . . I think we learned to live with them. It is like I say, our cultures are so different that we are never going to be one, big, happy family, but just as they had to learn to tolerate us, we had to learn to tolerate them. (013)

Another Zulu-speaking participant who had grown up and been educated during apartheid pointed out the spatial differences in her life before and after the transition. She said, "That time [apartheid] and where we are now are like two different worlds. Where I am working now, I could not have imagined it before. Some of the places, you know you would not put your foot in before. Now, we can go where we want and work where we want" (103). These changes, she said, were not only vital to her ability to provide for her family, but integral to her notion of freedom. The removal of the apartheid laws regulating movement and space have dramatically changed the character of urban centers in South Africa. Now city centers in South Africa are open to all.

The integration of space is not only physical but also symbolic, and expressed through places such as public museums, statuary, and the ways in which people, history, and symbols inhabit such spaces. For the Zulu-speaking South Africans with whom I spoke, the idea that their history is now being incorporated into public spaces through new programming, names, statuary, and educational initiatives is a vital redress of past erasure. These programs of redress also took the form of reconstructing black history in South Africa in the National and Provincial Archives, through the collection and curation of new and diverse sets of documents (Harris 2002). According to one museum worker, "Here in the archives, white people and Indians come to look for their family. We didn't have the time to do that. We don't have those documents [for black South Africans]. The importance of family history, but the lack of documents is what we are dealing with. That is what we are trying to fix now" (097). There was also a general sense, among almost all of the Zulu speakers who participated in interviews, that the public money being spent to replace statuary, rename streets, and supplement the historic and cultural facets of life in Durban was worthwhile.

At the same time, the shift in this balance caused a good deal of anxiety for Afrikaans-speaking interview participants in the Free State. On many occasions during interviews, people expressed fear or anxiety over the loss of history. One Afrikaans-speaking museum worker noted that in the last ten years, the museum industry had become increasingly racialized. She said, "It is now about black history and white history. White people are not included in this [new] history, purely based on the color of their skin" (071). This recalibration of resources and emphasis constituted racial hostility for this participant.

Another participant, unaffiliated with the tourism or culture industries, noted that the perceived disappearance of "his" history from public spaces was profoundly alienating for him, saying

I live here. For 300 years, my family has been here. I do not call myself South African because my history does not count. It does not count anymore with the new dispensation. Really, there were only about 50 years when things went haywire. 50 years of apartheid. Your standing and viewpoint on the country does not really matter. We renamed things. They are renaming things. History is disregarded. When you look at the past, you are infringed upon. You feel disowned. It is not about the money. It is about a frame of mind. You are outside now. (049–050)

The initiatives that are publically billed as integrating, then, end up being hostile to those who share this frame of mind. Rather than sharing public space, the renaming or inclusion of new memorial objects constitutes a substitution, and thereby, a displacement. That sense of what one interview participant called "the dominant culture [of] Black African-ness" (032) was perceived as alienating. It signals, for many interview participants like the one quoted above, that they do not have a symbolic place, and therefore a literal home, in the South African nation.

The removal of prohibitions on movement and the integration of space mark a major shift from the apartheid era. The fact that people can and do inhabit space in far less constrained ways than before is meaningful to many people. So too are the changes made to the representativeness of public space, for both good and bad. While often met with resistance, the integration of public space in South Africa represents a fundamental change in South African life. This change can be seen in both the character of public spaces and the ways in which people think about the character of the nation.

While public spaces have notably changed their character, the private geographies of apartheid segregation have remained "resilient" in the post-apartheid era in terms of both the boundaries that demarcated provinces and the racial makeup of constituent municipalities (Ramutsindela 2007). But such resilience can also be seen in the patterns of individual land ownership and tenure, both rural and urban (Berrisford 2011; Walker et al. 2010; O'Laughlin et al. 2013). This continuity can be seen in the ways that "near-segregation still dominates so many areas of everyday life in South Africa, manifested in racialized patterns of employment, residence, transport, shopping, music, worship, friendship, health care, education and voting" (O'Laughlin et al. 2013, 8).

Where integration has occurred, it has happened in two very different types of communities: informal settlements in affluent, formerly whites-only areas, and the partial integration of middle-class neighborhoods in the context of major urban areas (Lemanski 2006; Ballard 2002; Murray 2017). Informal or shack settlements have been established through land occupations of vacant spaces; their legal status has been largely uncertain since the 1970s, but they have grown and become politically organized, in the last two decades. Informal settlements throughout the country contain almost 1.25 million households, and such areas house almost 6.4 percent of the population, according to the 2011 census (Housing Development Agency of South Africa 2013), though activist organizations have claimed the number to be as high as 2.4 million households. Scholars estimate that between one-quarter and one-third of urban residents live in informal settlements (Levenson 2014). Despite the government having built more than three million homes since 1994, the number of informal settlement dwellers has remained almost unchanged in the same period (Housing Development Agency of South Africa 2012).

Such settlements have been widely protested by affluent residents of these areas in terms that evoked apartheid-era race categorizations and prejudices. Ballard has argued that part of the resentment over the appearance of informal settlements in such areas stems from the fact that they challenged the "sense of place and therefore [affected residents'] self-perception as western, modern, civilised people" (Ballard 2004, 49). Thus, although space writ large is potentially integrated, there is no real sharing in practice.

Integration of middle-class suburbs, by contrast, has been seen as the epitome of the "new" South Africa, and a signal of the increasing tolerance of the population. Yet the results of such integration, according to interview evidence, have been mixed (Horn and Ngcobo 2003). In terms of residents' sense of belonging, the phenomenon of desegregation has different effects, conditioned by race. New black residents of middle- and upper-class neighborhoods "do not have an equal sense of 'belonging' to the cultural space as their 'white' neighbours and thus are constantly striving to fit into white spaces rather than experienc[ing] an equal 'right' to shared cultural space" (Lemanski 2006, 433). In many ways, then, there has been resistance, even within integrated areas, to the sharing of space within privileged communities.

Another resistance to the freedom of movement and increasing integration of residential areas can be observed in the proliferation of gated communities and security estates throughout affluent areas of South Africa (Murray 2017). Gated communities, although not expressly race-segregated, are only open to people who can pay for the privileges of private security, and partly for this reason have mostly white residents. This privatization of living spaces is sometimes done in direct contravention of the law through the unauthorized closing of streets and the erection of security booms. As of 2002, there were about 500 illegal road closures for security purposes within the city of Johannesburg (Landman and Schönteich 2002). As of 2008, there were 49 legal road closures, 37 with expired permits, 188 illegal closures, and 265 pending applications with the city government (Lemanski, Landman, and

Durington 2008, 146). Interview evidence from people who manned these barriers or lived behind them suggests that they were erected as preventative security measures (Clarno 2014). Between 2001 and 2011, the number of private security companies in South Africa increased by more than 61 percent, while the number of people employed as guards or security officers increasing by 111 percent (Carter 2013).

Whether lawful or unlawful, the broad term "security estate" has become the accepted nomenclature for office parks, universities, or private homes that have, among other things, a complete security perimeter, monitoring mechanisms for the premises and surrounding area, and a guarded entrance. Such zones, and the fear of crime that legitimates them, seem to aid in creating a fear of the outside world in the minds of the residents and workers in such zones. By understanding the public sphere as fundamentally dangerous, residents feel they have the right to divorce themselves, and exclude others from the spaces they inhabit (Hook and Vrdoljak 2002, 218). The fact that securitized spaces are available only to those who have the ability to pay for them further exacerbates the already-present social cleavages of class and race. It is also not incidental that such securitized spaces arose quickly after the end of influx-control laws in South Africa. Though crime was a constant fear among the white and affluent populations under apartheid, with advent of multiracial democracy the policing structures that explicitly privileged and protected white South Africans changed. The privatized security industry, as such, is a product of the post-apartheid order.

Paradoxically, however, greater levels of security in such estates creates for residents a sense of safety through access control, and a sense of community within, but "this feeling of safety inside ironically contribute[s] to greater anxiety outside, through the juxtaposition of the 'safe inside' versus 'dangerous outside'" (Lemanski, Landman, and Durington 2008, 148). Such contrasts, in turn, have detrimental effects in terms of individuals' perception of the public as "outside" of their secure zones, in terms of public spaces, public goods, and where the responsibilities of citizens begin and end.

South African scholar Richard Ballard has labeled the phenomenon of physical and social distancing through securitization "semigration" (Ballard 2005). Ballard describes this phenomenon as an

> attempt to have the best of both worlds. Through mechanisms such as gated communities, one is able to opt out of urban life, and with it uncontrolled mixing and what is seen as the increasingly "African" and "Third World"

character of the city. . . . In the absence of the state's attempts to manage social
diversity, smaller groups of "like minded" individuals would have to band together to restore a level of homogeneity, and thus predictability and security,
in their lives. . . . Gated communities are, thus, simply suburbs that no longer
trust the state to be performing a series of functions on their behalf . . . the
prospect of racial and class mixing going unmanaged by the state is leading
many to resolve the problem with their private resources. (Ballard 2005, 17)

Thus, the retreat behind walls is a disengagement from both the social and
the political fabric of the newly integrated city. Indeed, a particularly affluent
gated community north of Durban, called Zimbali ("flowers," in isiZulu), has
advertised for new residents to "Emigrate to Zimbali," or to "Become a citizen
of Zimbali." This notion that moving behind walls is in some way analogous
to emigration, or to a change in citizenship, details just how radically separate
this community proposes to be from the nearby diverse urban centers.

A real estate firm in Johannesburg has apparently used a similar strategy
to promote moving to Cape Town, encouraging people to "semigrate" to the
Cape. The idea behind this push was related to the Western Cape's distinct
demographics, as the only province with a black minority, and therefore, the
idea that "moving to Cape Town was, more or less, just as good as leaving
Africa itself" (Fairbanks 2018).

Part of the detachment is in the form of privatized security. Zimbali
advertises itself as a "refuge," one of the benefits of residence being twenty-
four-hour guarded entrances to the gated estate, as well as electrified perimeter fencing with foot patrols and CC-TV monitoring. One ethnography of
this community, by Dixon et al. (1994), details the intricate security measures
taken within those security perimeters, including booms that can be lowered
at many intersections, codes for guest entrance, and similar measures. The
authors characterize Zimbali as

a veritable fortress, but once you are in, it is like being in a time warp reminis-
cent of the old white South Africa—no security on any of the houses, children
playing in the street, private property left lying about without risk of being
stolen, black staff working on the grounds and gardens and in the kitchens.
The only sense of time having moved on and of this being South Africa today
is the occasional presence of black families living in this "village." In part,
there is an overlap between race and class as elites seek to protect themselves
from the (racial) underclass around them. (Dixon et al. 1994, 52)

Other scholars examining such communities have reported that, indeed, the racial makeup of those living in these estates has remained largely unchanged in the twenty years of democracy (Durington 2006; Morange et al. 2012).

Of course the very concept of semigration has both racial and class dimensions. The entire geography of South Africa has, as explained above, been overdetermined by race for decades. Yet in the post-apartheid era of desegregated public spaces and multiracial cities, white South Africans have remained both affluent and remarkably resistant to integration of their residential spaces.

Indeed, on several occasions, the topic of semigration and security came up during conversations with interview participants regarding emigration (discussed in greater detail in chapter 4). For participants, there were obvious parallels between the forces that drove some people to feel they needed to leave the country and made others feel the need to securitize and detach their residential spaces from a wider community. One Afrikaans-speaking woman in Bloemfontein, when asked about what she thought about the process of emigration, responded, "I have never considered leaving, but my children will definitely leave. I do not mind. It is not unpatriotic. They can just go explore the world. My oldest child lives in Johannesburg. The crime gets to him and his family. He does not like the lifestyle. We did not grow up that way, but now we all live in our own little worlds. It is the walls and the fear" (071). A fifty-seven-year-old Afrikaans-speaking man said, when asked the same question, "All of us know people who have left. I would like to stay and make a contribution . . . but I know I cannot force my children to stay. . . . But you must know . . . people emigrate inwardly. They detach with walls and fences" (078).

Yet these kinds of security interventions are not limited to gated communities in South Africa. South Africans have the largest number of private security guards per capita of any country in the world, and private security personnel outnumber the official police force by three to one (Carter 2013). The total outlay for private security for homes and businesses in South Africa in 2013 was R70 billion, or about $7 billion (Shaikh 2014).

The urban landscape of affluent neighborhoods is one of walls and fences when seen from the street or the sidewalk. Figure 4 is a picture of a residential road in Durban, close to where I lived in 2013. This picture was captured in 2009 by Google Maps, but the security interventions below are still there, and most have been strengthened. Different security interventions are highlighted in different colors. Black squares indicate electrified fences, which are

Fig. 4. Typical road in
the Berea in Durban,
from Google Maps.

constantly armed, and angled out to deter people scaling the walls. White squares are placards posted outside of the perimeter walls announcing to passers-by that certain residences have security systems and companies that monitor the houses electronically and by physical patrol. White circles indicate the presence of either razor wire or metal spikes placed along the top of residential walls to deter climbing. Finally, the black circle indicates the location of the guard post, which is constantly manned by an individual, paid for collectively by the residents of the street. The vast majority of these houses also have security bars built in to their windows and doors.

Such security interventions are not only present in residences, but, as noted above, in offices and on university campuses. The majority of South African university campuses are enclosed within security perimeters. Any individual entering campus needs to either present an official student ID to get through turnstyles, or to have an appointment with a university employee and be willing to write down their own name, official document numbers and contact details, and the name and affiliation of the person they are visiting.

The University of the Free State has a semi-open campus, which can be entered without presenting an ID. However, the campus is still surrounded by nine-foot metal fences and has five entrances, of which three or four are closed after dark. The entrances to the campus are open to pedestrians, but campus guards monitor them and inspect exiting cars, whose drivers are forced to stop by traffic booms. The open campus policy at the university arose in the period after the Reitz Incident, which significantly damaged the reputation of the university, especially among black Africans.[5]

Yet the policy of a semi-open campus caused significant anxiety among university staff. Several university employees, especially administrative and support staff, the majority of whom are white women, expressed fear because the university campus was potentially open to any foot or vehicular traffic. On several occasions, staff in multiple departments complained about feeling unsafe in their offices, especially if colleagues needed to leave work early. In one particularly memorable instance, an interview had to be rescheduled because a particular staff member's colleague had gone home sick. When I asked her to clarify why the interview had to be rescheduled, she said that she was also leaving work with sick time because she did not feel safe in the office alone during the afternoon, or walking to her car alone after work.

Securitized space is rarely exited voluntarily by those who live in it.[6] This fact was thrown into relief one day when I was walking to the grocery store in Bloemfontein. The grocery store was less than a kilometer from the gate of the university, and along a major metropolitan road. The large sidewalks on either side of the four-lane road are often used by students of color, though rarely by people who are perceived as white, many of whom owned cars and used them. I regularly walked to get groceries for my on-campus living, though always in the daytime, and generally without detours. One day, while leaving the university and walking to the store, a car pulled up alongside me and stopped on the shoulder. I quickened my pace, because such an action was unusual, and because I was alone on the sidewalk. Yet the passenger in the car called out to me in Afrikaans, and I turned. The car was carrying two middle-aged, white Afrikaans speakers. They expressed concern for me, and where I was going. I responded that I was walking to the grocery store. They expressed concern again, asking me where my car was, and what had gone wrong. They insisted that I call a mechanic to come and attend to my car, and that I could sit with them while I waited. Again, I tried to explain that no, I had no car, and no, I was not in any trouble. I insisted that I was simply walking to the store to buy food. At a loss for what to say, the woman in the passenger seat exclaimed "But no, people do not walk here." During the course of our conversation, at least four people had walked by us, all of them people of color, both men and women. The anxiety she seemed to express was that people "like me" (probably understood as white women) do not walk here. Friends and colleagues echoed these sentiments on many occasions when, for example, they insisted that they could drive me to the store, and that it was too dangerous to walk there. After I politely responded to the car passenger indicating that I walked here often and was quite fine and that I appreciated their concern, the car drove off.

As discussed in chapter 5, crime is a major problem in South Africa, though the extent to which increases in crime rates since the mid-1990s are the result of greater reporting or an increase in the actual crime rate is under debate. The creation of gated communities is, in many ways, a response not only to the fact of high crime rates, but to public perceptions of crime and the threatening nature of outside space (Lemanski 2004). Some preliminary evidence from South Africa suggests that perhaps the flourishing of gated communities and security measures has actually attracted rather than deterred crime, resulting in overall unchanged levels of personal security (Breetzke, Landman, and Cohn 2014).

The voluntary segregation and securitization of private space, especially in the context of rapidly desegregating public space, is a curious one. Which of these trends actually characterizes the democratic era of spatial politics in South Africa? These processes have happened simultaneously, yet they do not directly contradict one another; they are, rather, in conversation. As pointed out above, the increasing integration of public space has led affluent, mostly white, South Africans to leave, in part because of fear. While the Zulu speakers who talked with me indicated that the public sphere changes meant they were welcome in South Africa after the transition, many Afrikaans speakers voiced a sense of alienation. Securitized private space, with its embedded conception of the public sphere as threatening, exacerbates these emotional responses. As with land reform, this is a zero-sum notion of who is welcome in the nation, both in public and in private.

WHERE IS SOUTH AFRICA?

During the period of transition from apartheid to democracy, several proposals were considered which would have substantially altered the geographic makeup of the country. The Constitution of 1996, which provided the framework for the new government and for the processes of transition, including the Truth and Reconciliation Commission, allowed for the establishment of the Volkstaat Council, whose aim was to study the feasibility of creating an autonomous and/or sovereign state for Afrikaners, separate from South Africa. The Volkstaat Council's final report, submitted to the Presidency in 1997, included maps with suggestions of regions suitable as potential *volkstaat* regions. These proposals were not the first time that groups in South Africa had proposed secession by Afrikaners to form their own state. Throughout the late 1980s and the mid-1990s, various activist groups, political parties, and labor unions had presented proposals to their constituents and to Parliament to form a *volkstaat*.

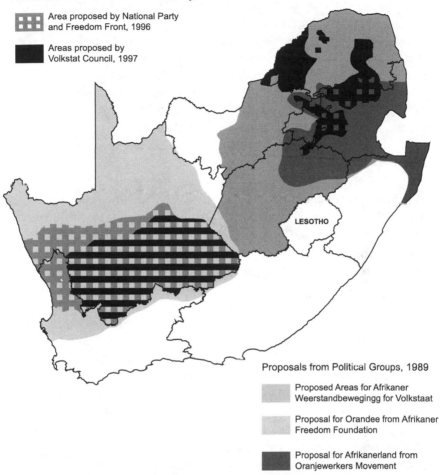

Proposed Areas for Afrikaner Volkstaat, Official Proposals
Submitted to Parliament and Presidency, mid-1990s

Area proposed by National Party
and Freedom Front, 1996

Areas proposed by
Volkstat Council, 1997

LESOTHO

Proposals from Political Groups, 1989

Proposed Areas for Afrikaner
Weerstandbewegingg for Volkstaat

Proposal for Orandee from Afrikaner
Freedom Foundation

Proposal for Afrikanerland from
Oranjewerkers Movement

Fig. 5. Map of possible *volkstaat* regions, from Final Report of Volkstaatraad, National Party
Documents, and three proposals from political groups (Christopher 2001; Jooste 1997).
Cross-hatch designs indicate overlapping regions that belong to multiple proposals.

The *volkstaat*, or people's state, has a long intellectual history in South
Africa, and has been variously interpreted since the late 1980s as either an
autonomous federal territory within a larger country, or an independent
republic exclusively for Afrikaners. Although there have been various territorial proposals for such a region, there is agreement on what a volkstaat would
symbolize, and what it would protect—the Afrikaans language and Afrikaner

culture. In 1993, the twenty-six-party Commission on the Demarcation/ Delimitation of States, Provinces and Regions heard testimony from volk-staat advocates insisting on the creation of such a region for the protection of Afrikaner *eiesoortigheid* (distinctiveness of ethnicity or identity) by insisting that "different races and nations have different value systems. The Afrikaner nation also has the right to unity and freedom in its own country with its own language" (Muthien and Khosa 1995, 308–9, translation by author).

Although the Volkstaat was never recognized by the central state, the town of Orania, founded by academic and activist Carel Boshoff, is one attempt to build such a community, and the town is still actively recruiting support-ers. Set along the banks of the Orange River on the far eastern side of the Northern Cape, Orania is home to just under 900 residents and was founded in 1990 within the evocatively named municipality of Thembelihle, or "the place of beautiful hope." The town is the logical extension of Boshoff's activist work with the Afrikaner-Vryheidstigting (Afrikaner Freedom Foundation), and was established based on the idea that "since black majority rule was unavoidable and white minority rule morally unjustifiable, Afrikaners would have to form their own volkstaat in a smaller part of South Africa" (Schön-teich and Boshoff 2003, 44). Built around a former government-constructed water purification outpost, the land area of Orania was purchased outright by a corporate body that would become the shareholders of the settlement.

The original shareholders and later residents who have bought land have the option to accept or refuse new applicants for landownership and resi-dence within the town, and local suffrage is restricted to landowners (Cava-nagh 2013). Town leaders claim that residency and ownership are based not on race, but rather on language and culture; however the 2011 census recorded the population of Orania as 97.2 percent white, with 98.4 percent saying their first language is Afrikaans (Frith 2012). Kleinfontein, another such commu-nity outside of Pretoria, is estimated to have approximately 1,000 residents, with 450 shareholders, all of whom identify themselves as white (van Zuydam 2013). Both towns have townships adjacent to them, housing a white work-force employed to do manual labor, either for private homes in town or for the town council (Lindner 2013; van Zuydam 2013).

This dream of a *volkstaat*, having its foundation in the long trajectory of Afrikaner nationalism, has come to be rooted in these towns and a handful of other "cultural communities"[7] on the peripheries of the 'new' South Africa. In a 2013 documentary, Boshoff outlined the basic idea of Orania, saying, "Good fences make good neighbors! And that is true. Give a people its own territory and it lives in peace with its neighbours. But trying to make a Rainbow Nation out of us in South Africa is the recipe for disaster and unnecessary bloodshed, [in] the long run. That is very normal" (Lindner 2013). Yet the public relations video that was shown to visitors in 2013 as part of the official tour of Orania is entitled "Nie 'n Volkstaat Nie" (This is not a Volkstaat), indicating a desire not for independence, but for autonomy and self-governance. Whether in terms of a federal system or as an independent republic, the organizing principle of this cultural community is that separateness is the only way to prevent violence and preserve identity.

Kleinfontein and Orania, with a combined population of approximately 1,900, are actually two very small towns in a country of more than fifty-four million. Yet these communities, especially Orania, came up often during the course of conversations with Afrikaans speakers in Bloemfontein, across the spectrum of ages, genders, and employment statuses. Those who brought up the subject were also largely in support of the concept of "self-determination" as established in the constitution, by which such communities defend their existence.[8]

Although some people, like one middle-aged Afrikaans-speaking man in Bloemfontein, connected Orania and other such exclusive communities to the survival of the Afrikaner as a *volk*,[9] others who discussed cultural threat were not quite so extreme in their language. According to one young Afrikaans-speaking man with whom I spoke, "[Orania is] very isolated up there, but people are ultimately forced into that kind of thing. Their culture, their safety is being threatened. . . . There is a threat to our culture now. People are leaving, they are changing the names of the streets. That is why you have Orania. People definitely feel the threat" (032). While in Orania, I spoke with a family at the restaurant area who were driving across South Africa in a camper van for vacation. They said that they made a habit of stopping in Orania every year because of the relaxed atmosphere, the opportunity to be "among [their] own," and the fact that they could camp outside during their time within the perimeter fencing. This combination of perceived threats, both against culture and in terms of physical safety, forms an interesting matrix of anxieties for such people. The contrast of Orania, as a safe space for culture and for physical bodies, to the apparent urban necessities of fortified houses was repeatedly highlighted, both during my visit and by interview participants.

While many individual houses do have chain-link fences, the majority, I was told, do not have security systems, though I could not verify this claim. There were children playing in yards unsupervised, and personal property was left in the open unguarded. Much like the gated communities referenced above, however, the citizens of the main town in Orania seem to have opted for a security perimeter rather than individualized security measures. The town itself is surrounded by a fence and has cameras at all entrance and exit points. An employee in the town office assured me that the security booms that crossed the entrance and exit roads were mostly unmanned (as they were when I entered). These booms, I was told, were only closed once a month in a drill and to make sure they operated correctly, in the words of my tour guide "just to show that we are here." When I asked a follow-up question regarding the reasons for the cameras, I was quickly redirected to another topic of conversation.

During another conversation with an Orania resident, a man in his early thirties referred several times to the fact that "outsiders" had many misperceptions about Orania. When I asked him what they were, he said,

> Everyone seems to think that all Afrikaners are racist or bad. That Orania is a right-wing place. That we have high walls or something. . : . People always ask me why there are only white people in Orania. I say that we are only Afrikaners here. That we do not define by race. They think that the founding here is related to what happened in 1994, that we wanted to get away. It is not that. Even in the 1970s and 1980s, we knew that apartheid was not sustainable. We looked to become part of South Africa where Afrikaners could become the majority. Is that wrong? Can you say it is wrong for us to live our culture?

Yet the question of whether Orania was part of South Africa, as such, was not one on which there seemed to be widespread agreement, even among residents of the town. Among the people with whom I spoke in Orania, there was debate over whether they lived in South Africa. While many said that they did vote for internal Orania elections, they chose not to vote in the wider South African elections. Although "affiliated" with South Africa, or other communities, they were "autonomous" within a larger state. Others said that they were proudly South African, but wanted to live "freely" and among their own people, without the concerns for security that were there in the big cities. The same conversation seemed to occur around whether Orania could be considered a *volkstaat*, as referenced above. Even residents of Orania, then, do not have a consensus on whether their project is, at its core, about separation or autonomy, and what the difference between those two might be.

The other topic that came up often during the discussions of Orania with nonresidents was the idea of self-sufficiency as the core virtue of such communities.[10] This aspect was particularly relevant to one Afrikaans-speaking woman, who said

> I have been [to Orania]. Have a lot of respect for the people there. They do everything for themselves. They build houses and factories. They do their own gardening. They do everything. When I was working [in politics], I was convinced of how good Orania was. It was part of the future that I saw. It is really nice there. People do feel safe. You can even sleep outside. . . . We held a youth conference for [a political party] in Orania. When we asked for keys to get into [the] hall for [a] conference, we were told there were no keys. The place is just left open. There is no logical reason that people react so badly to the project in Orania. It is not trying to hurt anyone. . . . The *tuisland* [homeland] system was seen as chasing people away. But that is not what was meant. [Verwoerd] gave people a space where they can be themselves. Orania is like a homeland for us. It is safe to go there. We can be ourselves. It is not new to be proud of where you come from. You can be for yourself, but not against anyone else. (019)

This wide-ranging set of comments, which took place over the course of the ninety-minute interview, seems to highlight, beyond the idea of self-sufficiency, the myriad ways that nonresident supporters of Orania identify with the goals of the community and view it with a kind of nostalgia.

There were also those who objected to projects like Orania within the group of Afrikaans speakers in Bloemfontein. One thirty-eight-year-old Afrikaans-speaking woman used the words "uncomfortable," "strange," and "undemocratic" to describe Orania (032), while a two-person focus group of a man and woman in their mid-forties agreed that Orania is "too separate" (030). Still others compared the individuals in Orania with the KKK (049–050) and the Amish (028). The people who critiqued Orania and other such settlements tended to be among the younger segment of people with whom I spoke, and they were all employed in high-status occupations, within the academy and as business owners. These critiques were important voices within the context of the discussion on Orania, in part because they did not engage with the autonomy/secession debate, but rejected both the ideals and practices of the community.

While separatist communities loom large in the imaginations of many people with whom I spoke, both the critics and the supporters, they do represent a very small proportion of the population of South Africa, even among Afrikaans speakers. Even when I went to the town to visit, I was struck by the smallness of the town, and the ways in which it was set up as a performative space. The fact that the town has a set of employees dedicated to public relations, an entire repertoire to show to visitors including an official tour in a town vehicle that itself advertises the town on its exterior, and a welcome video and tourist shop, seems to indicate that the town is as much a showpiece as a place of residence.

This impression was strengthened when I was told before visiting that to conduct research in town, it would be necessary to get a permit from the town office. I acquired this permit, which required me to present my consent forms and all contact information to the town office, only after I explained in English to the assistant at the desk what my purpose was and with whom I had already spoken. She then asked me how to translate "research permit" into Afrikaans. I was startled and failed to respond. Luckily, an older gentleman standing behind me in line, a resident of the town, helpfully provided the translation (*navorsing permit*).

The importance of this town seems to be not so much in its actual size or its effects on South Africa as a whole, but in its role as a living archive and testing site in the new South Africa. The fact that it exists is, for nonresident supporters, both sufficient to ensure that somewhere there is an authentic Afrikaner space, where it is possible to live according to "our own rules and our own game" (053), and that such a lifestyle will be, at minimum, tolerated by the central state. The example of Orania and other separatist communities being accepted and protected by the state provides an exit strategy for those anxious about living in "new" South Africa, but also proof that their lifestyle is tolerated by those in power. In other words, for those within the Afrikaans community who believe, in whole or in part, that state-sponsored, immanent, and particularized threats to their community do exist, the continued existence and growth of Orania and Kleinfontein provides a counterpoint. By acting, then, as archive, potential refuge, and litmus test, such communities allow South Africa to remain safe and unified for individuals who admire, but do not reside in, such communities.

But there are obvious connections here, in terms of demands for security, to the de facto segregated and securitized estates discussed above. In both the separatist community and in the literature on security estates, protection of private property and the demand for safety form a critical part of the legitimizing rhetoric. Both involve placing physical barriers between their communities and the larger South African public. Both are also, by implication or explicit design, segregated spaces. The cardinal differences then, are in the invocation of culture and the general public perception of such communities, and in the ways such communities propound a cross-class identity. Whereas many aspire to live in a security estate, separatist communities were often seen as a backward or inherently racist way of living by participants.

The case study of the history and current manifestations of the volkstaat is at the nexus of the discussions of private and public space in South Africa. The resilience of separatist communities, or even autonomous cultural communities, demonstrates how South Africa as a geographic marker, as well as a symbolic public sphere, has been consistently under debate. Even if they are a small minority, the supporters of such communities are proposing an alternative mode of (dis)engagement with a national public, or in its most extreme example, of the creation of a new and more homogenous nation. The justifications for such claims, made in terms of both public existence and private security, implicate the nature of integration and what it means to be South African in an era of multiracial democracy.

CONCLUSION

The politics of space in South Africa, emerging from decades and centuries of governmental policies aimed at complete segregation and spatial control, are obviously still fractured in the twenty years since the democratic transition. Many reminders of segregation inherited from the old regime stand in place alongside newly implemented technologies of segregation developed and maintained in the democratic era. And yet, the meaningful integration of public space, the development of more diverse symbolic representations, and freedom of movement reflect a massive break with the past and a reminder of just how much has changed. Through the above examination of the politics of space, this chapter sought to explore how contestation over space in legally integrated South Africa both recreates and challenges the borders between subnational communities. Although major strides have been made in dismantling petty and grand apartheid, the lack of transformation of property ownership and the fear of public space inherent in security discourses means that although the policies of apartheid have been abolished, the apartness that was its aim remains largely unreformed.

Gated communities and securitized office parks challenge the possibility of meaningfully shared public spaces in South Africa, and flag difference in new and increasingly varied ways. The retreat behind such walls, sometimes likened to emigration, constitutes a near-exit from the integrated public sphere. The anxieties expressed by many Afrikaans-speaking participants about the state of public safety reinforce findings from other scholars about how such security affects the psyches of those who implement it.

Related to securitization of physical private property such as homes is the discussion of land reform and the difficulty in squaring the incommensurable claims to ownership, belonging, and citizenship tied up with the issue of land. Because of the symbolic resonance of land in both self-definition for Afrikaans speakers and citizenship-nationalism for Zulu speakers, the debate over the policies aimed at ameliorating past dispossessions (collective and individual) often bypasses policy completely in favor of a larger debate about belonging and home.

The *volkstaat* discussion combines the dynamics of both public and private space, insofar as the proposals for autonomous or separatist communities are made based on justifications that span both communal survival and individual safety. The resilience of such discussions, and the toleration of such communities by the South African state, point to the ongoing contestation over the meaning of South Africa as a symbolic and literal space for Afrikaners.

The transition from apartheid to multiracial democracy was premised on the idea of inclusion, in national symbols and spaces, of communities that had been deeply segregated. That inclusion was intended as a way to make coequal citizens, and to overcome the divisions of the past through the sharing of space. Yet because of the interface of integrated public space and increasingly securitized and segregated private space, there is an open question about the degree to which integrated space is meaningfully shared or serves to elide the divisions of the past in favor of a greater sense of national community.

CHAPTER 8

The Medium and the Message

Language and Communal Identity

Language is a basis for communal identity that is both practical and ideological. While there are certainly pragmatic barriers to communication across linguistic divides, the history of nationalist development shows that political and cultural entrepreneurs, through both active effort and as an externality of economic and social change, shore up those divisions and make them central to group identities. The codification of language, especially with the help of mass media, has been central to the development of communities and their boundaries (Anderson 2006). In South Africa, with eleven official national languages recognized by the post-apartheid state, and a history of segregation based on state-reified linguistic-ethnic groups, language has been a source of identity and contention.

Starting in the nineteenth century, leaders in the communities that would later self-identify as Zulu and Afrikaner/Afrikaans began to standardize and promote codified versions of their languages for specifically political purposes. Elites from the Zulu Empire began endorsing the Zunda dialect (over competing regional variations of Tekela and Thefula) as a way to consolidate the rule of Shaka and his agnates in cooperation with the project of imperial expansion and assimilation (Mahoney 2012, 24, 30). The standardization of Afrikaans was a similarly self-conscious political initiative undertaken by groups such as the Genootskap van Regte Afrikaners (the Society of True Afrikaners) and later by the white minority state in its own operation, as well as through the church and other powerful social organizations (Deumert 2004, 1, 9, 55). Both languages are now spoken widely throughout the country, with isiZulu being spoken as a first language by more than 22 percent of the population and serving as an urban lingua franca for many black South

Africans. Afrikaans is spoken by both white and coloured communities, with 13.4 percent of the total South African population claiming it as a first language (Statistics South Africa, n.d.).

Language as a source of identity commands a powerful place in terms of defining South Africans' subnational identities, in part because of the historic deployment of language as a tool of segregation. With the development of the Union of South Africa and later the ideology of apartheid, language communities and the ethno-racial identities associated with them were promoted by the apartheid state as the foundational identity matrix for citizens in the sovereign state. Although the apartheid state's official policies of discrimination were framed in terms of race and ethnicity, the latter was deeply connected to primordialist conceptions of tribalism and linked with the foundational principle of language (Cook 2006).

Even in the post-apartheid era, language has remained an important way that South Africans express their identity. What has changed is the political context in which such identities are expressed. But to what extent is linguistic diversity consonant with or challenging to nation-building? How has the project of multilingualism, in the context of democratic South Africa, allowed language communities to flourish while also providing the basis for meaningful integration, possibly through the emergent lingua franca of English? Does language remind people of their differences, or provide the basis for eliding them?

This chapter examines language as a vector of identity politics and nationalism in South Africa, with reference to both the bridging and dividing possibilities of multilingualism. The chapter is divided into three sections, which examine how language is connected with communal and individual identity. The first addresses the connections between identity and language in South Africa as reported by interview participants, with reference to English as a potentially integrating force. The second addresses how language-based identifications have eclipsed race-based identities as constitutionally protected and socially acceptable bases of segregation, specifically for Afrikaans speakers. Examining the university classroom as a site of contention over the segregating potential of Afrikaans- and English-medium education, this section looks at the conversation about multilingual and monolingual education and how it is tied with Afrikaans communal identity. The third section is a case study of how linguistic diversity can be shored up through the everyday consumption of different language media, examining a flashpoint of violence, the Marikana massacre of 2012, in the Zulu and Afrikaans press. Whether reflecting different preferences or creating them, the multilingual media landscape in South Africa reinforces divides between language communities.

LANGUAGE AND IDENTITY

In many ways, the terms connected with language have eclipsed the terms of race in individuals' self-identificatory narratives in the post-apartheid context, especially for white Afrikaans speakers and black Zulu speakers (Alexander 2001, 145).

Although the racial categorizations inherited from the old regime are still salient and utilized by many South Africans in discussing their own and others' identities, the collapsing of racial and linguistic categories is common in ordinary speech. Language has become a more convenient, less polarizing point of identification.

Words such as *Afrikaanssprekende* (Afrikaans speaker), *Afrikaanses* (Afrikaans), and *Afrikaner* have been the subject of much debate within the Afrikaans-speaking press from the mid-2000s onward. Each of these terms defines a community by language, race, or both, to varying degrees. While Afrikaanses is often used to denote the Afrikaans-speaking community, regardless of race, this categorization has also been claimed by people who use the compound "Afrikaans speaker" to refer to themselves or others. The debates over these terms have played out in many Afrikaans papers, asking questions such as "Afrikaner, Afrikaans-speaking, African—Who are we?" (Malan 2005), questioning whether the Afrikaans-speaking category is becoming extinct (du Plessis 2011), or giving accounts of the myriad ways these terms have been deployed to overcome, deny, or elide the problematic past of Afrikaner nationalism (Brand 2005). Yet in many cases, Afrikaans-speaking interview participants in Bloemfontein often used such words as synonyms. One young woman with whom I spoke, when asked about Afrikaans music and cultural festivals (discussed in greater detail in chapter 6) such as the Vryfees, responded by saying

> I think [the festivals are important], yes, because that is where we can let out our culture . . . the Afrikaner culture, Afrikaans music, Afrikaans shows, that type of things. That is where you can say, "I am Afrikaans and I am proud of it." Because a lot of people who are Afrikaans say they do not like to be associated with it, they would rather speak English. I am the other way around.

Proud to speak Afrikaans, proud to be Afrikaans. So, for those festivals, I can be proudly Afrikaans . . . a proud Afrikaner. (010)

Language then, plays a foundational role in how this young woman lives her life and defines her community, and the linguistic identification of the boundaries of her community is interchangeable with terms that are more historically rooted in racial and ethnic conceptions of community.

Zulu-speaking participants in Durban expressed similar sentiments, by linking fluency in "indigenous languages" to being South African, as well as belonging to a group called "Zulu" (106).[1] In the words of one interview participant, "I am a speaker of the Zulu language. I was born in Zululand, and it was my only language until school. Now I live in the city, though, and we speak English. But I want to go back. Most people I know plan to go back" (094). Language provided an important link between place, race, identity, and history for many Zulu-speaking interview participants, who said that speaking the language brought them a sense of identity, while speaking English or Afrikaans fluently was considered a betrayal by peers. In the words of one young woman, "We must speak proper Zulu. Speaking properly brings me closer to home. . . . But, then, if I speak in a posh English or Afrikaans accent, then I am a coconut.[2] So what should I do?" (105).

The loss of language through the dominance of English as a public-sphere language was, for some interview participants, seen as a loss of a more meaningful sense of community, whether in public places such as shops, or in private among younger generations. One Zulu-speaking participant, when asked whether she would call herself "Zulu," responded by saying "Yes, I would call myself a Zulu in most cases. But, we use the English language as the medium of communication. We have moved away from the vernacular. Even at home we are speaking English now" (093). Another Zulu-speaking man in his late fifties told me that he felt alienated when speaking to his children in isiZulu, because they clearly translated their isiZulu from English. He gave the example of his children coming home from a science lesson in which they learned about rhino conservation, using the phrases *ubhejane omhlope* and *ubhejane omnyama*, literally white rhinoceros and black rhinoceros, a difference in speciation that is not reflected in a terminological difference in isiZulu. To explain his frustration, he exclaimed "What is this nonsense? Zulu people do not speak like this. There is one *ubhejane*, which is *ubhejane* in Zulu. They are thinking in English. They are losing their language."[3] The accusation that "Zulu people" do not speak like this is followed up with the idea that losing language is akin to losing ethnic identification.

But language, and the encroachment of English, was also a pressing concern for Afrikaans speakers. An Afrikaans-speaking young man, asked if he felt under threat, answered, "Definitely. There is the whole thing about English. It is everywhere. My mother only speaks Afrikaans. It is difficult for her to get around. . . . There is no attempt from the ANC to preserve language. It is a difficult problem. Even the SABC does not have much Afrikaans anymore" (039). Another young man, in an unconnected interview, in response to the same question, said "Language is a big issue. Afrikaners and Boers feel like they are marginalized because of the political past, and the university has become more English. I can understand it because Afrikaans gets marginalized and that is a big problem, it makes people feel scared" (076). A middle-aged woman, who was involved in local politics in Bloemfontein, when asked about what issues she cared about said that the protection of local languages was an important issue for her. Rather than citing a cultural threat as the important issue, she explained that for her, "It is not just a question of being unable to speak English. You cannot express yourself authentically in a language that is not yours. Look at the leaders in the government. They read very closely from a pre-written English text, but when they start speaking in Sotho or Afrikaans, they are dynamic speakers. They speak from the heart, from their soul" (011). This distinction, language as a driver of identity versus language as a medium of communication, is critical. English does not seem to command the same emotional connection.

But English has become an urban lingua franca, and the most commonly spoken second language reported in the 2011 census, even though fewer than 10 percent of South Africans speak English as a first language (Statistics South Africa 2012). In many cases, English is the medium of major parts of the public sphere in South Africa, including business, government, and street signs. It has enabled communication, and increasingly become a second language alongside of, rather than replacing, other languages such as Zulu or Afrikaans (Posel and Zeller 2016).

Monolingualism is still prevalent, however, and while it has declined since the 1990s, more than half of the South African population report speaking no second language (Statistics South Africa, n.d.). Moreover, monolingualism is far from random. It is most prevalent among low-income groups, with 39 percent of the 2011 census sample being both monolingual and in the lowest third of income categories.[4] Those who report only speaking one language are also geographically concentrated in peri-urban and rural areas. So while English may be an increasingly common medium of communication in affluent and urban populations, the bridging possibilities of English are limited by class and geography. Moreover, the connections between belonging, language, and identity supersede the question of multilingualism as a practical matter. Language is a matter of identity when speaking of Afrikaans and Zulu in a way that English is not.

LANGUAGE, NATIONALISM, AND THE UNIVERSITY— PARALLEL-MEDIUM UNIVERSITIES

The identity politics of language is particularly striking in parallel-medium (English- and Afrikaans-language) universities in South Africa. The University of the Free State is one such institution. Because of its commitment to "fostering institutionalized functional multilingualism" as well as the project to "develop Afrikaans as an academic and scientific language," the University of the Free State offers the majority of its classes and university functions in both English and Afrikaans (UFS Council 2003, 3).[5] Advocates of Afrikaans language in universities have attempted to deracialize the project of linguistic nationalism through discussing Afrikaans as a uniquely African language vested in South Africa, regardless of race (Vestergaard 2001).

While living in Bloemfontein, however, I spoke with many people who worked with students and observed that the functional outcome of the parallel language policy is a largely segregated living and learning experience, with black African students in English-language classrooms and white students in Afrikaans-language classes. According to one Afrikaans-speaking man who interacted regularly with students,

> [Black students] come to this university, and then they have one choice, to go to an English class. They cannot ask for being educated in their mother tongue, so they go to an English class. [An] Afrikaans, or an Afrikaner student, comes to this university, and they are a minority at this university, and they get the option of whether they want to be taught in Afrikaans or in English. And the argument they will give is "mother tongue education." So the black student must be happy being taught in his 2nd or 3rd language, but the Afrikaners—and in most instances their English is quite good—say "No, no, no, we cannot be taught in our second language." And the implication . . . is that white and black students do not share the classroom, they do not learn together. Then you end up with [Afrikaner] students coming to this university, spending 4 years here, and do it all white . . . they will stay outside in a

student house, and go to classes with white lecturers, white classmates, all in Afrikaans. They will have their sport together, they will socialize together, have a braai at their house. And it will be all white, for 4 years at this university. (007)

In the *Mail and Guardian*, Irma du Plessis, then a senior lecturer at the University of Pretoria, echoed these concerns in an editorial entitled "Diversity, Not Division, in Lecture Halls," in which she argues for a suspension of Afrikaans-medium classes by saying

[University of Pretoria's] Afrikaans-medium classes are in effect racially, culturally and linguistically homogeneous. This produces a teaching encounter far removed from that offered in the diverse English medium classes, and entirely out of kilter with broader South African society. . . . At UP, I would argue, we need to pursue a kind of meaningful, everyday multilingualism underpinned by the primary use of English as the language of tuition and communication. This constitutes an act of courtesy to each other that disables the reproduction of institutions wholly defined on the basis of an ethnocentric, *volkseie*[6] logic, which, together with race, formed the cornerstone of a system internationally recognised as a crime against humanity. (du Plessis 2016)

Language cleavages that coincide with other social divisions, such as race, are then used as the primary lens through which students at the University of the Free State experienced their collegiate life. The classrooms in which I taught and observed generally followed this pattern. Although there were exceptions, such as Afrikaans-speaking students from mixed-race backgrounds attending Afrikaans sections, or white students choosing English-medium classes, the vast majority of the classrooms conformed to the patterns identified above.

Language remains a powerful organizing force in South African society, and in some dual-medium universities, it has become an acceptable logic for segregation, albeit with some controversy. What is clear, however, is that language is a key component of communal identity, as well as threat perception, for both Afrikaans and isiZulu speakers. These communal lines, drawn by the practical and relatively objective boundaries of language, are reinforced through the choice of monolingual spaces that are then segregated because of the mutually reinforcing nature of the social cleavages of language and race.

NEWSPAPERS, LANGUAGE, AND PRINT CAPITALISM

Daily news in South Africa is printed in three of the country's major languages: English, Afrikaans, and Zulu. While the English press has the largest circulation, the Zulu-language press in South Africa has seen sustained growth over the past decade, and the Afrikaans press has also managed to avert some of the more precipitous declines in readership seen by many English-language news outlets ("Magazine and Newspaper Readership, Jan–Dec 2012" 2013). In both the Afrikaans- and Zulu-speaking communities, these news sources have been the drivers of commodification and consolidation of their language in the post-apartheid state, reifying and monetizing ethnolinguistic identities in a nominally nonracial state (see for example Ndlovu 2011; Wasserman 2009). Because their readership spans the geographic area of the country, the news stories reach people who may never meet one another, but have the same experience of receiving the daily news, satisfying Anderson's conditions of print capitalism (Holmes 2015).

But, as with the division between different mediums of education discussed above, the segmentation of the reading publics in South Africa based on linguistic cleavages has segregating implications. Scholars of media in multilingual contexts have pointed out how different language outlets shape and reflect different community realities, in studies of radio stations in Kenya preceding the 2007 election violence (Ismail and Deane 2008), of newspapers in East Africa in the postcolonial period (Ogude 2001), and of press catering to African diaspora communities in the West (Ojo 2006). Journalistic accounts even suggest that the recent coverage of violence in rural areas against landowners, which some activists call "farm murders," presents a similar case, wherein the Afrikaans-language press covers the violence as a national epidemic, but it receives very little coverage in media in other languages (Jansen 2017). In each, the systematic differences between media in different languages represent significant divides in how their listening or reading public understood and processed key events in their history. Linguistically segmented media are therefore involved in creating and recreating identity in the quotidian process of the news cycle.

An analysis of a key point of national crisis in South Africa—the 2012 violence at Marikana as the single most lethal police action under the post-apartheid state—reveals the systematic differences in framing presented by different language media to their reading publics. These differences—in terms of attributions of blame, use of emotional language, and inclusion of political and economic angles of coverage—have the effect of creating a fragmented understanding of the violence and its implications. Starting from the facts of the violence, as explored by the commission of inquiry empaneled to investigate the incident, the discussion then systematically compares the initial coverage of the violence in Zulu and Afrikaans. Finally, the section examines how individual interview participants invoked the violence at Marikana, and how their understanding of the violence is consonant with the coverage published by the newspapers serving their language communities. Whether reflecting or creating these divides, the systematic differences in how different language presses covered the Marikana violence are consequential because of the political externalities of these differences. The ways in which different language communities understood and invoked a single national crisis, and how those differences are reflected in their evaluations of the crisis, has implications for the evaluation of the democratic government, as well as the nation-building project.

The Marikana Violence

In mid-August of 2012, outside a small town in the Northwest province, workers at the Lonmin Platinum mine went on strike, demanding higher wages. Beginning on 10 August 2012, thousands of workers engaged in a walkout. The miners demanded a substantial increase in pay to match the escalated market price of platinum, and to compensate them for the dangerous jobs they were performing. Within a week of the start of the strike action, 44 people had been killed, and more than 100 wounded. The strike itself occurred in contravention of the larger negotiations over workers' compensation at the mine, and along with the actions of police at the mine, was under investigation by a government-convened commission for almost three years (Marikana Commission of Inquiry, n.d.).

After a week of tension between police and miners, with intermittent violence leading to the killing of two police officers, two private security guards, and four miners, several politicians, including the minister of mineral resources, Susan Shabangu, and the premier of the province, Thandi Modise, expressed concern over the violence at the mine, and pushed police and mineworkers to negotiate a truce. The striking miners refused to disarm on the afternoon of 15 August, and the negotiations fell apart (Botes and Tolsi 2013). On the afternoon of 16 August, members of the South African Police Service opened fire on a crowd of striking miners, first with rubber bullets and tear gas, and then with live ammunition, after the strikers violently resisted crowd-control strategies. This engagement left thirty-four people dead, and at least seventy-eight more wounded. Yet at the time of initial coverage of these events, vastly different narratives emerged from different language presses.

The attributions of blame and sympathy, the construction of active and passive participants, and the presence of economic and political coverage all point to the fact that people who consume their news primarily through the lens of the so-called vernacular press in South Africa are receiving substantially different narratives of what happened and how it should be interpreted. The differences in coverage, which almost certainly reflect the predispositions of the readers as well as creating them, nonetheless form a kind of iterated point of identification within these networks of mutually reinforcing social cleavages.

Although the Farlam Commission has investigated and reported a single and authoritative version of events, the Marikana story presents an interesting case study in ongoing print nationalisms. Unlike the segregating effects of multilingual education as outlined above, the issue of language of media consumption as a community-reinforcing exercise is more subtle than the effectively segregated classrooms of the university. However, the creation of new sources of division, including the vocabulary to talk about points of national crisis, serves as a quotidian reinforcement of the divides through language, not only as medium, but as message. Compounded problems of incommensurability and untranslatability deprive people of the tools necessary to talk across the historically rooted boundaries of class and location, as well as the obvious divides of language.

Press Coverage by Language

The news coverage from 17 to 27 August 2012, in all Afrikaans and isiZulu daily newspapers is the subject of the analysis below. What this collection reveals is an interesting range of interpretations of the violence at Marikana. The Afrikaans newspapers, all owned by a single media company (Naspers) but published under different names in different cities, utilized much of the same content both before and after the violence because they published reports from a unified reporting team on the scene. The coverage in *iSolezwe*, the only Zulu-language daily newspaper in South Africa, was largely generated from its own reporting team, as well as translating some content from the South African Press Association news wire.

The major differences that arise from this coverage are in three key areas: (1) constructions of action and reaction, (2) points of blame and sympathy, and (3) coverage of political and economic factors. Each of these categories, discussed in detail below, signals a different way to interpret the events related to the violence at Marikana. Through constructing one or the other side as responsible for the violence because of their actions, or casting one sides' claims as sympathetic and the others as blameworthy, the reading public is encouraged to view one side as perpetrators of violence and the other side as the victims. This difference is key in understanding the violence, and potentially presents incommensurable accounts of the events at Marikana. The inclusion of political and economic factors in the coverage of the violence changes the frame through which the violence is viewed, and re-casts the story in terms of worldly effects, as opposed to human tragedy or police brutality.

Actors and Reactors

The first day in Afrikaans and Zulu news coverage provides some of the starkest contrasts between the Afrikaans and isiZulu newspapers' accounts of the basic facts of the violence. The headlines, included in table 1, illustrate some of the key differences.

Looking deeper into the coverage of these events only magnifies the initial differences. In *iSolezwe*, the article entitled "*Amaphoyisa alalise uyaca emayini*," or "Police Massacre Many in the Mines," opens with the following description of the events of the afternoon of 16 August:

Table 1. Headlines, 17 August 2012

Afrikaans News

Die Burger (Cape Town)	*Lyke in Lonmin moles ruk SA/ maak internasionaal opslae*	Corpses from Lonmin Troubles Stun SA/Make International Headlines[1]
Die Beeld (Johannesburg)	*Bloedbad: Polisie Skiet 18 myners dood*	Blood Bath: Police Shoot 18 Miners Dead[2]
Die Volksblad (Bloemfontein)	*Bloedbad: Tot 20 sterf toe hulle polisie aanval*	Blood Bath: Up to 20 Die When They Attack Police[3]

Zulu News

iSolezwe (Durban)	*Isibhicongo emayini: Amaphoyisa alalise uyaca emayini*	Catastrophe/Devastation/Destruction at the Mine: The Police Massacre Many in the Mines[4]

[1] (Verslagspan—Team Report 2012b)
[2] (de Lange and Vos 2012)
[3] (Verslagspan—Team Report 2012a)
[4] (Mkhize 2012)

The police of this country yesterday created destruction among striking miners at the Lonmin Marikana Platinum mine when they shot at the miners and wiped them away. At the time of writing yesterday evening it was not yet known/found the number of those who were killed and wounded in this disaster at the mine. In a report on television news channel E.TV, they confirmed the names of 12 people. Some of the miners were injured very badly, since it was necessary that a large number of ambulances hastened to come to help, and the hundreds of workers on strike made room for them at the mountain where the strike began. (Mkhize 2012, translation by author)

The coverage of these events in *Die Burger*, *Die Volksblad*, and *Die Beeld* is nearly identical, just with slightly different phrasing to indicate the employment of the reporting team (de Lange and Vos 2012). The article was printed with three different titles. Despite the different headlines, all of the newspapers' accounts begin by saying

Shock waves were sent around the world yesterday by the worst police violence since South Africa's political transition, in which 18 to 20 people at Lonmin's Marikana mine were shot. The shooting erupted yesterday just after 16:00 . . . on a hill behind the miner's Wonderkop hostel when a group of protesters, armed with machetes and spears, stormed a police line. The policemen were nervous because the strikers had stolen firearms from two policemen in [a] riot on Monday afternoon after strikers hacked a fellow hostel resident to death. As the miners stormed the group, the policemen opened fire on them with automatic rifles and pistols. Less than a minute later, the dry grass in the field at the hill's slope was strewn with corpses. Only here and there the wounded stirred. (Verslagspan—Team Report 2012b)

The major difference between these accounts lies in the use of active verbs, and the groups to which actions are attributed. Whereas *iSolezwe* begins its coverage with the phrase that police created destruction, the Naspers papers begin with a passive construction in the opening sentence, followed by the attribution of action to strikers: storming a police line. This characterization is also brought out in the human-interest coverage addressed above, by framing the violence as a "shootout," implying that there was an exchange of fire, rather than unarmed miners being shot by police.

By depicting the police as the party under attack, and contextualizing it in the events of the prior week, *Die Volksblad*, *Die Beeld*, and *Die Burger* present the police as having a limited range of possible reactions and as being under an imminent threat. These sentiments are reinforced in the following days' coverage, where both *Die Volksblad* and *Die Beeld* published an opinion piece defending the actions of police by saying that they were "likely within the rights" in opening fire on the protesting miners (van Wyk 2012a, 2012b).[7]

Points of Sympathy and Blame

In general, the coverage of the violence in *iSolezwe* was more sympathetic than the Afrikaans press content to the workers' strike claims, and to their perspective in the immediate aftermath. Rather than focusing on the economic impact of the strikes in the days leading up to the clash, *iSolezwe* focused on the violence of the preceding days and official reactions to it. The Naspers Afrikaans newspapers, on the other hand, chose to focus the prior coverage of the Marikana strike on mine-owners' reactions to the strike and the economic effects of the work stoppage.

The most striking contrast in coverage comes in the headlines from 17 August. Whereas *iSolezwe* framed the violence in terms of a police attack on miners, the Afrikaans newspapers were slightly more ambiguous. One Afrikaans newspaper, *Die Volksblad*, stands out in this regard in the sense that it actually reverses the blame, albeit subtly in translation, to say that the violence was the fault of the striking workers attacking police. *Die Beeld*, by contrast, places the blame with the police, like *iSolezwe*, in their headline. *Die Burger* neglects to put blame on any party, but uses less emotional language than the other two, characterizing the violence as *moles* or "troubles," rather than a massacre as in the other papers. Yet, as discussed above, in the opening paragraphs of the articles, issues of blame are somewhat muddied.

These articles, in addition to attributing blame, also differ in a key respect: the terminology used to describe the violence. *iSolezwe* uses the word *Isibhicongo* to describe the violence. This word, loosely translated, means catastrophe, devastation, or destruction. It is a very expressive term, and in *iSolezwe* has been used only a few times in recent publications, and almost exclusively to describe multiple human deaths in the context of violence.

The term used by *Die Volksblad* and *Die Beeld*, *Bloedbad*, can be translated as blood bath, massacre, or carnage, which is also an evocative term. However, this term cropped up numerous times in headlines in Naspers papers in the following year, to describe everything from the Rand's declining exchange rate (Blumenthal 2013) to the theft and slaughter of livestock (Black 2013).

The inclusion of articles based on the effects of the strike and violence on miners and their families also points to the reading publics' differences in sympathy and attachment to the miners, the police, and the mine owners. The articles listed below have been labeled as "human interest" articles because of their emphasis on putting "a human face and emotional angle to the presentation of an event, issue, or problem, so it makes people regard the crisis as serious, urgent, or dangerous" (Cho and Gower 2006, 420). All of these articles present the stories of the violence from the side of the workers and their families, incorporating interview testimony.

The characterizations of the effects of the violence in these stories were very similar. The opening paragraphs of the first published human-interest stories on 18 and 19 August record similar anxieties among the families of workers who, at that time, were uncertain of the identities of the people who had been killed or injured in the violence.

In *Volksblad* and *Beeld*, an article entitled "Loved Ones Still Wondering" leads by saying

> Residents of the shantytown at Lonmin mine yesterday did not know where to start looking for their loved ones. By Sunday afternoon, scores of people still did not know whether their relatives were among the 34 people who died Sunday in a shootout between miners and police or if they are among the 78 injured. Many were transported to hospitals as far away as Pretoria and Johannesburg, but it is not yet clear to which mortuaries the deceased have been brought. (Fourie and Vos 2012, translation by author)

The account given in the *iSolezwe* article, entitled "Sympathy for the Relatives of the Massacre," has many of the same facts, but with more emotional language:

> An eruption of sadness happened among the families of the workers who were a part of the protest in the Marikana mine in the North West, because relatives have not been able to find out from Lonmin who has died or been injured in the violence. (Mofokeng 2012, translation by author)

The opening phrase, "an eruption of sadness," as well as the blame placed on the mine (Lonmin) for the delay in identifying the dead and the wounded, give this story greater emotional intensity and urgency than the Afrikaans account. The differences in emotive language could be explained, however, by the fact that *iSolezwe* frequently uses metaphor and bombastic language in daily coverage. As explained above, the Naspers papers are not free of dramatic and symbolic language, as shown in the use of the words "blood bath" by *Die Volksblad* and *Die Beeld*.

Several of the human-interest stories were picked up by only two of the three Naspers Afrikaans papers. Yet generally speaking, human-interest pieces about the violence occurred about as often in the Afrikaans press as in the isiZulu press. A key difference, however, is in the angle of coverage. All three Naspers papers published an article on 21 August that included interview testimony from several police officers involved in the shooting, arguing that their point of view and their side of the story was being ignored. The story, as published in *Die Volksblad* and *Die Beeld*, opens with the evocative quote from an anonymous member of the police unit at Marikana: "No one gives a f**k about the two policemen who died."[8] The story focuses on the stresses of the police officers in trying to contain and respond to the violent strike action, as well as their unclear orders from their commanding officers and ill-defined standard operating procedures.

iSolezwe's human interest stories are told exclusively from the point of view of the miners and their families. They recount details not just of the violence of 16 August, but also of the dangerous working conditions for the miners and the hardships of migrant labor and squalid living conditions. In the article on 27 August, entitled "It is not new for us that people die in the mines," workers' families recount the problems they have had with mine companies failing to notify them of the deaths of their loved ones, as well as never receiving compensation for those deaths.

Political and Economic Factors Occurring in Coverage

In the years since August 2012, the violence in Marikana had widespread negative political and economic effects, for the exchange rate of the South African rand (Mbele 2014), output levels of precious metals from South African mines (Visser 2014), and investor confidence in the mining sector (Lakmidas 2013). Newspapers around the world covered these kinds of effects, yet in the days immediately following the violence, Afrikaans and isiZulu newspapers dealt very differently with the economic and political aspects of the Marikana story.

Die Beeld published an article on 17 August that detailed the kinds of economic effects the country could see from the Marikana violence. The article, entitled *"Is minister steeds net 'verontrus?'"* (Is the minister still only "disturbed?"), opens by saying

The bloodbath yesterday afternoon at the Lonmin mine in Marikana is not only a human tragedy, but it will affect South Africa politically and economically for quite a while. Investors in the mining industry have become wary of the politics of our country. Shocks like these, and questions about our country's political stability—and the safety of investments—cause concern with investors, which has only been inflamed under the current government. (*Beeld* 2012)

Similar, but distinct, articles were published in *Die Volksblad* on 18 an 22 August and in *Die Burger* on 25 August.

Additionally, in all three Afrikaans newspapers, an article published on 22 August entitled *Marikana-geweld "het dalk politieke motiewe"* (Marikana violence "may have a political motive") directly criticizes the government's and party politicians' roles in the strike action and the ensuing violence.

The violent protests at Lonmin's Marikana mine is not just the result of a wage dispute between the employer and rock drill operators and there may be political motives behind it. . . . According to Gideon du Plessis, general secretary of Solidarity, many of the nearly 3,000 demonstrators were sacked employees of Lonmin and Impala Platinum (Implats) mines, while others claiming to be members of the rock drill operators actually worked in other job categories or were unemployed community members. "It is clear that many of the protesting workers were not aggrieved rock drill operators, but that strike opportunists exploited the strike and the misdeeds that have been committed . . . Du Plessis said. (Vos 2012, translation by author)

The only comparable article in *iSolezwe*, entitled *Yimithonseyana ephumelele ukuzosebenza* (Only a Few Report for Work) deals with the continuation of the work stoppage, the fears of the workers after the violence, and their continuing demand for a wage of 12,500 rand per month. While there were articles dealing with the visits of political leaders to the Marikana area, such as the article entitled *Sebehlonziwe ababulawe ngamaphoyisa emayini* (People killed by police in the mine have been identified) on 22 August, these articles focus on leaders' advocacy on behalf of miners, rather than criticizing their motives.

Reactions to Marikana

Although not a specific subject of the interview, Marikana came up with both Zulu and Afrikaans speakers with some regularity, in part because of its persistence as a headline throughout the later parts of 2012 and into 2013. In some important respects, Zulu and Afrikaans speakers referenced Marikana in similar ways, specifically in terms of a breakdown in communication between elites and workers. Two older men, one Afrikaans-speaking and one Zulu-speaking, characterized the Marikana massacre in remarkably similar ways in interviews six months apart. The Zulu-speaking man, a labor organizer himself, said in response to a question about the political challenges the country was facing, "[Zwelenzina] Vavi[9] has betrayed the workers . . . look at Marikana, look at all of that. What is the role of the trade unions? The workers are suffering, they are dying in violence and in the mines, and people like Vavi do not see that" (090). The Afrikaans man, in a remarkably similar sentiment expressed in response to the same question, said, "There is a massive short circuit between the black elites and the people on the ground. They can speak Xhosa, but they all speak English. Those who govern are out of touch. . . . Marikana is a big indicator of these problems. This is a rupture, a fault line" (021). The disconnect, framed in terms of language for the second case and possibly implicated in terms of class in the earlier statement, has the same effect. The violence at Marikana is the result of the divide between elites and workers. Such a consistency of interpretation signals that perhaps the different frames presented in the media in different languages are not an insurmountable barrier to common interpretation of the events.

But interview participants replicated the frames of sympathy and blame that were used by different language presses. Zulu-speaking participants, like the man quoted above, tended to focus on the fact that Marikana resulted from and resulted in human suffering. One young man, when asked what people should know about his country, referenced the problems of crime and violence, saying "Look at the pictures from Marikana. The police brutality, the suffering. . . . It fits into [the] violent, backward image that people have of the country" (108). The focus on the workers' conditions, and on the police as the commissioners of the violence, mirrors the Zulu-language press framing of these issues.

Afrikaans-speaking participants invariably hearkened back to the political implications of the violence. One Afrikaans-speaking man in his thirties said, "Look at mining, all the troubles in Marikana. People in politics are making money, they are in it to make money. They do business with these mines, and that is why this happened. It is all so messy" (038). This interpretation, of Marikana as a result of politics and being characterized as "messy," is a vastly different orientation to the sympathy and blame for each of the contending sides. While blame is apportioned by both Zulu and Afrikaans speakers on the political leaders involved, the invocation of sympathy and emotional content is distinct.

Such problems are certainly not intractable, but the differences in orientation and interpretation do present a challenge to building a common understanding of the events at Marikana and their potential remedies. Certainly, the problem of media polarization plagues monolingual as well as multilingual states. Yet the divisions that are reflected or created by a multilingual press, coinciding with the already deep cleavages of class and location along with the high prevalence of monolingualism in South Africa, present a uniquely troublesome problem of untranslatability to the already-present difficulties of incommensurability and isolation. Whereas a media consumer in a monolingual nation could conceivably understand or engage with the language presented by different news sources, the multilingual press does not provide such access without fluency across multiple languages.

The nature of the social cleavages of South Africa means that the frames presented in media servicing Afrikaans- and isiZulu-speaking communities are not in competition with one another. At best, they are in competition with the frames presented in the English-language media, but often consumers of so-called vernacular media do not regularly consume news from English-language sources (Ndlovu 2011; Wasserman and Botma 2008). Of course, translation is always difficult, especially between languages with radically different grammatical structures and idioms. Yet the difficulty in understanding across language divides that are reinforced by so many other social divisions, such as class and physical location, compounds these problems.

CONCLUSION

South Africa has been a multilingual country since its beginnings as a sovereign state. The consolidation of both Zulu and Afrikaans occurred because of nationalist and imperial impulses among elites, but the divides between language communities were re-inscribed under apartheid through Bantustan policies and education policies. Because of this long history of both internal and external definition of language communities, these divisions, inherited from the colonial and apartheid eras, have remained salient into the democratic era, but are also being revitalized. For both black Zulu and white Afrikaans speakers, linguistically vested identities have overshadowed the terms of race to talk about identity. As speakers of two of the eleven official languages of the new state, these linguistically defined communities have thrived. In part, this is because of their representation in both universities and print media, both critical connections between the consolidation of language and the creation of communal identity for theorists of language and nationalism, such as Anderson (2006).

This vibrant multilingualism presents some challenges to the nation-building project, however. Through both active choice and more passive externality, the self-selection of South Africans into language communities that coincide with geographic, racial, and class-based cleavages has the potential to keep certain spaces and experiences segregated under a new guise. The racially segregating potential of language-based categorizations is played out in harshest relief in dual-medium universities. While the ostensible choice available to students between an Afrikaans or an English curriculum is framed in terms of language, the reality is that such a choice allows students to self-select into not only linguistically, but racially distinct spaces.

Less obviously commissioned self-segregation by language comes in the form of the different language media in South Africa that serve these communities. These different-language presses present the news daily to reading publics whose ability to consume different-language media is limited. What is more noteworthy, however, is the systematic differences between different-language presses' accounts of key points of national importance. The case study in this chapter, of the violence at the Marikana mine in 2012, illustrates some of these differences. While the Afrikaans press muddied issues of blame and sympathy, and talked about the event mostly in terms of economic and political implications, the Zulu press primarily understood the event through the lens of human tragedy affecting the miners as a population to which they were sympathetic. These differences, mirrored in the ways that interview participants invoked the Marikana violence, could be interpreted either as a creation or a reflection of the predispositions of the communities that the various newspapers are serving. What is certainly true, however, is that the systematic differences in coverage result in different language communities experiencing what Anderson has called the "simultaneity of nationalist history" within subnational communities in ways that potentially interrupt the formation of a broader sense of national belonging.

Linguistic diversity, as a practical barrier to understanding, is both a fact of social life and an observable, iterated process of quotidian social division in South Africa. It flags difference, and reminds people of boundaries. Language can be seen as an affiliative identity, as with many attendees of Afrikaans music and culture festivals discussed in chapter 6, but there are practical and cultural barriers to entry in the case of the communities discussed above, especially when language becomes an analogue for race. Where countervailing forces exist, such as the possibilities of English as a common medium of communication, they are often perceived as threatening to communities that see language as a primary identifier.

CHAPTER 9

Conclusion

Democracy depends on more than the institutions of representative government. It depends on citizens upholding democratic values, such as tolerating electoral losses, protecting minority rights, and accepting the peaceful turnover of power. Nation-building is more than the cessation of hostilities. It involves creating a community of sentiment that is more or less equivalent to the legal-bureaucratic boundaries of citizenship. Both nation building and democratization are contingent on the ways that citizens relate to one another, in cooperation and in opposition. At their core, the ambitions of these two projects are also at odds: nations ask people to forget their differences, and democracies incentivize remembering them.

Yet much of the literature on both postconflict nation-building and democratization is overwhelmingly institutionalist in orientation, focusing on democratic institutional design as the central project of nation-building. Scholars have proposed varieties of institutional power-sharing and federalism arrangements (e.g., Lijphart 1969, 1977; Hartzell and Hoddie 2003; McGarry and O'Leary 2005; Lemarchand 2007; Selway and Templeman 2012), or ways of structuring elections (Norris 2012; Lyons 2004), all of which propose to mitigate previous violence. This approach is vested in the idea that democratic institutions, if properly designed, can peacefully channel conflict between factions. Consequently, this peace will help to build a national community.

This book, in taking the grounded, micro-level approach to studying nationhood and democratization, has examined the ways that even in the face of remarkable institutional change, divisions in society can, and do, remain resilient and reproduce themselves, even in the absence of institutional incentives. In part, the durability of societal division can be explained in terms of the opposing projects of nation-building and democratization. While nations seem to be predicated on the selective forgetting of social divisions, the ongoing processes of democracy incentivize the flagging and recreation of social divisions for partisan ends.

The forgetting implicated in the nation-building project does not always take the form of the total erasure of such divides, but rather the reduction of their salience, and the creation of cross-cutting ties between citizens. Even those "state-nations" that foster "multiple but complementary sociocultural identities," rather than a single overriding national identity, nonetheless rely on "strong identification and loyalty from their citizens . . . [and] crafting a sense of belonging (or 'we-feeling') with respect to the state-wide political community" (Stepan, Linz, and Yadav 2011, 4–5). This basic sense of unity undergirds the daily legitimacy of the state and the sustainable practices of democracy. Yet in postconflict societies, such a sense of unity must spring from a forgetting, or at least a softening, of the salience of the divides associated with past conflict.

By contrast, democracies, in conducting elections, incentivize political entrepreneurs to flag and maintain difference as a way to build electoral constituencies. This is all the more true in postcolonial and postconflict democracies, wherein citizens are asked to choose from among parties without reference to a history of policymaking or platforms that are hastily erected in the aftermath of transition (Randall and Svåsand 2002). Often, parties utilize identity politics, as has been the case in South Africa, as a heuristic to help build constituencies. Whether conceived of as "ethnic outbidding," which threatens democratic functioning (Geertz 1973, 255–310; Horowitz 1991, 2000; Sisk 1994), or as more benign agents of mobilization (Chandra 2005; Ishiyama 2009; Elischer 2008), this periodic flagging of difference means that divides in the national community are made relevant in new contexts in each election cycle. Whether identity-based political parties sustain or undermine democracy, they have regular, national platforms in which there is the option, and even the incentive, to remind partisans of what makes them different.

It would seem that there is a tension between the goals of nation-building—amalgamating society on the basis of a shared, even if not singular, identity—and democratization—institutionalizing contestation among factions to produce popular, representative government. But nationalism and democracy are, in their unifying and divisive tendencies, held in productive tension. An excess of the fractiousness of democratic contestation certainly undermines stability and unity, whereas an excess of nationalistic unity is almost certainly undemocratic. On the other hand, a basic sense of political community makes democratic contestation sustainable, lending legitimacy to political institutions and helping to establish key democratic norms, such as respect for minority rights.

The tension between these two poles is not necessarily resolvable. It is, however, ignored by the ways in which the extant literature on postconflict peace-building, which involves both the cultivation of national communities and the installation of democratic processes, has focused on institutionalism to the exclusion of the social and personal dimensions of each. In failing to account for the diverse, and sometimes contradictory, imperatives of building a national community and building a functioning democracy, these literatures potentially recommend policy prescriptions that undermine both.

POLICY IMPLICATIONS

These conclusions have a number of implications. This section addresses four major classes of policy-relevant conclusions that can be drawn from the analysis. The first implication revolves around the interpretation of history through the truth-commission process. Scholars such as James Gibson and Amanda Gouws have discussed the need for complex narratives to understand conflict, to avoid re-entrenching identities that were prior drivers of conflict. The evidence presented here does not necessarily indicate that either now, or in the past, the transition process produced such complex narratives. In many ways, the language interview participants used to discuss both their recollections of the transition process and the current state of the reconciliation project do not reflect a high degree of complexity regarding identity characteristics such as race. The narratives people used to talk about race in my interviews tended to reveal rather simplistic dualities of belonging/opposition, perpetrators/victims, and good/bad, in which they affiliated themselves largely with their own ethnolinguistic and racially defined in-group and opposed those outside of it.

This discussion does not, in any way, assume the moral equivalence of perpetrators of violence and victims, or of the fight between the apartheid state and anti-apartheid organizations, but rather that individuals of all affiliations and from all identity backgrounds did participate in violence and did apply for amnesty under the auspices of the TRC. But even in the face of widely publicized and complex evidence arising from the TRC, written sources from the time and interview evidence produced years later indicate that individuals experienced and interpreted the commission through simplistic narratives arising from their race and gender positionalities going into the commission process.

The second implication of this book is that the implementation of electoral democracy has been insufficient for many South Africans to feel that their lives have been changed. In the absence of meaningful social and economic change, the process of nation-building has been largely hollow for many poor and disenfranchised South Africans. The other side of this argument, however, is obviously that many wealthy South Africans, including some I interviewed, saw even the changes that had taken place as inherently menacing, and directly contributing to their perceptions of threat, despite the limited redistribution measures that have taken place. The difficulty, then, is in balancing these various tendencies. However, it seems clear that the continuity of socioeconomic experience from the apartheid to the post-apartheid era, and the relatively fast abandonment of economic programs aimed at meaningfully transforming the economy, have hindered the legitimacy of the state in the eyes of the majority of the population. Scholars and policymakers must address the interface between the economic and social dimensions of nation-building in the analysis of South Africa as a historical case, as well as in terms of the South African "model" for transitions to democracy.

The third set of implications stemming from this research concerns the role of time in the process of nation-building. Many individual South Africans, as well as scholars of South African politics, have suggested that the passage of time will lend itself to the nation-building process. My research suggests that, in many ways, the passage of time does not unquestionably contribute to that process. Because many interview participants in my study understood the public sphere as being "re-racialized" through the detrimental effects of party politics, redistributive measures, or security concerns, there is a sense in which the passage of time is reaffirming the perception of threat from other groups, rather than contributing to their amelioration. Additionally, since the first democratic elections, a number of ceremonies, historical interpretations, and spaces have sprung up that create new and more present modes of in-group affirmation. The flourishing of, for example, the Reed Dance or the Afrikaans music and language festivals in the post-apartheid era signals a desire on the part of many in their target constituencies for spheres of in-group interaction and identification.

By contrast, of course, the emergence of a black middle class, and the integration of middle- and upper-class suburbs, schools, and security parks, signals a potential for greater integration of the middle and upper classes of

South Africa, though the evidence is mixed. On the lower end of the socioeconomic spectrum, however, residents of townships and informal settlements are still living in almost entirely un-integrated spaces. The fact that race and class still overlap to such a startling degree, as discussed above, inhibits the nation-building process. These correlations have spatial dimensions as well. For many poor people, the process of time has not meaningfully changed how people in the poorest areas live, or the degree of interracial contact or relationships that they could have. In the words of one Zulu-speaking interview participant, a man in his early fifties, "If you ask one white South African a question, 'Have you been to a township?' They will all say no. Even twenty years later, they have not even set foot here. That is how you know reconciliation has failed" (087). The combination of spatial politics, lack of change, and the ineffectiveness of the passage of time are all reflected in this quote, insofar as this man has not seen his landscape change, nor does he believe that the change has occurred for others.

The final policy implication of this research is that despite the fact that it governs a highly divided society, the South African government functions with a high degree of regularity. Although waves of protest from among the poorest sectors of the population have challenged local government, and although many from among the most privileged sectors have left the country or retreated into securitized compounds, the South African economy is growing; regular, free, and fair elections are held; and the public protector and constitutional court have the ability and power to check the executive.

Conflicts over and investigations into presidential spending under the Zuma administration, altercations between parties at the State of the Nation address, as well as violence around workers strikes, service delivery protests, and university demonstrations have signaled emerging conflicts that have led some observers to argue that this stability should not be taken for granted. Additionally, the reliance on internal ANC governance as a mechanism to effect changes in leadership—as with the transitions from Mbeki to Motlanthe, and then from Zuma to Ramaphosa—has led some observers to express concern about the lack of general electoral success at replacing the executive, and about the quality of democracy (Goodman 2018; Dlamini 2010). Yet in each of these cases, the institutions of South African democracy—the judiciary, the parliament, etc.—have remained resilient. This fact undermines some of my own conclusions regarding the need for underlying unity to lend legitimacy and durability to democratic governance. However, the fact that many astute observers of South African politics have noted these conflicts, over party politics or work conditions or service delivery, as important signals about the tolerance levels of the South African public or the legitimacy of the government, do lend credence to my overall arguments.

AREAS OF FUTURE RESEARCH

Several avenues of future research can stem directly from this project, as extensions of the study of South African nationalism. There are possibilities for conducting interviews with other population groups, or in other areas. Because of the peculiar demographics of the Western Cape, in which more than 60 percent of the people speak Afrikaans as a first language, but where many more Afrikaans speakers would probably not consider themselves "white," conducting interviews with Afrikaans speakers could yield interesting results regarding the role of language as an organizing principle of identity. By comparing those interviews with those already conducted, or adding in interview populations from Pretoria and Johannesburg, it might be easier to draw widespread conclusions about the nature of Afrikaans speakers as a language group, or the persistence of racialized divisions within that category. Another extension of the interview pool could include South Africans from other language groups, such as isiXhosa or Sesotho speakers, or South Africans who are first-language English speakers. It may also be useful to conduct comparisons over time, with interviews under different circumstances, in order to ascertain the peculiar effects of the 2012–2013 time frame on the responses.

Another mode of comparison that could be used, especially as regards the analysis of chapter 5, could be a more ethnographically informed project on ceremonies in South Africa. This could involve attending virginity-testing ceremonies leading up to the Reed Dance, which happen in small communities throughout KwaZulu-Natal. Another site of comparison could be the various places in which the Day of the Vow is celebrated, such as at the Bloedrivier Museum in KwaZulu-Natal, the Women's Monument in Bloemfontein, or the churches in Stellenbosch where they hold the celebrations in the Western Cape. The difficulty in this design lies in the fact that the Day of the Vow is celebrated only on one day per year. Such a project would probably require a team of researchers. Perhaps a more feasible comparison for an individual researcher would be ethnographies of the various music and language festivals outlined in chapter 6, which could shed light on the ways in which Afrikaans-speaking people enact such festivals, and how they serve as identity creators.

The analysis in this manuscript could also be extended in comparison to other postconflict democratizing societies that specifically had truth commissions, such as Rwanda, Liberia, Sierra Leone, East Timor, Chile, or the former Yugoslavia. Although not all aspects of the analysis could be applied because of the social or linguistic landscapes of the countries, it could be useful to have a comparative study of the impact of truth commissions as nation-building tools. A comparative study of the different structures of the commissions or the levels of publicity they received could shed light on their effectiveness in mitigating the detrimental effects of identity politics in such societies. Such an analysis could involve interviews and archival evidence to discuss how truth commissions play a role in fostering the creation of nation-hood, and the various ways in which the revelations made by a truth commission effect participants and audience members.

Additionally, the analysis could be broadly brought to bear on postconflict democracies such as Iraq, Afghanistan, Rwanda, or Liberia, in which democracy and postconflict reconstruction were pursued simultaneously. In each of these circumstances, researchers have observed the persistence and renewal of sectarian divides in the postwar period. Yet in some cases, as in Liberia, where the various sides of the conflict were not strictly associated with identity-based groups, the salience of conflict-era divisions has faded. The differences between these countries and South Africa could shed light on the role of outside intervention or whether the severity of violence associated with the conflicts affects the outcomes of nation-building and democratization.

Another avenue for comparative study could be more consolidated democratic systems—such as Spain with the recent renewal of Catalan separatism, or the Basque region, or the Flemish separatists in Belgium, or the Scottish independence referendum—to examine the extended timeline of these tensions between nationalism and democratization in divided societies. Analysis of similar areas of nationalist and subnationalist identity formation in longer-standing states could give credence to the conclusions here in terms of the general theory that democracies revitalize such social divisions, rather than simply inheriting them from past conflict.

From a methodological point of view, the insights of Adida, Ferree, Posner, and Robinson (2016) on coethnicity effects on survey research could be extended to interview-based research, looking at both the ethics and effectiveness of more ethnographically informed interview-based research by researchers who can blend in with the populations they study rather than standing apart from them. Such positionality presents both ethical and practical challenges and opportunities for the researcher in terms of access and consent. Exploring such matters is crucially important in terms of developing research standards in qualitative research that take into account the influence of the researcher on the kinds of research they can and do conduct.

CONCLUSIONS: A TROUBLED BRIDGE OVER WATER

So, we return to the same field in the northern KwaZulu-Natal, with the museums that stand, poised for a confrontation or a conversation, across the Ncome River from one another. The new, democratic government in South Africa has allowed the space for both museums to exist, and for the versions of history that they portray to be protected. The process of the political transition made the reconciliation bridge linking these two museums possible, and the bridge over the river metaphorically and literally spans the distance between the two institutions, and by implication, their supporters. These changes are important, and represent a meaningful difference from the past. From a purely institutional point of view, these changes constitute a new order. The bridge makes it possible to cross the river. But if the bridge is locked, either literally or in the metaphorical sense, what meaning does it hold? What does it actually bridge if no one walks across it?

The bridge and the museums are a metaphor for how institutionalist approaches to understanding nation- and democracy-building fall short. The frozen battle fifty miles outside of Dundee holds the museums and the bridge in a kind of stasis between remembering the schisms that have divided South Africa and celebrating the bridges that span them. This tension, between the bridge and the parallel museums, is the same tension inherent in the distinct projects of nation-building and democracy-building.

Going forward, will South African democracy find itself characterized by the bridge or the museums? Does the institutional change, in terms of either democratic representation (the parallel museums) or formal, state-led nation-building (the bridge), constitute a fundamentally different order? While the different institutional context provides for the possibility of new ways of relating that are constitutive of nation- and democracy-building, they do not ensure such changes. Both democracies and nations are made meaningful and sustainable by the ways that individual citizens relate to one another, and how they think about their similarities and differences.

Each of the preceding chapters has examined a facet of the nation or of democracy, drawn from interviews and grounded theorizing, whether space, ceremony, symbols, or language, and looks at how South Africans discuss or inhabit their identities in relation to themselves and to one another. Each chapter has examined a different arena in which the official attempts to build democracy or nationhood in South Africa have interfaced with the individual choices, affiliations, and separations made by the lived experience of South African citizens. Each thematic chapter has addressed the tensions between remembering and forgetting, signals of sectarian identities and their national complements.

What are the locks on the bridges that span, for example the integration of neighborhoods, or the symbolic repertoires of nationhood? In what ways have the newly integrated spaces of South Africa been meaningfully shared after the advent of multiracial democracy? That symbolically resonant bridge, while important, is still often inaccessible. The existence of the bridge is important, but the locks on it are also a reality. Whether they are the literal locks of gated communities or the symbolic boundaries of affiliation that dictate who is welcome at public observances, the subnational barriers of affiliation inherited from the apartheid and colonial eras are being recreated in the democratic era. The bridge itself becomes meaningful, not as a structure spanning the river, but when it becomes an actual connection between both sides.

Interview Guide and Interview Index

INTRODUCTORY QUESTIONS:

Which of the following words best describes you? *Feel free to choose more than one.*
- umZulu _____
- Black _____
- African _____
- Zulu Speaker _____
- South African _____
- Isibongo or Isithakazelo sami _____
- I don't think of myself in those terms _____

What is the primary language spoken in your home?
- Zulu _____
- English _____
- Other (Please provide _____)

Did you vote in the last Municipal Election (2011)?
- Yes _____
- No _____
- Wasn't Eligible _____
  - If Yes: in which municipality?

  _____

Did you vote in the last National Election (2009)?
- Yes _____
- No _____
- Wasn't Eligible _____
  - If Yes: in which municipality?

  _____

OPEN-ENDED QUESTIONS:

Section 1
- What makes a person South African?
- What do you think it means for South Africa to be a "rainbow nation"? Do you think this is an accurate description of South Africa?
- If you identify as South African, are you proud to be South African? Why?
  ◦ Are there specific occasions you can think of, or particular times when you felt proud to be South African?
- When do you feel most South African?
- Do you feel you belong in South Africa?

Section 2
- What makes a person Zulu?
- Are you proud to be Zulu? Why?
- When do you feel most Zulu?
  ◦ Alternative: What makes you feel the most like an Afrikaner/Zulu?
- Do you know people who have attended the umKhosi womHlanga?
  ◦ Have you attended them?
  ◦ Do you think they are important? Why or why not?
- Do you belong to any groups that you think represent Zulus? Which ones? How do they represent you?

Section 3
- What are the major problems in South Africa right now?
- What are the good things the government is doing now?
- Of the problems you have named, do you see anyone working in politics right now to solve them?
  ◦ Are there any political actors that you believe are trustworthy?
  ◦ Who do you feel speaks on behalf of your interests in politics?
- If you did vote in the last election, do you think your vote was effective?

Section 4
- Did you follow the proceedings of the Truth and Reconciliation Commission?
  ◦ If yes: Do you think that the commission had a positive or a negative effect?
- Do you think that reconciliation is a useful thing to talk about in South Africa now? Why or why not?
- What do you think a "reconciled" South Africa would look like?

Code	Location	Date	Home Language	Gender	Age	Vote '09 (Natl)	Vote '11 (Mun.)
001	Bloemfontein	7/9/12	Afrikaans, English	Female	24	Yes	Yes
002	Bloemfontein	7/12/12	Afrikaans	Female	23	No	No
003	Bloemfontein	7/13/12	Afrikaans	Male	61	Yes	Yes
004	Bloemfontein	7/16/12	Afrikaans	Male	60–70	Yes	Yes
005	Bloemfontein	7/27/12	Afrikaans	Female	20–30	Yes	Yes
006	Bloemfontein	7/31/12	Afrikaans	Male	40–50	Yes	Yes
007	Bloemfontein	8/1/12	Afrikaans	Male	25–35	Yes	Yes
008	Bloemfontein	8/1/12	Afrikaans	Female	29	No	No
009	Centurion	8/10/12	Afrikaans	Male	65	Yes	Yes
010	Bloemfontein	8/13/12	Afrikaans	Female	19	Not Eligible	Not Eligible
011	Bloemfontein	8/14/12	Afrikaans	Female	50	Yes	Yes
012	Bloemfontein	8/16/12	Afrikaans	Male	60–70	Yes	Yes
013	Bloemfontein	8/16/12	Afrikaans	Female	27	Yes	Yes
014	Bloemfontein	8/19/12	Afrikaans	Male	20–30	Yes	Yes
015	Bloemfontein	8/23/12	Afrikaans, English	Female	50–60	Yes	Yes
016	Bloemfontein	8/24/12	Afrikaans	Female	20–30	Yes	Yes
017	Bloemfontein	9/6/12	Afrikaans	Male	67	Yes	Yes
018	Bloemfontein	9/7/12	Afrikaans	Male	20–30	No	Yes
019	Bloemfontein	9/10/12	Afrikaans	Female	20–30	Yes	Yes
020	Bloemfontein	9/11/12	Afrikaans	Female	22	No	No
021	Bloemfontein	9/11/12	Afrikaans	Male	40–50	Yes	No
022	Bloemfontein	9/12/12	Afrikaans	Male	30–40	Yes	Yes
023	Bloemfontein	9/17/12	Afrikaans	Female	20–30	Yes	Yes
024	Bloemfontein	9/18/12	Afrikaans	Female	35	Yes	No
025	Bloemfontein	9/18/12	Afrikaans	Male	30–40	Yes	No
026	Bloemfontein	9/18/12	Afrikaans	Male	32	Yes	No
027	Bloemfontein	9/19/12	Afrikaans	Female	35–45	Yes	Yes
028	Bloemfontein	9/20/12	Afrikaans	Female	27	Yes	Yes
029	Bloemfontein	9/20/12	Afrikaans	Female	27	Yes	Yes
030	Bloemfontein	9/21/12	Afrikaans	Female	22	Yes	Yes
031	Pretoria	9/26/12	Afrikaans	Male	20–30	Yes	Yes
032	Pretoria	9/27/12	Afrikaans	Female	39	Yes	Yes
033	Pretoria	9/28/12	Afrikaans	Male	50–60	No	No
034	Pretoria	9/29/12	Afrikaans	Male	20–30	No	No
035	Bloemfontein	10/1/12	Afrikaans	Male	60	Yes	Not Eligible
036	Bloemfontein	10/1/12	Afrikaans	Male	43	Yes	Yes
037	Bloemfontein	10/1/12	Afrikaans	Female	35–45	Yes	Yes

Code	Location	Date	Home Language	Gender	Age	Vote '09 (Natl)	Vote '11 (Mun.)
038	Bloemfontein	10/3/12	Afrikaans, S. Sotho	Male	30	Yes	Yes
039	Bloemfontein	10/3/12	Afrikaans	Male	26	Yes	Yes
040	Bloemfontein	10/4/12	Afrikaans	Male	21	Yes	Yes
041	Bloemfontein	10/4/12	Afrikaans	Female	23	No	No
042	Bloemfontein	10/11/12	English	Female	20–30	Yes	Yes
043	Bloemfontein	10/15/12	Afrikaans	Female	42	Yes	Yes
044	Bloemfontein	10/16/12	Afrikaans	Female	81	Yes	Yes
045	Bloemfontein	10/17/12	Afrikaans	Male	43	Yes	Yes
046	Bloemfontein	10/17/12	Afrikaans	Male	28	Yes	Yes
047	Bloemfontein	11/5/12	Afrikaans	Male	24	No	No
048	Pretoria	10/19/12	Afrikaans	Male	50–60		
049	Bloemfontein	10/31/12	Afrikaans	Male	47	Yes	Yes
050	Bloemfontein	10/31/12	Afrikaans	Female	36		
051	Bloemfontein	10/31/12	Afrikaans	Female	23	Yes	No
052	Bloemfontein	10/31/12	Afrikaans	Male	36	Yes	Yes
053	Bloemfontein	11/1/12	Afrikaans	Male	27	Yes	Yes
054	Bloemfontein	11/1/12	Afrikaans	Male	26	Yes	No
055	Bloemfontein	11/2/12	Zulu	Male	29	No	No
056	Bloemfontein	11/7/12	Afrikaans	Female	54	Yes	Yes
057	Bloemfontein	11/7/12	Afrikaans, English	Male	28	Yes	Not Eligible
058	Bloemfontein	11/7/12	Afrikaans	Female	35	Yes	Yes
059	Bloemfontein	11/7/12	Afrikaans	Female	52	Yes	Yes
060	Bloemfontein	11/7/12	Afrikaans	Female	44	Yes	No
061	Bloemfontein	11/7/12	Afrikaans	Male	56	Yes	Yes
062	Bloemfontein	11/7/12	Afrikaans	Female	56	Yes	Yes
063	Bloemfontein	11/7/12	Afrikaans	Male	26	Yes	Yes
064	Bloemfontein	11/12/12	Afrikaans	Female	36	Yes	No
065	Bloemfontein	11/12/12	Afrikaans	Female	62	Yes	Yes
066	Bloemfontein	11/13/12	Afrikaans	Male	45	Yes	Yes
067	Bloemfontein	11/13/12	Afrikaans	Female	61	Yes	No
068	Bloemfontein	11/13/12	Afrikaans	Female	43	Yes	Yes
069	Bloemfontein	11/14/12	Afrikaans	Male	42	Not Eligible	Not Eligible
070	Bloemfontein	11/14/12	Afrikaans	Male	55	Yes	No
071	Bloemfontein	11/21/12	English, Afrikaans	Female	51	Yes	Yes
072	Bloemfontein	11/26/12	Afrikaans	Female	24	No	No
073	Bloemfontein	11/26/12	Afrikaans	Male	38	Yes	Yes
074	Bloemfontein	11/26/12	Afrikaans	Female	47	Yes	Yes

Code	Location	Date	Home Language	Gender	Age	Vote '09 (Natl)	Vote '11 (Mun.)
075	Bloemfontein	11/26/12	Afrikaans	Female	45	Yes	Yes
076	Bloemfontein	11/26/12	Afrikaans	Male	34	Yes	Yes
077	Bloemfontein	11/30/12	Afrikaans	Male	53	Yes	Yes
078	Bloemfontein	12/3/12	Afrikaans	Male	57	Yes	Yes
079	Bloemfontein	12/6/12	Afrikaans	Male	34	Yes	Yes
080	Bloemfontein	12/7/12	Afrikaans	Female	42	Yes	Yes
081	Durban	1/29/13	Zulu	Male	25	Yes	Yes
082	Durban	2/9/13	Zulu, English	Female	35	No	No
083	Durban	2/9/13	Zulu	Female	27	Yes	Yes
084	Durban	2/9/13	Zulu, South Sotho	Female	86	Yes	Yes
085	Durban	2/9/13	Zulu	Female	50–60	Not Eligible	Not Eligible
086	Durban	2/15/13	Zulu, English	Male	35	Yes	Yes
087	Durban	2/13/13	Zulu	Male	53	Yes	No
088	Durban	3/19/13	Zulu	Male	60	Yes	Yes
089	Durban	3/26/13	Zulu	Male	38	Yes	Yes
090	Durban	3/26/13	Zulu	Male	68		
091	Durban	3/26/13	English	Male	42	Yes	Yes
092	Pretoria	4/3/13	Zulu	Male	45		
093	Durban	4/8/13	Zulu	Female	50	Yes	Yes
094	Durban	4/8/13	Zulu	Male	35	Yes	Yes
095	Durban	4/10/13	Zulu	Female	38		
096	Durban	4/15/13	Zulu	Female	35	Yes	Yes
097	Durban	4/16/13	Zulu	Female	35		
098	Durban	4/17/13	Zulu	Male	56	Yes	Yes
09	Durban	4/17/13	Zulu, English	Female	53	Yes	Yes
100	Durban	4/18/13	Zulu	Male	40	Yes	Yes
101	Durban	4/19/13	Zulu	Male	25	Yes	Yes
102	Durban	4/22/13	Zulu	Male	23	Yes	Yes
103	Durban	4/22/13	Zulu	Female	53	Yes	Yes
104	Durban	4/23/13	Xhosa	Female	29	Yes	No
105	Pretoria	4/29/13	Zulu	Female	23	No	No
106	Durban	5/22/13	Zulu	Male	45	Yes	No
107	Durban	5/23/13	Zulu	Male	30	Yes	Yes
108	Durban	5/28/13	Zulu	Male	39	Yes	Yes
109	Pretoria	6/2/13	Ndebele	Male	35–45	Not Eligible	Not Eligible

NOTES

CHAPTER 1

1. Zulu Nationalist public figures and historians, including King Goodwill Zwelithini, hotly contest this version of the history. At the commemoration of the Reconciliation Bridge across the Ncome River, the king said "It's not true that the river turned into blood. If we keep saying that our children will spit on our graves" (Dzanibe 2014).

2. Malan said of South Africa, "there's no such thing as a true story here. The facts might be correct, but the truth they embody is always a lie to someone else. My truths strike some people as racist heresies. Nadine Gordimer's strike me as distortions calculated to appeal to gormless liberals on the far side of the planet. A lot of South Africans can't read either of us, so their truth is something else entirely. Atop all this, we live in a country where mutually annihilating truths coexist entirely amicably" (Malan 2009, 4).

3. A parliamentary committee heard testimony about the closures in 2016, and representatives from both the Voortrekker Monument and the Bloedrivier Museum cited as a primary reason for their budgetary constraints the fact that the Department of Arts and Culture could not transfer funds regularly to their institutions because neither is a Declared Cultural Institution. Both institutions are funded primarily by private donations rather than government funding. Both Freedom Park and the Ncome River Museum are Declared Cultural Institutions, and therefore receive the majority of their operating budgets from governmental funds.

4. The strategy of creating new monuments and museums in spaces that had previously been occupied by Afrikaner nationalist and colonial monuments was a key move in the transition, because of the idea that such new monuments would complicate the memorialization of white nationalist figures and promote representation of the majority population. But this strategy also assumed that there would be a connection between and conversation about the new monuments and the old monuments occupying the same space. The #RhodesMustFall movement called into question this "multiplicative logic" of the transition period because, the student activists argued, the contextualization of monuments to majority rule was an insufficient and unsuccessful attempt to transform public spaces and university campuses (Holmes and Loehwing 2016).

5. These polite fictions about the organic development of the state from demands by self-defined communities are possible in the context of early-forming states in the

developed world (see, for example, Weber 1976). However, in much of the postcolonial world, the imposition of authority predates any articulation of nationalism because of the experience of colonialism and the external definition of borders. This order of events is especially true on the African continent, where colonial imposition of borders was at its farthest remove from the realities on the ground. Yet with the anticolonial movements of the mid-twentieth century, articulations of nationalism grounded many resistance efforts, at least among elites. Although they had a more complex relationship to the idea of self-determination, nationalist movements on the continent did self-consciously articulate the idea of self-determination and the illegitimacy of outside rule as key components of the anticolonial struggle.

6. The transition itself was not completely peaceful. Much of the violence of the transition was geographically concentrated in KwaZulu-Natal and Gauteng and fought along partisan and ethnolinguistic lines (Donham and Mofokeng 2011; Taylor 2002).

7. Primordialism has lost much of its sway as an independent theory of nationalism, because it largely lacks evidentiary support. As such, it has been roundly dismissed by prominent scholars of nationalism (see, for example, Brubaker 1996; Chandra 2006; Wimmer 2013). Even if the primordial tradition is not independently influential, it represents an important element in the combined repertoire of nationalist thinking (Coakley 2018).

8. Grant funding through the Fulbright program, where I originally applied for research funds—though the grant was later funded by the Andrew W. Mellon Foundation after the defunding of Fulbright programs by the federal government in 2011—was unavailable for projects primarily concentrated in the Cape. The region was already considered "well-studied."

CHAPTER 2

1. Although during the Social Cohesion Summit in Kliptown there were many working definitions of what "social cohesion" meant, the official conference report defines the term as "the extent to which a society is coherent, united and functional, providing an environment within which its citizens can flourish" ("Social Cohesion and Social Justice in South Africa" 2012, i).

2. Giliomee quotes a contemporary travel diary, which says of the white settlers at the Cape of Good Hope, "Although the first colonists here were composed of various nations, they are, by the operation of time, now so thoroughly blended together, that they are not to be distinguished from each other; even most of such as have been born in Europe, and who have resided here for some years, changed their national character, for that of this country" (Stavorinus 1798, quoted in Giliomee 2010, 51).

3. A kind of white supremacy founded on hierarchical divine right, with whites as masters and any nonwhite others as servants.

4. The standard orthography for these proper nouns has changed, but original spellings have been maintained in quotes.

5. Many of these cooperatives still exist today and are major providers of financial services (Sanlam and Santam), electricity (Eskom), or wine and spirits (KWV).

6. The electoral competition between the Unionist/South African Party led by Botha and Smuts and the National Party dominated the first thirty years of electoral politics in the South African Republic. The short-lived merger of these two parties, into the United Party, was dissolved by Hertzog over South Africa's proposed entry into World War II against Nazi Germany in 1939. Although the party managed to hold control of the government until the 1948 elections, they then lost to the National Party, which held power until the inauguration of Nelson Mandela in 1994.

7. The effects of this act, however, are still evident. The frustrations with continuity of land tenure and ownership patterns are discussed in greater detail in chapter 7.

8. The official name for the policy of separating black South Africans into different "nations," territorially defined as Bantustans or homelands, in which they would be granted the rights and privileges of citizenship. Through the Promotion of Bantu Self-Government Act of 1959, and later the Bantu Homeland Citizens Act of 1970, the apartheid government created the ten homelands for eight "nations," and divided the black African population among them. This policy allowed the National Party government to claim that no black majority existed in South Africa, while also further alienating black Africans from procedural citizenship or affective belonging in the national community of South Africa.

9. Among historians of South Africa there is some debate about the extent to which apartheid differed from earlier forms of segregation and repression. Some scholars argue that by 1924, the major pillars (and boundaries) of racial segregation had already been enacted, and that apartheid itself was different only in degree, rather than in character, from these earlier policies (for example, see Cell 1982, 58; Omer-Cooper 1994). Other scholars argue that in fact apartheid did differ in a significant way from segregation policies because the apartheid state pursued a policy of purposeful underdevelopment in the Bantustans, which forced workers into labor migracy to ensure a cheap labor supply (see, for example, Wolpe 1972, 428; Burawoy 1976). Regardless of this important debate, however, there is little disagreement on the idea that South Africa, as a unit, sought to territorially and ideologically separate black and white citizens from the earliest days of the union.

10. It was true that "all the homelands [were] so greatly dependent on South Africa for aid in economic development, defense, and internal security, that they enjoy[ed] little more than the degree of political freedom the South African government wants them to enjoy" (Giliomee and Schlemmer 1985, 47). Nonetheless, there were major differences in population, territory, and capacity between such homelands as the 45,000-square-kilometer area of Transkei and the 655-square-kilometer area of QwaQwa, or between contiguous homelands such as Ciskei, and the territorially dispersed KwaZulu or Bophuthatswana.

11. In an ANC press release from August 1952, Nelson Mandela wrote, "We are not in opposition to any government or class of people. We are opposing a system which

has for years kept a vast section of the non-European people in bondage. . . . We welcome true-hearted volunteers from all walks of life without consideration of colour, race or creed. . . . The unity between the Africans, Indians, and coloured people has now become a living reality" (Mandela 1952).

12. The Congress of Democrats was a group of South African whites, formed in collaboration with the African National Congress. This organization sought to publicize the ANC's intentions and policy among the white population.

13. Biko, in his essay "Black Souls in White Skins," on the subject of nonracialism, says "Nowhere is the arrogance of the liberal ideology demonstrated so well as in their insistence that the problems of the country can only be solved by a bilateral approach involving both black and white. . . . Hence the multiracial political organisations and parties and the 'nonracial' student organisations, all of which insist on integration not only as an end goal but also as a means . . . the people forming the integrated complex have been extracted from various segregated societies with their inbuilt complexes of superiority and inferiority and these continue to manifest themselves even in the 'nonracial' set-up of the integrated complex. As a result the integration so achieved is a one-way course, with the whites doing all the talking and the blacks the listening. . . . It is rather like expecting the slave to work together with the slave-master's son to remove all the conditions leading to the former's enslavement" (Biko 2002, 20–21).

14. This is not to say that Black Consciousness was "anti-white." In the SASO manifesto of July 1971, the organization ratified the following policy positions vis-à-vis the white population in South Africa: "SASO Believes: a) South Africa is a country in which both Black and White live and shall continue to live together, b) That the Whiteman must be made aware that one is either part of the solution or part of the problem, c) That, in this context, because of the privileges accorded to them by legislation and because of their continual maintenance of an oppressive regime, Whites have defined themselves as part of the problem, d) That, therefore, we believe that in all matters relating to the struggle towards realizing our aspirations, Whites must be excluded, e) That this attitude must not be interpreted by Blacks to imply 'anti-Whitism' but merely a more positive way of attaining a normal situation in South Africa f) That in pursuit of this direction, therefore, personal contact with Whites, thought it should not be legislated against, must be discouraged, especially where it tends to militate against the beliefs we hold dear" (Karis and Gerhart 1997, 481).

15. Many of which only came out with testimony before the Truth and Reconciliation Commission, as covered in chapter 3.

16. In 1995, the Gini coefficient, a statistical measure of income inequality ranging from zero (total equality) to one (total inequality), of South Africa was the second highest in the world at 0.58. Income inequality had been rising for the previous twenty years; "the income share accruing to the poorest 40% of African earners fell by a disquieting 48%, while the share accruing to the richest 10% rose by 43%" between 1975 and 1991 ("Poverty and Inequality in South Africa: Final Report" 1998, 24).

CHAPTER 3

1. It states "We, the people of South Africa, declare for all our country and the world to know: that South Africa belongs to all who live in it, black and white . . ."

2. When asked her thoughts on the current government, she said "[Politicians] are not in touch with what we need. Politicians still think about apartheid. Now we are liberated. We need to grow economically. They are comfortable. They have forgotten about us. Now, it is just about self-enrichment. They have forgotten about how they got there" (095).

3. When pressed further about why he thinks that, he responded, "A rainbow, in the end, is one thing and the different colors work together in creating that spectacular thing. Obviously, we are not there. I think what happened was, the more you say something, the more you believe it. So, a lot of people talk about the rainbow nation. . . . I think it detracts from the real issues. I do not like it" (007).

4. The invocation of "Kill the Boer" is in reference to ANC spokesperson Julius Malema's singing of a song by that name at a 2010 rally, invoking apartheid-era imagery of killing off the "foreign" whites to drum up support (Marrian 2012; Allen 2010). The ANC defended Malema in court, saying that the song itself was a legacy of the anti-apartheid struggle. In late 2012, they promised not to use the song in rallies anymore. After a political fallout with then-president Zuma, Malema was suspended from his position as ANC Youth League president and kicked out of the party in 2012. He now heads an opposition political party, the Economic Freedom Fighters, and has continued to use the song in political rallies.

5. *Braai*, the Afrikaans word for grilling, is a typical weekend entertainment for young people in South Africa. These parties, which generally occur outside, center around alcohol and grilling meat and are a central part of weekend culture. There is even a public holiday, Heritage Day, colloquially referred to as Braai Day, because that is assumed to be a unique part of South African heritage. This topic is covered in more detail in chapter 6.

6. When asked to elaborate on this point, the young man referenced the biblical story of the Tower of Babel as an explanation. He explained that God had created people differently, and intended for them to live separately. This biblical justification for separation was commonly used under apartheid by Afrikaner Nationalists and leaders in the Dutch Reformed Church. Interestingly, however, it is being invoked here by a member of generation that came of age after the end of apartheid.

7. *Kwaito*, a style of music closely related to house/trance music, incorporates a whole tradition of "vernacular and fashion norms" associated with township life and black youth (Steingo 2005, 333).

8. Steve Hofmeyr is an Afrikaans-language country music singer and actor who is politically very active, for example with the Red October campaign to end white genocide and the Expedition for Afrikaner Self-Determination, or *Onafhanklike Afrikaner-Selfbeskikkingsekspedisie*. His music is associated mainly with a rural ideal and white Afrikaners.

9. These hostels are the university dormitories, which were integrated by the vice chancellor of the University of the Free State in 2008. This young man had been on campus in 2008 when the integration occurred. The integration was contentious, and sparked varied student protests (Tromp and Molosankwe 2008), but I could not find any corroborating documents for this claim.

10. To tell complicated histories about apartheid and resistance to it is not the same as making the various parties of the conflict morally equivalent. As Archbishop Desmond Tutu asserts in the foreword to the final report by the TRC, the commission did make moral judgments about the causes for which perpetrators of violence were fighting, and weighted them differently. He characterized this discerning stance by saying, "A venerable tradition holds that those who use force to overthrow or even to oppose an unjust system occupy the moral high ground over those who use force to sustain that same system. That is when the criteria of the so-called 'just war' come into play. . . . This does not mean that those who hold the moral high ground have carte blanche as to the methods they use. Thus, to hold this particular view is not to be guilty of a bias. It is to assert that we move in a moral universe where right and wrong and justice and oppression matter" (Truth and Reconciliation Commission of South Africa 2002, 12, para. 54).

11. Umkhonto weSizwe, the Spear of the Nation. This group constituted the armed wing of the ANC, founded by ANC youth league leaders in the wake of the Sharpeville Massacre in 1961.

12. The Azanian People's Liberation Army, the armed wing of the Pan Africanist Congress, also founded in 1961.

13. This conflation of the ANC, which had an explicitly armed wing in Mkhonto we Sizwe, and the UDF, which had nonviolence at the core of its mission, is an interesting one. The view of the two organizations as a single unified and violent front belies a very particular conception of the "sides" of the conflict over apartheid.

14. A common Zulu and Xhosa interjection to express disbelief, resignation, or exasperation. In this particular interview, it was a particularly resigned, sighing expression of the word.

15. Krog writes, "For us all; all voices, all victims: / because of you / this country no longer lies / between us / but within . . . / I am changed forever. I want to say: / forgive me / forgive me / forgive me / You whom I have wronged, please / take me / with you" (Krog 2000, 364–65).

16. In English: "I know we were wrong / It was on BBC, CCN and all over the TV / Now the facts are on the table / Can we please move on sir? / For I will no longer say that I am sorry. / I will go to the back of the queue, / I will wear our rainbow on my sleeve, / But I will not apologize any longer. / The fact that I do not always agree / Does not make me a "racist." / Look for the splinter in your own eye [Look at your own faults first], / Because I will not say I am sorry any longer" (Translation by author).

17. Referring to a March 2013 investigation, which included the exhumation of the bodies of two young men in a Soweto cemetery. It was alleged that the bodies were those of two ANC activists who disappeared in 1988. Reportedly, these young men were last

seen with Winnie Madikizela-Mandela (see for example Tay 2013). These young men, and others, were discussed during Madikizela-Mandela's testimony at the TRC. Bishop Tutu, who chaired the session, broke into tears, begging Madikizela-Mandela for information on the fate of these young men, and she gave only very short answers, none leading to the exhumation or repatriation of the young men's bodies.

18. Afrikaans for despondant, crestfallen, dejected, dispirited. It is an evocative and emotional word, and distinct from *hopeloos* (hopeless).

CHAPTER 4

1. Voter turnout in the most recent rounds of elections has fallen, and some scholars have noted that the decline is most precipitous in the youngest cohort of voters, which some say is cause for concern (Schulz Herzenberg 2014). Turnout in the 2019 election was 65.1 percent (Scholtz 2019).

2. The last election that many scholars rate as truly competitive was in 1953, and had a minimum voting age of twenty-one (Berman 2010), which would mean that voters in that election had to be both white and born in 1932 or before. As of 2015, that would mean that the voters would have to be eighty-three years old or older to have participated in a competitive election. As of the 2011 census, those who are both white and over the age of eighty comprise approximately 0.25 percent of the total population (Statistics South Africa 2012, 30).

3. This is a reference to the promotion of then-premier of KwaZulu-Natal, Zwele Mkhize, who was promoted to the role of treasurer-general of the ANC in 2013.

4. A reference to then-party leader, Helen Zille.

5. Although not overtly racial, such invocations of the "majority" among Afrikaans speakers were often, as I believe is the case here, a coded reference to racialized constituencies.

6. A conservative party that caters mostly to a white, Afrikaner constituency.

7. As will be discussed below, other scholars, such as Elke Zuern (2011), have argued that the working definition of democracy for many poor South Africans is more closely related to a politics of socioeconomic equality than one of multiparty democracy, and in this conception of the term, there is strong support for it.

8. This evolution, in which opposition parties have become suspect, mirrors the evolution of the ANC's official stance on opposition parties and their role in democracy, discussed in detail in chapter 2.

9. This is not to say, however, that South Africans from different racial or ethnolingusitic backgrounds see the political challenges in their country in entirely incommensurate ways. In fact, when asked what the biggest challenge facing their country was, Afrikaans and Zulu speakers identified a similar set of issues. Overwhelmingly, across both Afrikaans and Zulu speakers, interview participants identified corruption (or a synonym of corruption, such as cronyism or nepotism) as the most pressing issue in South Africa. Yet despite similarities in identifying the problem of corruption and the

language used to discuss the problem, Afrikaans and Zulu speakers' views of the solution diverged significantly. For most Afrikaans speakers, the solution to the problem of corruption lay in supporting opposition parties and voting against the ANC. For Zulu speakers, the prescriptions were either an emphasis on unity or stressing the intractability of the problem.

10. In the words of Mkhabela, "Though not entirely fluent, he speaks Zulu when he's in KwaZulu-Natal, Xhosa in the Eastern Cape, Tsonga and Sepedi in Limpopo. He hardly speaks Venda, his mother tongue" (Mkhabela 2017).

11. This is a reference to a department store, Woolworth's, advertising job openings to which "Africans, coloureds and Indians" were welcome to apply (SAPA 2012). In response, several groups, such as the historically white Afrikaans trade union Solidarity, organized a boycott of the upmarket chain store, including calling for supporters to enter Woolworth's grocery stores, fill their carts with goods, and then abandon them in the store. The protest was meant to simultaneously destroy perishable food products and to demonstrate to management how much revenue was lost because of their "discriminatory practices" (Hermann 2012).

12. Julius Malema, referenced above, is the former president of the ANC Youth League. He was brought up on charges of hate speech and incitement to violence because of his repeated singing of an anti-apartheid struggle song entitled "Dubul' iBhunu" (Kill the Boer or Farmer) (Allen 2010). In part because of the case, Malema was expelled from the ANC and ended up forming his own political party, as discussed above.

13. The issue of farm attacks and farm murders is very politically charged in South Africa. The violence is commonly understood as violence against white landowners in rural or peri-urban settings. Activist groups such as Afriforum allege that these incidents constitute a targeted and widespread campaign of racially targeted violence. However, several scholarly analyses have suggested that, in fact, farmers in general are statistically less likely to be targeted than other groups of South Africans (du Plessis 2018; Wilkinson 2017; Holmes 2019a).

14. This is a reference to the shooting of former heavyweight boxing champion Corrie Sanders in Cape Town in September 2012. Sanders was shot during a robbery of a restaurant where he and his family were celebrating his nephew's birthday (*News24* 2012b).

15. As an example, nearly 30 percent of South Africa–trained health professionals have left the country, and 58 percent of those who remain say that they intend to leave if possible (Mayosi and Benatar 2014).

CHAPTER 5

1. A form of internal passports used to control the movement of black South Africans under apartheid, specifically to "control the freedom of movement of the African population and to circumscribe their access to labour markets in both urban and rural

areas . . . the pass laws have occupied the central position in the process of policing the African population and directing them into places dictated by whites. In short they are a key part of the legal-administrative apparatus of maintaining white domination" (Savage 1986, 181).

2. Both historically and presently, domestic workers, the overwhelming majority of whom are black women, are subject to harassment and sexual violence at the hands of their employers (du Plessis 2011). Although the details of the situation referenced here are unknown, it should be acknowledged that many such encounters between domestic servants and their employers involve violence, rape, and coercion.

3. Black Economic Empowerment programs were undertaken by the ANC-led government with the intent of redressing the economic inequalities arising and inherited from the apartheid era. These programs aimed to transform the economy through the use of certain standards in hiring and ownership of large firms, as well as their practices of procurement and management. While critics have accused these measures of enriching a small elite at the expense of the larger black population, evidence indicates that the 2003 reforms, labeled Broad-Based Black Economic Empowerment, have begun to have a positive effect on capital accumulation and equity among black households (Patel and Graham 2012).

4. This young woman was referring to the controversy over an ad run in several national newspapers by the department and grocery store chain Woolworth's. In some versions the advertisement included text indicating that the jobs available were open exclusively to black Africans, while others invited "Africans, coloureds and Indians" to apply (SAPA 2012).

5. While it is true that the percentage of white households occupying top income brackets in South Africa has fallen in the last decade (*Economist* 2017), that is largely due to the increasing diversity of the middle and upper rungs of income earners, and the ways in which the income distribution spectrum has been skewed toward the top earners since apartheid (Iheduru 2004). The average white-headed household is significantly wealthier than its black counterparts, and white South Africans are more uniformly prosperous than any other population group (Orthofer 2016; Leibbrandt, Finn, and Woolard 2012).

6. This word, derived from an Arabic word meaning "infidel," has been used since the early days of settlement in the Cape colony to refer to black Africans in South Africa. Its usage, which has been compared to the word "n****r" in the United States, has a particularly violent and hateful history. It has been identified as hate speech by the South African Department of Justice and Constitutional Development.

7. In the 2012 Statistics South Africa "Victims of Crime Survey," of a total of 13,423,000 crimes, 1,650,000 were reported by households whose head was classified as "white," a rate of 12.29 percent (Statistics South Africa 2012b). The 2011 South African census reported that 8.9 percent of the population in 2011 was classified as white (Statistics South Africa 2012a).

CHAPTER 6

1. The mythologized vow of the Voortrekker *kommandos* after the Battle of Ncome River, as described in the Introduction. The vow, according to nationalist historians, bound the Voortrekkers to commemorate the day of their military victory over the Zulu *impi* and to build a church. The military victory and the vow are central parts of the nationalist myth of divine election of Afrikaners (Murray 2013; Giliomee 2010).

2. The amendment resulted from several cases of "extreme hardship," in which children who did not appear to conform to the physical standards of the classified race of their parents were rejected from schooling or other public services on the basis of their appearance. The highest-profile case was brought by Abraham Laing, patriarch of a white Afrikaner family from the Transvaal, whose daughter had been reclassified as coloured based on her physical appearance. The amendment modified the earlier Population Registration Act of 1950, and linked the race of children and parents more closely, while also accounting for language, appearance, "general acceptance," and "deportment" (Horrell 1968, 20–21, 24–25).

3. Now called the Battle of Ncome River, discussed in the introductory chapter.

4. Regiment or army.

5. Warriors or heroes.

6. An Afrikaans expression for "Oh, no," which does not actually connote negativity. It is often used to take up space, in much the same way that "like" or "yeah, no" do for native English speakers.

7. This particular word, *geestehesittinge*, is a particular and somewhat heavy word in Afrikaans that comprises the spiritual and the intellectual aspects of thought. It implies both the individual and the communal as well as the divine and the rational.

8. Voortrekkers are a youth organization that was formed in the 1930s as an alternative to the Boy Scouts, which were seen as a British organization, and therefore hostile to Afrikaner interests. The founding ABCs of the Voortrekkers organization are *Afrikanerskap* (Being Afrikaner), *Burgerskap* (Citizenship), and *Christenkap* (Christianity).

9. The numbers all come from newspaper reports published in major, mainstream Afrikaans-language outlets, rather than activist or organizing groups.

10. AWB stands for Afrikaner Weerstandsbeweging (Afrikaner Resistance Movement), a far-right political organization in South Africa. The group has symbolic and literal ties to the neo-nazi movement, and openly supports armed opposition to and secession from the multiracial democracy in South Africa.

11. This is a reference to the farmer/paramilitary uniform of khaki shirt, shorts, and knee socks. Such dress is associated with the Afrikaner right wing, including the AWB. There were many people at the Voortrekker Monument in such dress on the Day of the Vow 2012.

12. Earlier in the interview, he said of these group names (Afrikaner and Boer) "*Ag*, but there is a lot of political baggage with these words. I am conservative, but that is not the problem. . . . I do not like to be associated with their extremeness. My politics are also to the right, but not like that" (076).

13. There is debate over whether virginity testing in its present form is actually a revival of Zulu tradition or a modern invention.

14. Stepan, Linz, and Yadav also discuss the need for institutional arrangements that support limited ethnofederalism to undergird such identities. Such arrangements are largely absent in South Africa, although they were discussed as possibilities during the transitional period, in part because of a strong ANC preference for centralized authority, and worries about the influence of traditional leaders who had been associated with the apartheid regime and the Bantustan leadership (see for example Sisk 1994, 272–73).

15. For more on discourses of threat and bodily integrity, as well as a discussion of farm violence, please see chapter 4.

16. Literally, farmers' music. A kind of instrumental folk/traditional music, mostly led by a concertina, that was meant for country dances.

17. *Braai*, the Afrikaans word for grilling or barbecue, is a social practice that involves the full range of grilling activities. It is imbued with gendered scripts (men tend the fire and women prepare the side dishes), and regularly lasts from early afternoon through late in the night. Often staged as pitch-ins, such social gatherings are held in private residences or public parks and involve copious quantities of grilled meat, side dishes, and, quite often, alcohol. Some braais last upwards of twelve hours, serving essentially two full meals throughout the course of the gathering.

CHAPTER 7

1. Such connections have been made across Southern Africa in anticolonial and anti-apartheid struggles, such that "the idea of land has been mobilized as a source of alternative *nationalist* narratives based on the desire for repossession—not just of land, but of the idea of land *as* nation: '*the* land'" (Graham 2009, 2, emphasis in original text).

2. There is quite a lot of debate over these exact numbers. The figures this participant quoted more accurately describe the land ownership situation in 1994, but as stated above, because very little has changed in the patterns of land ownership, it is not remarkable that people use these figures to make their point.

3. There is significant debate in the scholarly literature on the long-term effects of Zimbabwean land reform. Some scholars argue that certain of these consequences have been ameliorated by the passage of time, with agricultural output on the rise since 2006 (Moyo 2011; Kinsey 1999), or that such reforms have reduced inequality (Chitiga and Mabugu 2008). Others, however, argue that labor relations in Zimbabwe have remained unchanged, and hence that little transformation has taken place (Moyo 2011).

4. This characterization is, in many important ways, historically untrue. As is covered in chapter 5, there was extensive contact between black and white South Africans under the apartheid regime, especially in the domestic sphere. But many Afrikaans-speaking participants, especially those old enough to recall the apartheid living conditions, did not report this as "contact."

5. This incident involved young, white, Afrikaans male students who lived in a particularly heritage-laden residence on campus forcing older members of the cleaning

and security staff of their residence to engage in physical fitness tests, and to eat food on which they seemed to have urinated. The young men taped this "test" and the video leaked, causing an international scandal on campus. There were ensuing riots in 2008, and the vice chancellor of the university was asked to step down. A new vice chancellor, Jonathan Jansen, was hired. He implemented the open-campus policy as one of many interventions aimed at healing the relationship between the university and the black community in Bloemfontein (see, for example, Bryson 2014).

6. See also the penultimate section of chapter 5, which draws from a confrontation between vigilantes and a young black man in a white suburb after dark.

7. This term is used by the South African government's Human Rights Commission to designate those zones in which exclusionary policies might be adopted to ensure the rights of communities defined by culture, language, or religion (Strydom 1996; Henrard 2002). Orania and Kleinfontein have been recognized as cultural communities because of their mission to protect Afrikaans language and culture (FF+ 2013).

8. Self-determination was not a regular interview topic, but rather was brought up in the cases discussed below. This could very easily lead to an overrepresentation of supporters within the population with whom I spoke. It is, however, interesting that such a wide swath of individuals did support the efforts, in whole or in part, of such separatist communities.

9. "The project [in Orania] is fine, but there must be more Oranias. If you have a community that is predominantly Afrikaner you can build institutions, like universities. We must be a majority somewhere, if we are to survive. . . . We must be self-governing. Afrikaners cannot survive without being in the majority somewhere. . . . There must be balance between openness and closedness. You must be sufficiently open to allow for growth, but not so open that you lose your sense of self" (021).

10. "[Orania is] all about self-reliance. They are postindustrial, focusing on green development. Also, they have very direct democratic town governance. . . . What Orania really understood is that the tendency toward centralism is very strong. They will not go into war. They are proposing a form of re-territorialization; the making of place in a new way" (069).

CHAPTER 8

1. Some Zulu-speaking interview participants also identified themselves as "Zulu by language, but not by tribe" (087) because of the difference between the descendants of the Zulu royal house, whose surname is Zulu, and those who belong to groups that were militarily absorbed into the *amaZulu* (Zulu nation) during the imperial wars of the mid-nineteenth century (Hamilton 1995, 1998).

2. A derogatory slang term that indicates someone who is black but "acts white," as a coconut is dark on the outside and white on the inside.

3. This man was not denying the existence of different species of rhinoceros, but rather that the difference was expressible in English using the terms "white" and "black"

(themselves corruptions of the original terms of speciation, denoting a wide-mouthed [white] rhino) and then translated back into isiZulu.

4. These income categories are those that report earning less than ZAR 19,200 per annum. Those people who report having no income and are also monolingual are, by themselves, 19.7 percent of the total census sample.

5. While the official university policy addresses a desire to "support the development and frequency of the use of Sesotho as a scientific language," in my interactions with Sesotho-speaking academics, they did not see this as a credible commitment by the university. They stated that the only university courses offered in the language are those that teach Sesotho as a second language (UFS Council 2003, 3).

6. A nationalist identifier meaning the people's own, or belonging to the *volk*.

7. The headline of *Die Beeld*'s article was *Polisie "tree op binne sy regte met reaksie"* (Police "acting within their rights with reaction"). *Die Volksblad*'s headline was *Dít is kriteria vir optrede: Polisie "was waarskynlik binne regte"* (These are the criteria for action: "The Police were likely within their rights").

8. Original text: ""Niemand gee 'n f** om oor die twee polisiemanne wat dood is nie." *Die Burger*'s article started with a slightly sanitized version of the same quote, "Nobody cares about the two policemen who died." (*"Niemand gee om oor die twee polisiemanne wat dood is nie."*)

9. Then general secretary of the Congress of South African Trade Unions (COSATU). He was expelled from the position in a vote of the executive council in 2015.

BIBLIOGRAPHY

Abrahams, Caryn. 2016. "Twenty Years of Social Cohesion and Nation-Building in South Africa." *Journal of Southern African Studies* 42 (1): 95–107. https://doi.org/10.1080/03057070.2016.1126455

Adam, Heribert. 1971. *Modernizing Racial Domination: South Africa's Political Dynamics.* Berkeley: University of California Press.

Adam, Heribert, and Hermann Giliomee. 1979. *The Rise and Crisis of Afrikaner Power.* Cape Town: David Philip.

Adida, Claire L., Karen E. Ferree, Daniel N. Posner, and Amanda Lea Robinson. 2016. "Who's Asking? Interviewer Coethnicity Effects in African Survey Data." *Comparative Political Studies* 49 (12): 1630–60. https://doi.org/10.1177/0010414016633487

Adler, Glenn, and Eddie Webster. 1995. "Challenging Transition Theory: The Labor Movement, Radical Reform, and Transition to Democracy in South Africa." *Politics & Society* 23 (1): 75–106. https://doi.org/10.1177/0032329295023001004

Alden, Christopher, and Maxi Schoeman. 2015. "Reconstructing South African Identity through Global Summitry." *Global Summitry* 1 (2): 187–204. https://doi.org/10.1093/global/guw001

Alexander, Neville. 2001. "Language Politics in South Africa." In *Shifting African Identities,* edited by Simon Bekker, Martine Dodds, and Meshack M. Khosa, 141–52. Pretoria: Human Science Research Council Press.

Alfred, Luke. 2015. "No Easy Road between Voortrekker Monument and Freedom Park." *Mail and Guardian Online,* April 24. https://mg.co.za/article/2015-04-23-no-easy-road-between-voortrekker-monument-and-freedom-park

Allen, Karen. 2010. "Black Liberation Slogan 'Frightens Us.'" *BBC,* April 3. http://news.bbc.co.uk/today/hi/today/newsid_8601000/8601436.stm

ANC Women's League. 2015. "Preparations to 6th National Conference." http://www.anc.org.za/wl/show.php?id=11362

Anderson, Benedict. 2006. *Imagined Communities: Reflections on the Origin and Spread of Nationalism.* New York: Verso.

Andrucki, Max J. 2010. "The Visa Whiteness Machine: Transnational Motility in Post-Apartheid South Africa." *Ethnicities* 10 (3): 358–70.

Atuahene, Bernadette. 2011. "South Africa's Land Reform Crisis: Eliminating the Legacy of Apartheid." *Foreign Affairs* 90: 121.

Backer, David. 2010. "Watching a Bargain Unravel? A Panel Study of Victims' Attitudes about Transitional Justice in Cape Town, South Africa." *International Journal of Transitional Justice* 4 (3): 443–56. https://doi.org/10.1093/ijtj/ijq015

Ballard, Richard. 2002. "Desegregating Minds: White Identities and Urban Change in the New South Africa." Swansea: University of Wales. http://www.ukzn.ac.za/CCS/files/Ballard%202002%20Desegregating%20Minds.pdf

Ballard, Richard. 2004. "Middle Class Neighbourhoods or 'African Kraals'? The Impact of Informal Settlements and Vagrants on Post-Apartheid White Identity." *Urban Forum* 15 (1): 48–73.

Ballard, Richard. 2005. "Bunkers for the Psyche: How Gated Communities Have Allowed the Privatisation of Apartheid in Democratic South Africa." In *Dark Roast Occasional Paper Series*. Vol. 24. Isandla Institute.

Ballard, Richard, Adam Habib, Imraan Valodia, and Elke Zuern. 2005. "Globalization, Marginalization and Contemporary Social Movements in South Africa." *African Affairs* 104 (417): 615–34.

Barrington, Lowell W. 1997. "'Nation' and 'Nationalism': The Misuse of Key Concepts in Political Science." *PS: Political Science and Politics* 30 (4): 712–16.

Beall, Jo, Stephen Gelb, and Shireen Hassim. 2005. "Fragile Stability: State and Society in Democratic South Africa." *Journal of Southern African Studies* 31 (4): 681–700. https://doi.org/10.1080/03057070500370415

Beeld. 2012. "Is Minister Steeds Net 'Verontrus'?" August 17. http://152.111.1.88/argief/berigte/beeld/2012/08/17/B1/12/pkhoferkie.html

Beresford, Alexander. 2015. "Power, Patronage, and Gatekeeper Politics in South Africa." *African Affairs* 114 (455): 226–48. https://doi.org/10.1093/afraf/adu083

Beresford, Alexander. 2016. *South Africa's Political Crisis: Unfinished Liberation and Fractured Class Struggles*. London: Palgrave Macmillan.

Berman, Dan. 2010. "Apartheid Was Helped by a Twisted Election System." *FiveThirtyEight* (blog). May 22. http://fivethirtyeight.com/features/apartheid-was-helped-by-twisted/

Berrisford, Stephen. 2011. "Unravelling Apartheid Spatial Planning Legislation in South Africa." *Urban Forum* 22 (3): 247–63.

Bezuidenhout, Andries. 2007. "From Voëlvry to De La Rey: Popular Music, Afrikaner Nationalism and Lost Irony." In *Department of History Seminar*. University of Stellenbosch. http://sun025.sun.ac.za/portal/page/portal/Arts/Departemente1/geskiedenis/docs/a_bezuidenhout.pdf

Biko, Steve. 2002. *I Write What I Like: A Selection of His Writings*. Edited by Aelred Stubbs. Chicago: University of Chicago Press.

Billig, Michael. 1995. *Banal Nationalism*. London: Sage.

Binns, Tony, and Ross Robinson. 2002. "Sustaining Democracy in the 'New' South Africa." *Geography* 87 (1): 25–37.

Black, Maryke. 2013. "Volksblad: Boer Verslae Ná Bloedbad Op Plaas." *Volksblad*, April 18. http://www.volksblad.com/nuus/2013-04-18-boer-verslae-n-bloedbad-op-plaas

Blignaut, Charl. 2012. "The End of the Rainbow: Freedom Park." *City Press*, December 23. http://www.citypress.co.za/news/the-end-of-the-rainbow-freedom-park/

Blumenthal, Mari. 2013. "Rand-Bloedbad Duur Voort." *Volksblad*, May 30. http://www.volksblad.com/sake/2013-05-30-staatskas-baar-sorg

Booysen, Susan. 2015. *Dominance and Decline: The ANC in the Time of Zuma*. New York: NYU Press.

Boraine, Alex. 2001. *A Country Unmasked: Inside South Africa's Truth and Reconciliation Commission*. Cape Town: Oxford University Press.

Bosman, Frouwien, and Pierre Du Toit. 2011. "Electoral Systems and the Contest for Relative Group Status in Post-Conflict Societies: The Case of the 2009 Election in South Africa." *Politikon* 38 (2): 211–29.

Botes, Paul, and Niren Tolsi. 2013. "Marikana: One Year after the Massacre." *M&G Online*, August. http://marikana.mg.co.za/

Bottomley, Edward-John. 1990. "Public Policy and White Rural Poverty in South Africa, 1881–1924." PhD thesis, Queen's University at Kingston (Canada). http://search.proquest.com/pqdt/docview/220089748/abstract/140C13362B550D79BB8/1?accountid=11620

Bottomley, Edward-John. 2012. *Poor White*. Cape Town, South Africa: Tafelberg.

Bottomley, Edward-John. 2016. "Transnational Governmentality and the 'Poor White' in Early Twentieth Century South Africa." *Journal of Historical Geography* 54 (October): 76–86. https://doi.org/10.1016/j.jhg.2016.09.002

Brand, Gerrit. 2005. "Afrikaners, Afrikaanses en ander stories." *Rapport*, February 6, final edition. http://152.111.1.87/argief/berigte/rapport/2005/02/06/R1/14/01.html

Breetzke, Gregory D., Karina Landman, and Ellen G. Cohn. 2014. "Is It Safer Behind the Gates? Crime and Gated Communities in South Africa." *Journal of Housing and the Built Environment* 29 (1): 123–39. https://doi.org/10.1007/s10901-013-9362-5

Bremner, G. A. 2016. "Stones of Empire: Monuments, Memorials, and Manifest Authority." In *Architecture and Urbanism in the British Empire*, edited by G. A. Bremner, 86–125. New York: Oxford University Press.

Breytenbach, Breyten. 1993. *Return to Paradise*. London: Faber and Faber.

Brubaker, Rogers. 1996. *Nationalism Reframed: Nationhood and the National Question in the New Europe*. Cambridge: Cambridge University Press.

Bryson, Donna. 2014. *It's a Black-White Thing*. Cape Town: Tafelberg.

Burawoy, Michael. 1976. "The Functions and Reproduction of Migrant Labor: Comparative Material from Southern Africa and the United States." *American Journal of Sociology* 81 (5): 1050–87.

Burger, Rulof, and Rachel Jafta. 2010. "Affirmative Action in South Africa: An Empirical Assessment of the Impact on Labour Market Outcomes." CRISE Working Paper 76. London: United Kingdom Department of International Development. http://r4d.dfid.gov.uk/pdf/outputs/inequality/workingpaper76.pdf

Calpin, G. H. 1941. *There Are No South Africans*. London: Thomas Nelson and Sons.

Campbell, John. 2019. "What the ANC's Election Win Means for South Africa." *Council on Foreign Relations*, May 14. https://www.cfr.org/in-brief/what-ancs-election-win-means-south-africa

Carlin, John. 2008. *Playing the Enemy: Nelson Mandela and the Game That Made a Nation*. New York: Penguin Press.

Carter, Danielle. 2013. "Non-State Security, State Legitimacy and Political Participation in South Africa." PhD thesis, Michigan State University. http://search.proquest.com/pqdtglobal/docview/1492736556/abstract/A2CD1BB44E424BD8PQ/1?ac countid=11620

Carton, Benedict. 2009. "Introduction: Zuluness in the Post- and Neo-Worlds." In *Zulu Identities: Being Zulu, Past and Present*, edited by Benedict Carton, John Laband, and Jabulani Sithole, 3–22. New York: Columbia University Press.

Carton, Benedict, John Laband, and Jabulani Sithole. 2009. *Zulu Identities: Being Zulu, Past and Present*. New York: Columbia University Press.

Cavanagh, Edward. 2013. "The History of Dispossession at Orania and the Politics of Land Restitution in South Africa." *Journal of Southern African Studies* 39 (2): 391–407.

Cell, John Whitson. 1982. *The Highest Stage of White Supremacy*. Cambridge: Cambridge University Press.

"Cenotaph Hall | Voortrekker Monument." n.d. Accessed January 17, 2015. http://www.vtm.org.za/cenotaph-hall/

Chandra, Kanchan. 2005. "Ethnic Parties and Democratic Stability." *Perspectives on Politics* 3 (2): 235–52.

Chandra, Kanchan. 2006. "What Is Ethnic Identity and Does It Matter?" *Annual Review of Political Science* 9 (1): 397–424.

Chandra, Kanchan. 2007. *Why Ethnic Parties Succeed: Patronage and Ethnic Head Counts in India*. Cambridge: Cambridge University Press.

Chipkin, Ivor. 2007. *Do South Africans Exist? Nationalism, Democracy and the Identity of "the People."* Johannesburg: Witwatersrand University Press.

Chipkin, Ivor, and Bongani Ngqulunga. 2008. "Friends and Family: Social Cohesion in South Africa." *Southern African Studies* 34 (1): 61–76.

Chisale, Sinenhlanhla Sithulisiwe, and Deirdre Cassandra Byrne. 2018. "Feminism at the Margins: The Case of the Virginity Bursaries in South Africa." *African Identities* 16 (4): 1–12. https://doi.org/10.1080/14725843.2018.1439729

Chitiga, Margaret, and Ramos Mabugu. 2008. "Evaluating the Impact of Land Redistribution: A CGE Microsimulation Application to Zimbabwe." *Journal of African Economies* 17 (4): 527–49.

Cho, Seung Ho, and Karla K. Gower. 2006. "Framing Effect on the Public's Response to Crisis: Human Interest Frame and Crisis Type Influencing Responsibility and Blame." *Public Relations Review* 32 (4): 420–22.

Christopher, A. J. 2001. *The Atlas of Changing South Africa*. 2nd ed. London: Routledge. http://site.ebrary.com/lib/iub/Doc?id=10017809

Clarno, Andy. 2014. "Beyond the State: Policing Precariousness in South Africa and Palestine/Israel." *Ethnic and Racial Studies* 37 (10): 1725–31. https://doi.org/10.1080/01419870.2014.931984

Coakley, John. 2018. "'Primordialism' in Nationalism Studies: Theory or Ideology?" *Nations and Nationalism* 24 (2): 327–47. https://doi.org/10.1111/nana.12349

Coan, Stephen. 2013. "Bridging a River of Blood." *The Witness*, November 14. https://www.news24.com/Archives/Witness/Bridging-a-river-of-blood-20150430

Cock, Jacklyn. 1980. *Maids & Madams: A Study in the Politics of Exploitation*. Johannesburg: Ravan Press.

Cohen, Nissim, and Tamar Arieli. 2011. "Field Research in Conflict Environments: Methodological Challenges and Snowball Sampling." *Journal of Peace Research* 48 (4): 423–35. https://doi.org/10.1177/0022343311405698

Cohen, Shari J. 1999. *Politics Without a Past: The Absence of History in Postcommunist Nationalism*. Durham: Duke University Press.

Cole, Catherine M. 2009. *Performing South Africa's Truth Commission: Stages of Transition*. Bloomington: Indiana University Press.

Comaroff, Jean, and John L. Comaroff. 1993. "Introduction." In *Modernity and Its Malcontents: Ritual and Power in Postcolonial Africa*, edited by Jean Comaroff and John L. Comaroff, xi–xxxvii. Chicago: University of Chicago Press.

Cook, Susan E. 2006. "Language Policies and the Erasure of Multilingualism in South Africa." In *Silence: The Currency of Power*, edited by Maria-Luisa Achino-Loeb. New York: Berghahn Books.

Coombes, Annie E. 2003. *History after Apartheid: Visual Culture and Public Memory in a Democratic South Africa*. Durham: Duke University Press.

Coombes, Annie E. 2005. "Translating the Past: Apartheid Monuments in Post-Apartheid South Africa." In *Hybridity and Its Discontents: Politics, Science, Culture*, edited by Avtar Brah and Annie Coombes, 173–97. New York: Routledge.

Crampton, Andrew. 2001. "The Voortrekker Monument, the Birth of Apartheid, and Beyond." *Political Geography* 20 (2): 221–46. https://doi.org/10.1016/S0962-6298(00)00062-7

Crapanzano, Vincent. 1985. *Waiting: The Whites of South Africa*. New York: Random House.

Daneel, Roeline. 2008. "Still Evolving: The 14th Klein Karoo Nasionale Kunstefees." http://reference.sabinet.co.za/sa_epublication_article/theatre_v22_a11

De Juan, Alexander, and Eva Wegner. 2019. "Social Inequality, State-Centered Grievances, and Protest: Evidence from South Africa." *Journal of Conflict Resolution* 63 (1): 31–58. https://doi.org/10.1177/0022002717723136

De Klerk, V. A, and G. Barkhuizen. 2004. "Pre-Emigration Reflections: Afrikaans Speakers Moving to New Zealand." *Southern African Journal of Linguistics and Applied Language Studies* 22 (3–4): 99–109.

DeGelder, Mettje Christine. 2004. "After Apartheid: 'Contradictory Consciousness' among White South African Immigrants to Canada." Master's thesis, Memorial University of Newfoundland (Canada).

Department of Arts and Culture, Republic of South Africa. 2016. "Closure of Reconciliation Bridge and Road in Pretoria and Ncome: Voortrekker Monument, Freedom

Park, Msunduzi Museum and DAC Briefing; Status and Future of Ncome Museum: DAC Briefing." Parliamentary Monitoring Group, February 2. https://pmg.org.za/committee-meeting/21966/

Deumert, Ana. 2004. *Language Standardization and Language Change: The Dynamics of Cape Dutch*. Amsterdam: John Benjamins.

Dixon, John A., Don H. Foster, Kevin Durrheim, and Lindy Wilbraham. 1994. "Discourse and the Politics of Space in South Africa: The 'Squatter Crisis.'" *Discourse & Society* 5 (3): 277–96. https://doi.org/10.1177/0957926594005003002

Dlamini, Jacob. 2009. *Native Nostalgia*. Johannesburg: Jacana Media.

Dlamini, Jacob. 2010. "The Root of the Matter: Scenes from an ANC Branch." *African Studies* 69 (1): 187–203. https://doi.org/10.1080/00020181003647280

Dolby, Nadine. 2001. *Constructing Race: Youth, Identity, and Popular Culture in South Africa*. Albany: State University of New York Press.

Donham, Donald L, and Santu Mofokeng. 2011. *Violence in a Time of Liberation: Murder and Ethnicity at a South African Gold Mine, 1994*. Durham, NC: Duke University Press.

Du Plessis, Elmien. 2018. "AfriForum's Own Farm Murder Stats Don't Support Their Claims." *News24*, May 7. https://www.news24.com/Columnists/GuestColumn/afri forums-own-farm-murder-stats-dont-support-their-claims-20180507

Du Plessis, Irma. 2011. "Nation, Family, Intimacy: The Domain of the Domestic in the Social Imaginary." *South African Review of Sociology* 42 (2): 45–65.

Du Plessis, Irma. 2016. "Diversity, Not Division, in Lecture Halls." *The Mail & Guardian Online*, April 29. http://mg.co.za/article/2016-04-29-diversity-not-division-in-lec ture-halls/

Du Plessis, Tim. 2011. "'Afrikaanses' Aan't Uitsterf." *Rapport*, December 12. http://152.111.1.87/argief/berigte/rapport/2011/12/13/RH/2/politiekerapport.html

Du Preez, Max. 2007. "De La Rey Lives Again." *Carte Blanche*. Johannesburg: MNet TV. http://legacy-mnet.dstv.com/carteblanche/Article.aspx?Id=3251&ShowId=1

Dubin, S. 2016. *Transforming Museums: Mounting Queen Victoria in a Democratic South Africa*. New York: Palgrave Macmillan.

Dugard, John. 1980. "South Africa's Independent Homelands: An Exercise in Denationalization." *Denver Journal of International Law and Policy* 10: 11.

Duminy, James. 2014. "Street Renaming, Symbolic Capital, and Resistance in Durban, South Africa." *Environment and Planning D: Society and Space* 32 (2): 310–28. https://doi.org/10.1068/d2112

Dunning, Thad, and Lauren Harrison. 2010. "Cross-Cutting Cleavages and Ethnic Voting: An Experimental Study of Cousinage in Mali." *American Political Science Review* 104 (1): 21–39.

Durington, Matthew. 2006. "Race, Space and Place in Suburban Durban: An Ethnographic Assessment of Gated Community Environments and Residents." *GeoJournal* 66 (1–2): 147–60. https://doi.org/10.1007/s10708-006-9021-4

Dzanibe, Siyabulela. 2014. "Division Marks Opening of Reconciliation Bridge." *IOL*

News, December 17. https://www.iol.co.za/news/south-africa/kwazulu-natal/divi
sion-marks-opening-of-reconciliation-bridge-1796622

The Economist. 2017. "South Africa's Inequality Is No Longer about Race," May 20. https://www.economist.com/news/middle-east-and-africa/21722155-democracy-has-brought-wealth-only-few

Eldredge, Elizabeth A. 1992. "Sources of Conflict in Southern Africa, c. 1800–30: The 'Mfecane' Reconsidered." *Journal of African History* 33 (1): 1–35. https://doi.org/10.1017/S0021853700031832

Elischer, Sebastian. 2008. "Do African Parties Contribute to Democracy? Some Findings from Kenya, Ghana and Nigeria." *Africa Spectrum* 43 (2): 175–201.

Esbenshade, Richard S. 1995. "Remembering to Forget: Memory, History, National Identity in Postwar East-Central Europe." *Representations*, no. 49: 72–96. https://doi.org/10.2307/2928750

Etherington, Norman. 1995. "Old Wine in New Bottles: The Persistence of Narrative Structures in the Historiography of the Mfecane and the Great Trek." In *The Mfecane Aftermath: Reconstructive Debates in Southern African History*, edited by Carolyn Hamilton. Johannesburg: Witwatersrand University Press.

Etherington, Norman. 2004. "A Tempest in a Teapot? Nineteenth-Century Contests for Land in South Africa's Caledon Valley and the Invention of the Mfecane." *Journal of African History* 45 (2): 203–19. https://doi.org/10.2307/4100464

Everatt, David. 2010. *The Origins of Non-Racialism: White Opposition to Apartheid in the 1950's*. Johannesburg: Witwatersrand University Press. http://witspress.co.za/cat alogue/the-origins-of-non-racialism/

Everatt, David. 2016. "The Era of Ineluctability? Post-Apartheid South Africa After 20 Years of Democratic Elections." *Journal of Southern African Studies* 42 (1): 49–64. https://doi.org/10.1080/03057070.2016.1116326

"Explaining the Official Crime Statistics for 2012/2013." 2013. Factsheet. Johannesburg: Institute for Security Studies. http://www.issafrica.org/iss-today/explaining-the-of ficial-crime-statistics-for-2012-13

Fairbanks, Eve. 2018. "The Unlikely Upside of Cape Town's Drought." *The Huffington Post*, April 19. https://highline.huffingtonpost.com/articles/en/cape-town-drought/

Feinberg, Harvey M. 1993. "The 1913 Natives Land Act in South Africa: Politics, Race, and Segregation in the Early 20th Century." *International Journal of African Historical Studies* 26 (1): 65–109. https://doi.org/10.2307/219187

Ferree, Karen E. 2006. "Explaining South Africa's Racial Census." *Journal of Politics* 68 (4): 803–15. https://doi.org/10.1111/j.1468-2508.2006.00471.x

Ferree, Karen E. 2010. *Framing the Race in South Africa: The Political Origins of Racial-Census Elections*. New York: Cambridge University Press.

FF+. 2013. "Kleinfontein Settlement Recognised as Cultural Community—FF+—PARTY." http://www.politicsweb.co.za/politicsweb/view/politicsweb/en/ page71654?oid=461494&sn=Detail&pid=71616

Fish, Jennifer N. 2006. "Engendering Democracy: Domestic Labour and Coalition-

Building in South Africa." *Journal of Southern African Studies* 32 (1): 107–27. https://doi.org/10.1080/03057070500493811

Fourie, Hilda, and Ügen Vos. 2012. "Geliefdes Wonder Nog." *Volksblad*, August 18, 2012. http://152.111.11.6/argief/berigte/volksblad/2012/08/18/VB/5/thfeerstestorie-myn_1834.html

"The Freedom Charter." 1987. *Third World Quarterly* 9 (2): 672–77. https://doi.org/10.2307/3991903

Fricke, Christine. 2013. "Protocol, Politics and Popular Culture: The Independence Jubilee in Gabon." *Nations and Nationalism* 19 (2): 238–56. https://doi.org/10.1111/nana.12018

Friedman, Steven. 1993. *Long Journey: South Africa's Quest For A Negotiated Settlement.* Braamfontein, South Africa: Ravan.

Friedman, Steven. 2009. "An Accidental Advance? South Africa's 2009 Elections." *Journal of Democracy* 20 (4): 108–22. https://doi.org/10.1353/jod.0.0114

Frith, Adrian. 2012. "Orania SP." Sub Places from Census 2011. 2012. http://census2011.adrianfrith.com/place/374003001

Geertz, Clifford. 1973. *The Interpretation of Cultures: Selected Essays.* New York: Basic Books.

Gellner, Ernest. 2008. *Nations and Nationalism.* Ithaca: Cornell University Press.

George, Leanne. 2014. "Voortrekkermonument: Duisende Trotseer Eendeweer Vir Versoeningsdagvieringe." *Netwerk24*, December 16. http://www.netwerk24.com/nuus/2014-12-16-voortrekkermonument-duisende-trotseer-eendeweer-vir-verso eningsdagvieringe

Gerhart, Gail M., and Clive L. Glaser. 2010. *From Protest to Challenge.* Vol. 6, *A Documentary History of African Politics in South Africa, 1882–1990, Challenge and Victory, 1980–1990.* Bloomington: Indiana University Press.

Gibson, James L. 2003. "The Legacy of Apartheid Racial Differences in the Legitimacy of Democratic Institutions and Processes in the New South Africa." *Comparative Political Studies* 36 (7): 772–800. https://doi.org/10.1177/0010414003255104

Gibson, James L. 2004. "Does Truth Lead to Reconciliation? Testing the Causal Assumptions of the South African Truth and Reconciliation Process." *American Journal of Political Science* 48 (2): 201–17.

Gibson, James L. 2006. *Overcoming Apartheid: Can Truth Reconcile a Divided Nation?* New York: Russell Sage Foundation.

Gibson, James L., and Amanda Gouws. 2003. *Overcoming Intolerance in South Africa: Experiments in Democratic Persuasion.* New York: Cambridge University Press.

Giliomee, Hermann. 2007. "De La Rey, FNB and Unwanted Guardians." *Politics Web.* March 1. http://www.politicsweb.co.za/politicsweb/view/politicsweb/en/page71619?oid=82396&sn=Detail

Giliomee, Hermann. 2010. *The Afrikaners: Biography of a People.* Expanded and updated ed. Charlottesville: University of Virginia Press.

Giliomee, Hermann, James Myburgh, and Lawrence Schlemmer. 2001. "Dominant

Party Rule, Opposition Parties and Minorities in South Africa." *Democratization* 8 (1): 161–82.

Giliomee, Hermann, and Lawrence Schlemmer, eds. 1985. "The Changing Political Functions of the Homelands." In *Up Against the Fences: Poverty, Passes and Privilege in South Africa*, 39–56. New York: St. Martin's Press.

Giollabhuí, Shane Mac. 2017. "The Fall of an African President: How and Why Did the ANC Unseat Thabo Mbeki?" *African Affairs* 116 (464): 391–413. https://doi. org/10.1093/afraf/adx003

Girshick, Paula. 2004. "Ncome Museum/Monument: From Reconciliation to Resistance." *Museum Anthropology* 27 (1–2): 25–36. https://doi.org/10.1525/mua.2004.27.1-2.25

Goodin, Robert E. 1975. "Cross-Cutting Cleavages and Social Conflict." *British Journal of Political Science* 5 (4): 516–19. https://doi.org/10.1017/S000712340000836X

Goodman, Peter S. 2018. "South Africa Sees Fresh Start for Economy, with the Same Challenges." *New York Times*, February 15, sec. Business Day. https://www.nytimes. com/2018/02/15/business/south africa-economy-ramaphosa.html

Gordimer, Nadine. 1983. "Living in the Interregnum." *New York Review of Books*, January 20. http://www.nybooks.com/articles/archives/1983/jan/20/living-in-the-inter regnum/

Graham, James. 2009. *Land and Nationalism in Fictions from Southern Africa*. New York: Routledge.

Graybill, Lyn S. 2002. *Truth and Reconciliation in South Africa: Miracle or Model?* Boulder: Lynne Rienner.

Griffiths, Dominic, and Maria L. C. Prozesky. 2010. "The Politics of Dwelling: Being White/Being South African." *Africa Today* 56 (4): 22–41.

Grundlingh, Albertt, and Hilary Sapire. 1989. "From Feverish Festival to Repetitive Ritual? The Changing Fortunes of Great Trek Mythology in an Industrializing South Africa, 1938–1988." *South African Historical Journal* 21 (1): 19–38. https://doi. org/10.1080/02582478908671645

Gubler, Joshua R., and Joel Sawat Selway. 2012. "Horizontal Inequality, Crosscutting Cleavages, and Civil War." *Journal of Conflict Resolution* 56 (2): 206–32. https://doi. org/10.1177/0022002711431416

Gumede, Halala. 2013. "No South Africans in South Africa." Halala Siyanda. May 10. http://halalagumede.wordpress.com/2013/05/10/no-south-africans-in-south-af rica/

Guy, Jeff. 2013. *Theophilus Shepstone and the Forging of Natal: African Autonomy and Settler Colonialism in the Making of Traditional Authority*. University of KwaZulu-Natal Press.

Haas, Mary de, and Paulus Zulu. 1994. "Ethnicity and Federalism: The Case of KwaZulu/Natal." *Journal of Southern African Studies* 20 (3): 433–46.

Habib, Adam. 1997. "South Africa—The Rainbow Nation and Prospects for Consolidating Democracy." *African Journal of Political Science* 2 (2): 15–37.

Habib, Adam, and Collette Schulz Herzenberg. 2011. "Democratization and Parliamentary Opposition in Contemporary South Africa: The 2009 National and Provincial Elections in Perspective." *Politikon* 38 (2): 191–210. https://doi.org/10.1080/0258934 6.2011.580121

Habib, Adam, and Rupert Taylor. 1999. "Parliamentary Opposition & Democratic Consolidation in South Africa." *Review of African Political Economy* 26 (80): 261–67.

Hamber, Brandon. 1998. "'Dr Jekyll and Mr Hyde': Problems of Violence Prevention and Reconciliation in South Africa's Transition to Democracy." In *Violence in South Africa: A Variety of Perspectives*, edited by Elirea Bornman, Rene van Eeden, and Marie Wentzel, 349–70. Pretoria: Human Sciences Research Council Press.

Hamilton, Carolyn, ed. 1995. *The Mfecane Aftermath: Reconstructive Debates in Southern African History*. Bloomington: Indiana University Press.

Hamilton, Carolyn. 1998. *Terrific Majesty: The Powers of Shaka Zulu and the Limits of Historical Invention*. Cambridge, MA: Harvard University Press.

Hammond, Nicol. 2010. "The Gendered Sound of South Africa: Karen Zoid and the Performance of Nationalism in the New South Africa." *Yearbook for Traditional Music* 42 (January): 1–20.

Hancock, Sir Keith. 1966. "Are There South Africans?" Lecture presented at the The Alfred and Winifred Hoernle Memorial Lecture, South African Institute of Race Relations. http://www.disa.ukzn.ac.za/webpages/DC/boo19660000.028.058/boo19660 000.028.058.pdf

Harris, Verne. 2002. "The Archival Sliver: Power, Memory, and Archives in South Africa." *Archival Science* 2 (1): 63–86. https://doi.org/10.1007/BF02435631

Hartzell, Caroline, and Matthew Hoddie. 2003. "Institutionalizing Peace: Power Sharing and Post-Civil War Conflict Management." *American Journal of Political Science* 47 (2): 318–32. https://doi.org/10.1111/1540-5907.00022

Hauptfleisch, Temple. 2006. "Eventifying Identity: Festivals in South Africa and the Search for Cultural Identity." *New Theatre Quarterly* 22 (2): 181–98. https://doi. org/10.1017/S0266464X0600039X

Hayner, Priscilla B. 2002. *Unspeakable Truths: Confronting State Terror and Atrocity*. New York: Routledge.

Hazlett, Thomas W. 1988. "Economic Origins of Apartheid." *Contemporary Economic Policy* 6 (4): 85–104. https://doi.org/10.1111/j.1465-7287.1988.tb00549.x

He, Yinan. 2007. "Remembering and Forgetting the War: Elite Mythmaking, Mass Reaction, and Sino-Japanese Relations, 1950–2006." *History and Memory* 19 (2): 43–74.

Henrard, Kristin. 2002. *Minority Protection in Post-Apartheid South Africa: Human Rights, Minority Rights, and Self-Determination*. Westport, CT: Greenwood Publishing.

Hermann, Dirk. 2012. "Politicsweb—Woolworths Must Withdraw 'Blacks Only' Job Ad—Solidarity—PARTY." News. *PoliticsWeb*. September 4. http://www.politicsweb. co.za/politicsweb/view/politicsweb/en/page71654?oid=324051&sn=Detail

Hermanowicz, Joseph C., and Harriet P. Morgan. 1999. "Ritualizing the Routine:

Collective Identity Affirmation." *Sociological Forum* 14 (2): 197–214. https://doi.org/10.1023/A:1021462511364

Hirschmann, David. 1990. "The Black Consciousness Movement in South Africa." *Journal of Modern African Studies* 28 (1): 1–22. https://doi.org/10.2307/160899

Holmes, Carolyn E. 2015. "Marikana in Translation: Print Nationalism in South Africa's Multilingual Press." *African Affairs* 114 (455): 271–94. https://doi.org/10.1093/afraf/adv001

Holmes, Carolyn E. 2019a. "Analysis | Tucker Carlson, Those South African White Rights Activists Aren't Telling You the Whole Truth." *Washington Post*, May 15, sec. Monkey Cage. https://www.washingtonpost.com/politics/2019/05/15/tucker-carlson-those-south-african-white-rights-activists-arent-telling-you-whole-truth/

Holmes, Carolyn E. 2019b. "The Politics of 'Non-Political' Activism in Democratic South Africa." *Comparative Politics* 51 (4): 561–80.

Holmes, Carolyn E., and Melanie Loehwing. 2016. "Icons of the Old Regime: Challenging South African Public Memory Strategies in #RhodesMustFall." *Journal of Southern African Studies* 42 (6): 1207–23. https://doi.org/10.1080/03057070.2016.1253927

Holmes, Carolyn E., and Brian D. Shoup. 2013. "Framing the Democratic Narrative: Local and National Voting Patterns in South Africa." *Commonwealth & Comparative Politics* 51 (1): 56–75. https://doi.org/10.1080/14662043.2013.752177

Hook, Derek, and Michele Vrdoljak. 2002. "Gated Communities, Heterotopia and a 'Rights' of Privilege: A 'Heterotopology' of the South African Security-Park." *Geoforum* 33 (2): 195–219. https://doi.org/10.1016/S0016-7185(01)00039-2

Horn, André, and June-Rose Buyisiwe Ngcobo. 2003. "The Suburban Challenge: (De) Segregation, Opportunity, and Community in Akasia, City of Tshwane." *Urban Forum* 14 (4): 320–46. https://doi.org/10.1007/s12132-003-0017-6

Horowitz, Donald L. 1991. *A Democratic South Africa? Constitutional Engineering in a Divided Society*. Berkeley: University of California Press.

Horowitz, Donald L. 2000. *Ethnic Groups in Conflict, Updated Edition with a New Preface*. Berkeley: University of California Press.

Horrell, Muriel. 1968. "A Survey of Race Relations in South Africa 1967." Johannesburg: South African Institute of Race Relations. http://www.sahistory.org.za/sites/default/files/SAIRR%20Survey%201967.pdf

Housing Development Agency of South Africa. 2012. "South Africa: Informal Settlements Status (2001)." Research Reports. Johannesburg. http://www.thehda.co.za/uploads/images/HDA_Informal_settlements_status_South_Africa.pdf

Housing Development Agency of South Africa. 2013. "South Africa: Informal Settlements Status (2013)." Research Reports. Johannesburg. http://www.thehda.co.za/uploads/images/HDA_South_Africa_Report_lr.pdf

"Identity: Are There Any South Africans?" 2010. Quarterly Report Fourteenth Issue. Roundtable. Parktown, Johannesburg: Helen Suzman Foundation. http://hsf.org.za/resource-centre/roundtable-series/QRSMar14thweb.pdf/view

Iheduru, Okechukwu C. 2004. "Black Economic Power and Nation-Building in Post-Apartheid South Africa." *Journal of Modern African Studies* 42 (1): 1–30. https://doi.org/10.1017/S0022278X03004452

Independent Electoral Commission of South Africa. 2014. "Voter Turnout." Independent Electoral Commission of South Africa. http://www.elections.org.za/content/NPEPublicReports/291/Voter%20Turnout/National.pdf

Independent Electoral Commission of South Africa. 2019. "2019 National and Provincial Elections Results Dashboard." Independent Electoral Commission of South Africa. https://www.elections.org.za/NPEDashboard/app/dashboard.html

Ishiyama, John. 2009. "Do Ethnic Parties Promote Minority Ethnic Conflict?" *Nationalism and Ethnic Politics* 15 (1): 56–83. https://doi.org/10.1080/13537110802672388

Ismail, Jamal Abdi, and James Deane. 2008. "The 2007 General Election in Kenya and Its Aftermath: The Role of Local Language Media." *International Journal of Press/Politics* 13 (3): 319–27. https://doi.org/10.1177/1940161208319510

James, Deborah. 2001. "Land for the Landless: Conflicting Images of Rural and Urban in South Africa's Land Reform Programme." *Journal of Contemporary African Studies* 19 (1): 93–109. https://doi.org/10.1080/02589000125070

James, Deborah. 2007. *Gaining Ground? Rights and Property in South African Land Reform.* London: Routledge.

Jansen, Jonathan. 2017. "Two Sides to Murder Story." *HeraldLIVE,* November 2. http://www.heraldlive.co.za/opinion/2017/11/02/two-sides-murder-story/

Johnson, R. W. 2004. *South Africa: The First Man, The Last Nation.* London: Weidenfeld & Nicolson.

Jooste, C. J. 1997. *Selfbeskikking Vir Afrikaners—Self-Determination for Afrikaners.* Pretoria: Verslag van Die Volkstaatraad.

Jung, Courtney. 2000. *Then I Was Black: South African Political Identities in Transition.* New Haven: Yale University Press.

Karim, Aisha Abdool, and Sandisiwe Shoba. 2019. "KwaZulu-Natal: Old Kid on Block Back with a Vengeance." *Daily Maverick,* May 13. https://www.dailymaverick.co.za/article/2019-05-13-kwazulu-natal-old-kid-on-block-back-with-a-vengeance/

Karis, Thomas G., and Gail M. Gerhart. 1997. *From Protest to Challenge.* Vol. 5, *A Documentary History of African Politics in South Africa, 1882–1990: Nadir and Resurgence, 1964–1979.* Bloomington: Indiana University Press.

Kedourie, Elie. 1993. *Nationalism.* New York: Wiley.

Keegan, Tim. 1997. *Colonial South Africa: Origins Racial Order.* Charlottesville: University Press of Virginia.

Keepile, Karabo. 2010. "Reed Dance Keeps Traditions Alive." *M&G Online,* September 22. http://mg.co.za/article/2010-09-22-reed-dance-keeps-traditions-alive/

Kinsey, Bill H. 1999. "Land Reform, Growth and Equity: Emerging Evidence from Zimbabwe's Resettlement Programme." *Journal of Southern African Studies* 25 (2): 173–96. https://doi.org/10.1080/030570799108650

Krog, Antjie. 2000. *Country of My Skull: Guilt, Sorrow, and the Limits of Forgiveness in the New South Africa.* New York: Three Rivers Press.

Krog, Antjie, Nosisi Mpolweni, and Kopano Ratele. 2009. *There Was This Goat: Investigating the Truth Commission Testimony of Notrose Nobomvu Konile.* Scottsville, South Africa: University of KwaZulu-Natal Press.

Lahiff, Edward. 2007. "'Willing Buyer, Willing Seller': South Africa's Failed Experiment in Market-Led Agrarian Reform." *Third World Quarterly* 28 (8): 1577–97. https://doi.org/10.1080/01436590701637417

Lakmidas, Sherilee. 2013. "Lonmin Miners Strike in South Africa, Unnerving Investors." *Reuters*, March 5. http://www.reuters.com/article/2013/03/05/us-lonmin-marikana-idUSBRE9240LH20130305

Landman, Karina, and Martin Schönteich. 2002. "Urban Fortresses: Gated Communities as a Reaction to Crime." *African Security Review* 11 (4): 71–85. https://doi.org/10.1080/10246029.2002.9628147

Lange, Jan de, and Ügen Vos. 2012. "Bloedbad: Polisie Skiet 18 Myners Dood." *Die Beeld*, August 17. http://152.111.1.88/argief/berigte/beeld/2012/08/17/B1/1/HB.html

Langner, Danie. 2014. "Leef Trots!" *Federasie van Afrikaanse Kultuurvereniginge* (blog). December 16. http://www.fak.org.za/blog/leef-trots/

Laremont, Ricardo Rene, ed. 2005. *Borders Nationalism and the African State.* Boulder: Lynne Rienner.

Lefko-Everett, Kate. 2012. "Leaving It to the Children: Non-Racialism, Identity, Socialisation and Generational Change in South Africa." *Politikon* 39 (1): 127–47.

Leibbrandt, Murray, Arden Finn, and Ingrid Woolard. 2012. "Describing and Decomposing Post-Apartheid Income Inequality in South Africa." *Development Southern Africa* 29 (1): 19–34. https://doi.org/10.1080/0376835X.2012.645639

Lemanski, Charlotte. 2004. "A New Apartheid? The Spatial Implications of Fear of Crime in Cape Town, South Africa." *Environment and Urbanization* 16 (2): 101–12. https://doi.org/10.1177/095624780401600201

Lemanski, Charlotte. 2006. "The Impact of Residential Desegregation on Social Integration: Evidence from a South African Neighbourhood." *Geoforum* 37 (3): 417–35. https://doi.org/10.1016/j.geoforum.2005.09.002

Lemanski, Charlotte, Karina Landman, and Matthew Durington. 2008. "Divergent and Similar Experiences of 'Gating' in South Africa: Johannesburg, Durban and Cape Town." *Urban Forum* 19 (2): 133–58. https://doi.org/10.1007/s12132-008-9030-0

Lemarchand, René. 2007. "Consociationalism and Power Sharing in Africa: Rwanda, Burundi, and the Democratic Republic of the Congo." *African Affairs* 106 (422): 1–20. https://doi.org/10.1093/afraf/adl041

Levenson, Zachary. 2014. "We Are Humans and Not Dogs." *Berkeley Journal of Sociology* 58 (October). http://berkeleyjournal.org/2014/10/we-are-humans-and-not-dogs/

Levitsky, Steven, and Daniel Ziblatt. 2018. *How Democracies Die.* New York: Crown.

https://www.penguinrandomhouse.com/books/562246/how-democracies-die-by-steven-levitsky-and-daniel-ziblatt/9781524762933

Lewis, Anthony. 1994. "Abroad at Home; Miracle with Reasons." *New York Times*, April 29, sec. Opinion. http://www.nytimes.com/1994/04/29/opinion/abroad-at-home-miracle-with-reasons.html

Lijphart, Arend. 1969. "Consociational Democracy." *World Politics* 21 (02): 207–25. https://doi.org/10.2307/2009820

Lijphart, Arend. 1977. *Democracy in Plural Societies: A Comparative Exploration.* New Haven: Yale University Press.

Lindner, Tobias. 2013. *Orania.* Digital Media. Dreamtrader Fils. http://www.orania-film.de/about.html

Linz, Juan J., and Alfred Stepan. 2011. *Problems of Democratic Transition and Consolidation: Southern Europe, South America, and Post-Communist Europe.* Baltimore: Johns Hopkins University Press.

Linz, Juan J., and Alfred C. Stepan. 1996. "Toward Consolidated Democracies." *Journal of Democracy* 7 (2): 14–33. https://doi.org/10.1353/jod.1996.0031

Lipton, Merle. 1972. "Independent Bantustans?" *International Affairs* 48 (1): 1–19. https://doi.org/10.2307/2613623

Lodge, Tom. 2003. "How the South African Electoral System Was Negotiated." *Journal of African Elections* 2 (1): 71–76.

Lodge, Tom. 2014. "Neo-Patrimonial Politics in the ANC." *African Affairs* 113 (450): 1–23. https://doi.org/10.1093/afraf/adt069

Lyons, Terrence. 2004. "Post-Conflict Elections and the Process of Demilitarizing Politics: The Role of Electoral Administration." *Democratization* 11 (3): 36–62. https://doi.org/10.1080/1351034042000238167

Mabandu, Percy. 2012. "The End of the Rainbow: Voortrekker Monument." *City Press*, December 23. http://www.citypress.co.za/news/the-end-of-the-rainbow-voortrekker-monument/

MacDonald, Michael. 2006. *Why Race Matters in South Africa.* Cambridge, MA: Harvard University Press.

"Magazine and Newspaper Readership, Jan–Dec 2012." 2013. Sloane Park, Sandton: South African Audience Research Foundation. http://www.saarf.co.za/amps-readership/2012/AMPS%20DEC%202012-%20READERSHIP%20SUMMARY-with%20Non%20Pay-for%20SAARF.pdf

Maharaj, Brij. 1999. "The Integrated Community Apartheid Could Not Destroy: The Warwick Avenue Triangle in Durban." *Journal of Southern African Studies* 25 (2): 249–66.

Mahoney, Michael R. 2012. *The Other Zulus: The Spread of Zulu Ethnicity in Colonial South Africa.* Durham: Duke University Press.

Malan, Charles. 2005. "Afrikaner, Afrikaanse, Afrikaan—Wie Is Ons?" *Rapport*, February 27, Final edition. http://152.111.1.87/argief/berigte/rapport/2005/02/27/R1/30/01.html

Malan, Rian. 1990. *My Traitor's Heart: A South African Exile Returns to Face His Country, His Tribe, and His Conscience*. New York: Atlantic Monthly Press.

Malan, Rian. 2009. *Resident Alien*. Johannesburg: Jonathan Bell Publishers.

Mamdani, Mahmood. 2002. "Amnesty or Impunity? A Preliminary Critique of the Report of the Truth and Reconciliation Commission of South Africa (TRC)." *Diacritics* 32 (3): 33–59. https://doi.org/10.1353/dia.2005.0005

Mamdani, Mahmood. 2015. "Beyond Nuremberg: The Historical Significance of the Post-Apartheid Transition in South Africa." *Politics & Society* 43 (1): 61–88. https://doi.org/10.1177/0032329214554387

Mandela, Nelson. 1952. "We Defy—10,000 Volunteers Protest against Unjust Laws." African National Congress. http://www.anc.org.za/show.php?id=2592

Mandela, Nelson. 1994. "Nelson Mandela's Inaugural Speech—Pretoria May 10, 1994." University of Pennsylvania, African Studies Center Digital Archive. May 10. http://www.africa.upenn.edu/Articles_Gen/Inaugural_Speech_17984.html

Mangcu, Xolela. 2017. "Shattering the Myth of a Post-Racial Consensus in South African Higher Education: 'Rhodes Must Fall' and the Struggle for Transformation at the University of Cape Town." *Critical Philosophy of Race* 5 (2): 243–66. https://doi.org/10.5325/critphilrace.5.2.0243

Marcus, Tessa. 2009. "Virginity Testing: A Backward-Looking Response to Sexual Regulation in the HIV/AIDS Crisis." In *Zulu Identities: Being Zulu, Past and Present*, edited by Benedict Carton, John Laband, and Jabulani Sithole, 536–44. New York: Columbia University Press.

Maré, Gerhard. 2001a. "Race Counts in Contemporary South Africa: 'An Illusion of Ordinariness.'" *Transformation: Critical Perspectives on Southern Africa* 47: 75–93.

Maré, Gerhard. 2001b. "Race, Democracy and Opposition in South African Politics: As Other a Way as Possible." In *Opposition and Democracy in South Africa*, edited by Roger Southall, 85–102. London: Frank Cass.

Maré, Gerhard. 2001c. "Race, Democracy and Opposition in South African Politics: As Other a Way as Possible." *Democratization* 8 (1): 85–102. https://doi.org/10.1080/714000182

Maré, Gerhard. 2003. "'Non-Racialism' in the Struggle against Apartheid." *Society in Transition* 34 (1): 13–37.

Maré, Gerhard. 2005. "Race, Nation, Democracy: Questioning Patriotism in the New South Africa." *Social Research* 72 (3): 501–30.

Marikana Commission of Inquiry. n.d. "Marikana Commission of Inquiry—Documents." Daily Hearing Transcripts. Rustenburg: Marikana Commission of Inquiry. http://www.marikanacomm.org.za/documents.html

Marrian, Natasha. 2012. "Complaints against Malema Escalate." *Mail and Guardian Online*, March 11. http://mg.co.za/article/2010-03-11-complaints-against-malema-escalate

Marschall, Sabine. 2004. "Gestures of Compensation: Post-Apartheid Monuments and Memorials." *Transformation* 55: 78–95.

Marx, Anthony W. 1998. *Making Race and Nation: A Comparison of South Africa, the United States, and Brazil*. New York: Cambridge University Press.

Mattes, Robert. 2002. "South Africa: Democracy Without the People?" *Journal of Democracy* 13 (1): 22–36. https://doi.org/10.1353/jod.2002.0010

Mattes, Robert. 2004. "Voter Information, Government Evaluations and Party Images, 1994–2004." CSSR Working Paper No. 89. University of Cape Town. http://www.cssr.uct.ac.za/sites/cssr.uct.ac.za/files/pubs/wp89.pdf

Mattes, Robert. 2011. "Forging Democrats: A Partial Success Story?" In *After Apartheid: Reinventing South Africa?*, edited by Ian Shapiro and Kahreen Tebeau, 72–104. Charlottesville: University of Virginia Press.

Mattes, Robert. 2012. "The 'Born Frees': The Prospects for Generational Change in Post-Apartheid South Africa." *Australian Journal of Political Science* 47 (1): 133–53.

Mattes, Robert, and Jennifer Christie. 1997. "Personal versus Collective Quality of Life and South Africans' Evaluations of Democratic Government." *Social Indicators Research* 41 (1/3): 205–28. https://doi.org/10.2307/27522263

Mattes, Robert, and J. Piombo. 2001. "Opposition Parties and the Voters in South Africa's General Election of 1999." *Democratization* 8 (3): 101–28. https://doi.org/10.1080/714000211

Mattes, Robert, and Samantha Richmond. 2014. "South Africa's Youth and Political Participation, 1994–2014." CSSR Working Paper No. 338. Centre for Social Science Research, University of Cape Town. https://open.uct.ac.za/handle/11427/7905?show=full

Maylam, Paul. 2001. "The Politics of Adaptation and Equivocation: Race, Class and Opposition in Twentieth-Century South Africa." *Democratization* 8 (1): 103–16. https://doi.org/10.1080/714000190

Mayosi, Bongani M., and Solomon R. Benatar. 2014. "Health and Health Care in South Africa—20 Years after Mandela." *New England Journal of Medicine* 371 (14): 1344–53. https://doi.org/10.1056/NEJMsr1405012

Mbele, Lerato. n.d. "Marikana: Economic Impact One Year On." *BBC News—Africa Business Report*. Accessed March 30, 2014. http://www.bbc.co.uk/news/business-23710782

McClendon, Gwyneth H. 2016. "Race and Responsiveness: An Experiment with South African Politicians." *Journal of Experimental Political Science* 3 (1): 60–74. https://doi.org/10.1017/XPS.2015.10

McCusker, Brent, William G. Moseley, and Maano Ramutsindela. 2015. *Land Reform in South Africa: An Uneven Transformation*. Lanham, MD: Rowman & Littlefield.

McGarry, John, and Brendan O'Leary. 2005. "Federation as a Method of Ethnic Conflict Regulation." In *From Power Sharing to Democracy: Post-Conflict Institutions in Ethnically Divided Societies*, edited by Sid Noel, 263–96. Montreal: McGill-Queen's University Press.

McKaiser, Eusebius. 2010. "Saffer Politics: Why There Are No South Africans and It's

Ok." *Saffer Politics* (blog). March 12. http://safferpolitics.blogspot.com/2010/03/why-there-are-no-south-africans-and-its.html

McLaughlin, Eric S. 2007. "Beyond the Racial Census: The Political Salience of Ethnolinguistic Cleavages in South Africa." *Comparative Political Studies* 40 (4): 435–56. https://doi.org/10.1177/0010414006294420

Mkhabela, Mpumelelo. 2017. "Is Ramaphosa the Ethnic Unifier the ANC Needs?" *News24*, December 8. https://www.news24.com/Columnists/Mpumelelo_Mkhabela/is-ramaphosa-the-ethnic-unifier-the-anc-needs-20171208

Mkhize, John. 2012. "Amaphoyisa Alalise Uyaca Emayini." *ISolezwe*, August 17. http://www.iol.co.za/isolezwe/amaphoyisa-alalise-uyaca-emayini-1.1364751#.Ux8W8T-H8cs

Modiri, Joel. 2013. "Race, Realism and Critique: The Politics of Race and Afriforum v Malema in the (in)Equality Court: Note." http://reference.sabinet.co.za/sa_epublication_article/ju_salj_v130_n2_a5

Mofokeng, Motshwari. 2012. "Umunyu Befuna Izihlobo Zesibhicongo." *ISolezwe*, August 20. http://www.iol.co.za/isolezwe/umunyu-befuna-izihlobo-zesibhicongo-1.1365795#.Ux8U-j-H8cs

Møller, Valerie, Helga Dickow, and Mari Harris. 1999. "South Africa's 'Rainbow People,' National Pride and Happiness." *Social Indicators Research* 47 (3): 245–80. https://doi.org/10.2307/27522393

Morange, Marianne, Fabrice Folio, Elisabeth Peyroux, and Jeanne Vivet. 2012. "The Spread of a Transnational Model: 'Gated Communities' in Three Southern African Cities (Cape Town, Maputo and Windhoek)." *International Journal of Urban and Regional Research* 36 (5): 890–914. https://doi.org/10.1111/j.1468-2427.2012.01135.x

Moyo, Sam. 2011. "Changing Agrarian Relations After Redistributive Land Reform in Zimbabwe." *Journal of Peasant Studies* 38 (5): 939–66. https://doi.org/10.1080/03066150.2011.634971

Mozaffar, Shaheen, James R. Scarritt, and Glen Galaich. 2003. "Electoral Institutions, Ethnopolitical Cleavages, and Party Systems in Africa's Emerging Democracies." *American Political Science Review* 97 (3): 379–90. https://doi.org/10.1017/S0003055403000753

Msimang, Sisonke. 2017. "All Is Not Forgiven." *Foreign Affairs*, December 12, 2017. https://www.foreignaffairs.com/articles/south-africa/2017-12-12/all-not-forgiven

Murray, Martin J. 2013. *Commemorating and Forgetting: Challenges for the New South Africa*. Minneapolis: University of Minnesota Press. https://www.upress.umn.edu/book-division/books/commemorating-and-forgetting

Murray, Martin J. 2017. *Taming the Disorderly City: The Spatial Landscape of Johannesburg after Apartheid*. Ithaca: Cornell University Press.

Muthien, Yvonne G., and Meshack M. Khosa. 1995. "'The Kingdom, the Volkstaat and the New South Africa': Drawing South Africa's New Regional Boundaries." *Journal of Southern African Studies* 21 (2): 303–22.

"National and Provincial Labour Market Trends 2003–2013." 2013. Statistical Release P0211.4. Pretoria: Statistics South Africa. http://beta2.statssa.gov.za/publications/P02114/P021142013.pdf

"National Braai Day Mission and Vision." n.d. Accessed January 21, 2015. http://braai.com/national-braai-day-mission/

Nattrass, Nicoli, and Jeremy Seekings. 2001. "'Two Nations'? Race and Economic Inequality in South Africa Today." *Daedalus* 130 (1): 45–70. https://doi.org/10.2307/20027679

Ndletyana, Mcebisi, and Bavusile B. Maaba. 2010. "The African National Congress's Unprecedented Victory in KwaZulu-Natal: Spoils of a Resurgent Zulu Ethno-Nationalism." *Journal of African Elections*, South Africa Elections 2009: Special Issue, 9 (2): 123–41.

Ndlovu, Musa. 2011. "The Meaning of Post-Apartheid Zulu Media." *Communicatio* 37 (2): 268–90. https://doi.org/10.1080/02500167.2011.604172

Ndlovu-Gatsheni, Sabelo J. 2007. "Tracking the Historical Roots of Post-Apartheid Citizenship Problems: The Native Club, Restless Natives, Panicking Settlers and the Politics of Nativism in South Africa." Book (monograph). 66. 2007. https://openaccess.leidenuniv.nl/handle/1887/12905

Ndlovu-Gatsheni, Sabelo J. 2009. "Africa for Africans or Africa for 'Natives' Only? 'New Nationalism' and Nativism in Zimbabwe and South Africa." *Africa Spectrum* 44 (1): 61–78. https://doi.org/10.2307/40175270

News24. 2012a. "You Don't Understand Democracy, Zuma Told," September 14. http://www.news24.com/SouthAfrica/News/You-dont-understand-democracy-Zuma-told-20120914

News24. 2012b. "SA Boxing Champ Shot at Restaurant." September 23. http://www.news24.com/SouthAfrica/News/SA-boxing-champ-shot-at-restaurant-20120923

Ngwenya, Khaya. 2013. "Thousands Gather for Reed Dance." *City Press*, August 31, 2013. http://www.citypress.co.za/multimedia/pics-thousands-gather-for-reed-dance/

Norris, Pippa. 2012. *Making Democratic Governance Work: How Regimes Shape Prosperity, Welfare, and Peace.* Cambridge: Cambridge University Press.

Norris, Shane A., Robert W. Roeser, Linda M. Richter, Nina Lewin, Carren Ginsburg, Stella A. Fleetwood, Elizabeth Taole, and Kees van der Wolf. 2008. "South African-Ness Among Adolescents: The Emergence of a Collective Identity Within the Birth to Twenty Cohort Study." *Journal of Early Adolescense* 28 (1): 51–69.

Noy, Chaim. 2008. "Sampling Knowledge: The Hermeneutics of Snowball Sampling in Qualitative Research." *International Journal of Social Research Methodology* 11 (4): 327–44. https://doi.org/10.1080/13645570701401305

Oyedemi, Toks, and Desline Mahlatji. 2016. "The 'Born-Free' Non-Voting Youth: A Study of Voter Apathy Among a Selected Cohort of South African Youth." *Politikon* 43 (3): 311–23. https://doi.org/10.1080/02589346.2016.1160857

Ogude, James. 2001. "The Vernacular Press and the Articulation of Luo Ethnic Citizenship: The Case of Achieng' Oneko's Ramogi." *Current Writing* 13 (2): 42–55. https://doi.org/10.1080/1013929X.2001.9678104

Ojo, Tokunbo. 2006. "Ethnic Print Media in the Multicultural Nation of Canada: A Case Study of the Black Newspaper in Montreal." *Journalism* 7 (3): 343–61. https://doi.org/10.1177/1464884906065517

O'Laughlin, Bridget, Henry Bernstein, Ben Cousins, and Pauline E. Peters. 2013. "Introduction: Agrarian Change, Rural Poverty and Land Reform in South Africa Since 1994." *Journal of Agrarian Change* 13 (1): 1–15. https://doi.org/10.1111/joac.12010

Omer-Cooper, John D. 1966. *The Zulu Aftermath: A Nineteenth-Century Revolution in Bantu Africa*. Evanston, IL: Northwestern University Press.

Omer-Cooper, John D. 1994. *History of Southern Africa*. 2nd ed. Oxford: James Currey.

Orlowska, Izabela. 2013. "Forging a Nation: The Ethiopian Millennium Celebration and the Multiethnic State." *Nations and Nationalism* 19 (2): 296–316. https://doi.org/10.1111/nana.12021

Orthofer, Anna. 2016. "Wealth Inequality in South Africa: Evidence from Survey and Tax Data." REDI3x3 Working Paper 15. The Research Project on Employment, Income Distribution and Inclusive Growth. Southern Africa Labour and Development Research Unit, University of Cape Town. http://www.redi3x3.org/sites/default/files/Orthofer%202016%20REDI3x3%20Working%20Paper%2015%20-%20Wealth%20inequality.pdf

Oyedemi, Toks, and Desline Mahlatji. 2016. "The 'Born-Free' Non-Voting Youth: A Study of Voter Apathy among a Selected Cohort of South African Youth." *Politikon* 43 (3): 311–23. https://doi.org/10.1080/02589346.2016.1160857

Özler, Berk. 2007. "Not Separate, Not Equal: Poverty and Inequality in Post-apartheid South Africa." *Economic Development and Cultural Change* 55 (3): 487–529. https://doi.org/10.1086/511191

Patel, Kamna. 2016. "Sowing the Seeds of Conflict? Low-Income Housing Delivery, Community Participation and Inclusive Citizenship in South Africa." *Urban Studies* 53 (13): 2738–57. https://doi.org/10.1177/0042098015572090

Patel, Leila, and Lauren Graham. 2012. "How Broad-Based Is Broad-Based Black Economic Empowerment?" *Development Southern Africa* 29 (2): 193–207. https://doi.org/10.1080/0376835X.2012.675692

Pennington, Steuart. 2012. "Actually, There Are South Africans." *Business Day Live*. August 6. http://www.bdlive.co.za/articles/2010/03/17/actually-there-are-south-africans

Plaatje, Solomon Tshekisho. 1916. *Native Life in South Africa*. London: P.S. King and Co., Project Gutenberg. http://archive.org/details/nativelifeinsout01452gut

"The 'Poor-White' Problem In South Africa." 1933. *British Medical Journal* 2 (3788): 296–97. https://doi.org/10.2307/25318357

Posel, Deborah. 2001. "Race as Common Sense: Racial Classification in Twentieth-Century South Africa." *African Studies Review* 44 (2): 87–113. https://doi.org/10.2307/525576

Posel, Dorrit, and Jochen Zeller. 2016. "Language Shift or Increased Bilingualism in South Africa: Evidence from Census Data." *Journal of Multilingual and Multicultural Development* 37 (4): 357–70. https://doi.org/10.1080/01434632.2015.1072206

Pottie, David, and Shireen Hassim. 2003. "The Politics of Institutional Design in the South African Transition." In *Can Democracy Be Designed? The Politics of Institutional Choice in Conflict-Torn Societies*, edited by Sunil Bastian and Robin Luckham. New York: Zed Books.

"Poverty and Inequality in South Africa: Final Report." 1998. Pretoria: Government, Republic of South Africa. http://www.info.gov.za/view/DownloadFileAction?id=70499

Rademeyer, Alet. 2012. "'Moenie oor die land treur, onthou Gelofte.'" *Die Burger*, December 17, 2012. http://152.111.1.87/argief/berigte/dieburger/2012/12/17/SK/9/targelofte_1655.html

Ramutsindela, Maano F. 1997. "National Identity in South Africa: The Search for Harmony." *GeoJournal* 43 (1): 99–110. https://doi.org/10.2307/41147123

Ramutsindela, Maano F. 2007. "Resilient Geographies: Land, Boundaries and the Consolidation of the Former Bantustans in Post-1994 South Africa." *Geographical Journal* 173 (1): 43–55. https://doi.org/10.2307/30113492

Randall, Vicky, and Lars Svåsand. 2002. "Party Institutionalization in New Democracies." *Party Politics* 8 (1): 5–29. https://doi.org/10.1177/1354068802008001001

Rapport. 2008. "Diens Op 16 Des. by Die VTM," December 9, 2008. http://152.111.1.87/argief/berigte/rapport/2008/12/09/RG/6/mkgelof.html

Rassool, Ciraj, and Leslie Witz. 1993. "The 1952 Jan Van Riebeeck Tercentenary Festival: Constructing and Contesting Public National History in South Africa1." *Journal of African History* 34 (3): 447–68. https://doi.org/10.1017/S0021853700033752

Reilly, Benjamin. 2006. "Political Engineering and Party Politics in Conflict-Prone Societies." *Democratization* 13 (5): 811–27. https://doi.org/10.1080/13510340601010719

Renan, Ernest. 1882. "Qu'est-ce Qu'une Nation?" In *Oeuvres Completes*. Vol. 1: 887–90. Paris: Calmann-Levy.

Rich, Timothy S., and Carolyn E. Holmes. 2016. "Winning Is Not Everything: Public Perceptions of Losers and Non-Voters in South Africa." *Acta Politica* 51 (3): 328–45. https://doi.org/10.1057/ap.2015.17

Robinson, Amanda Lea. 2014. "National Versus Ethnic Identification in Africa: Modernization, Colonial Legacy, and the Origins of Territorial Nationalism." *World Politics* 66 (4): 709–46. https://doi.org/10.1017/S0043887114000239

Rooyen, Fanie van. 2010. "Geloftedag Is Nog Relevant, Hoor Skare." *Die Beeld*, December 17. http://152.111.1.88/argief/berigte/beeld/2010/12/17/B1/4/tfvrGelofte.html

Roy, Srirupa. 2006. "'A Symbol of Freedom': The Indian Flag and the Transformations of Nationalism, 1906–2002." *Journal of Asian Studies* 65 (3): 495–527.

RSA Legislature 1996. n.d. "Republic of South Africa Promotion of National Unity and Reconciliation Amendment Bill." Accessed February 5, 2011. http://www.justice.gov.za/trc/legal/b48b_98.htm

Sallaz, Jeffrey J. 2010. "Talking Race, Marketing Culture: The Racial Habitus In and Out of Apartheid." *Social Problems* 57 (2): 294–314.

SAPA. 2012. "Woolies Defends Employment Policy." *M&G Online*, September 9, 2012. http://mg.co.za/article/2012-09-09-woolies-defends-employment-policy/

SAPA. 2014. "R300m Tax Money for Royal Cultural Village." *Times LIVE*, May 4, 2014. http://www.timeslive.co.za/local/2014/05/04/r300m-tax-money-for-royal-cultural-village

Savage, Michael. 1986. "The Imposition of Pass Laws on the African Population in South Africa 1916–1984." *African Affairs* 85 (339): 181–205.

Scholtz, Dawie. 2019. "Demographics and Disappointment: Dawie Scholtz's Complete Election Post-Mortem | News24." *News24*, May 14, 2019. https://www.news24.com/Elections/Voices/demographics-and-disappointment-dawie-scholtzs-complete-election-post-mortem-20190514

Schönteich, Martin, and Henri Boshoff. 2003. "'Volk' Faith and Fatherland: The Security Threat Posed by the White Right." Monograph 81. Pretoria: Institute for Security Studies. http://www.iss.co.za/Pubs/Monographs/No81/Content.html

Schulz-Herzenberg, Collette. 2014. "Voter Participation in the South African Elections of 2014." Policy Brief 61. Pretoria: Institute for Security Studies. https://issafrica.s3.amazonaws.com/site/uploads/PolBrief61_Aug14.pdf

Schwartz-Shea, Peregrine, and Dvora Yanow. 2013. *Interpretive Research Design: Concepts and Processes*. New York: Routledge.

Scott, Duncan, Mohammed Vawda, Sharlene Swartz, and Arvin Bhana. 2012. "Punching Below Their Weight: Young South Africans' Recent Voting Patterns." *Human Sciences Research Council Review* 10 (3): 19–21.

Seekings, Jeremy. 1992. "'Trailing Behind the Masses': The United Democratic Front and Township Politics in the Pretoria-Witwatersrand-Vaal Region, 1983–84." *Journal of Southern African Studies* 18 (1): 93–114.

Seekings, Jeremy. 2007. "'Not a Single White Person Should Be Allowed to Go Under': Swartgevaar and the Origins of South Africa's Welfare State, 1924–1929." *Journal of African History* 48 (3): 375–94. https://doi.org/10.2307/40206586

Seekings, Jeremy. 2008. "The Continuing Salience of Race: Discrimination and Diversity in South Africa." *Journal of Contemporary African Studies* 26 (1): 1–25. https://doi.org/10.1080/02589000701782612

Seekings, Jeremy, and Nicoli Nattrass. 2008. *Class, Race, and Inequality in South Africa*. New Haven: Yale University Press.

Selway, Joel, and Kharis Templeman. 2012. "The Myth of Consociationalism? Conflict Reduction in Divided Societies." *Comparative Political Studies* 45 (12): 1542–71. https://doi.org/10.1177/0010414011425341

Seme, Pixley ka Isaka. 1911. "Native Union." *Imvo Zabantsundu*, October 24, 1911. http://www.sahistory.org.za/archive/native-union-article-pixley-ka-isaka-seme-october-24-1911

Senekal, Burgert A, and Cilliers van den Berg. 2010. "'n Voorlopige Verkenning van Postapartheid Afrikaanse Protesmusiek." *LitNet Akademies* 7 (2): 98–128.

Shaikh, Nabeelah. 2014. "Our R140bn Crime Rip-Off." *Sunday Tribune*, September 21. http://www.iol.co.za/news/crime-courts/our-r140bn-crime-rip-off-1.1754080#. VGvBYVfF_Uc

Sharp, John. 1998. "'Non-Racialism' and Its Discontents: A Post-Apartheid Paradox." *International Social Science Journal* 50 (156): 243–252. https://doi.org/10.1111/1468-2451.00127

Shore, Megan. 2009. *Religion and Conflict Resolution: Christianity and South Africa's Truth and Reconciliation Commission*. Farnham, UK: Ashgate Publishing.

Shoup, Brian D., and Carolyn E. Holmes. 2013. "Recrafting the National Imaginary and the New 'Vanguardism.'" *Democratization* 21 (5): 1–21. https://doi.org/10.1080/1351 0347.2013.777431

Simonsen, Sven Gunnar. 2005. "Addressing Ethnic Divisions in Post-Conflict Institution-Building: Lessons from Recent Cases." *Security Dialogue* 36 (3): 297–318. https://doi.org/10.1177/0967010605057017

Sisk, Timothy. 1994. *Democratization in South Africa*. Princeton: Princeton University Press.

Smith, Anthony D. 2010. *Nationalism: Theory, Ideology, History*. Cambridge: Polity.

Smith, Rogers M. 2003. *Stories of Peoplehood: The Politics and Morals of Political Membership*. Cambridge: Cambridge University Press.

"Social Cohesion and Social Justice in South Africa." 2012. Pretoria, South Africa: The Presidency of the Republic of South Africa. http://www.thepresidency.gov.za/peb ble.asp?relid=1103

South African Government. 2015. "Public Holidays in South Africa." http://www.gov.za/about-sa/public-holidays

South African Native National Congress. 1914. "Petition to King George V, from the South African Native National Congress, July 20." *Cape Argus*. https://www.sahis tory.org.za/archive/petition-king-george-v-south-african-native-national-con gress-july-20-1914

Southall, Roger. 2001. "Opposition in South Africa: Issues and Problems." *Democratization* 8 (1): 1–24. https://doi.org/10.1080/714000183

Stanley, Elizabeth. 2001. "Evaluating the Truth and Reconciliation Commission." *Journal of Modern African Studies* 39 (3): 525–46.

Statistics South Africa. 2012a. "2011: Census in Brief." Census 03-01-41. Pretoria: South African Census Bureau. http://www.statssa.gov.za/Census2011/Products/Cen sus_2011_Census_in_brief.pdf

Statistics South Africa. 2012b. "Victims of Crime Survey 2012." Statistical Release P0341. Victims of Crime Survey. Pretoria: Statistics South Africa. http://www.statssa.gov.za/Publications2/P0341/P03412012.pdf

Statistics South Africa. 2017. "Victims of Crime Survey 2016/2017." P0341. http://www.statssa.gov.za/?page_id=1854

Statistics South Africa. n.d. "Census 2011 Persons (10% Sample)." Nesstar. http://interac tive.statssa.gov.za:8282/webview/

Steingo, Gavin. 2005. "South African Music After Apartheid: Kwaito, the 'Party Politic,' and the Appropriation of Gold as a Sign of Success." *Popular Music and Society* 28 (3): 333–57. https://doi.org/10.1080/03007760500105172

Stepan, Alfred, Juan J. Linz, and Yogendra Yadav. 2011. *Crafting State-Nations: India and Other Multinational Democracies*. Baltimore: Johns Hopkins University Press.

Steyn, Melissa E. 2012. "'White Talk': White South Africans and the Management of Diasporic Whiteness." In *Postcolonial Whiteness: A Critical Reader on Race and Empire*, edited by Alfred J. Lopez, 119–36. Albany: State University of New York Press.

Stone, John. 1986. *Racial Conflict in Contemporary Society*. Cambridge, MA: Harvard University Press.

Strydom, H. A. 1996. "Minority Rights Issues in Post-Apartheid South Africa." *Loyola of Los Angeles International and Comparative Law Journal* 19: 873.

Suny, Ronald Grigor. 2004. "Why We Hate You: The Passions of National Identity and Ethnic Violence." In Berkeley Program in Soviet and Post-Soviet Studies Working Paper Series. Berkeley: University of California, Berkeley. http://iseees.berkeley.edu/sites/default/files/u4/bps_/publications_/2004_01-suny.pdf

Tay, Nastasya. 2013. "Bodies Exhumed in ANC 'Murder' Case Linked to Winnie Mandela." *The Independent*, March 12. http://www.independent.co.uk/news/world/africa/bodies-exhumed-in-anc-murder-case-linked-to-winnie-mandela-8531758.html

Taylor, Rupert. 2002. "Justice Denied: Political Violence in Kwazulu-Natal After 1994." *African Affairs* 101 (405): 473–508. https://doi.org/10.1093/afraf/101.405.473

Team Report. 2000. "Verdeeld Op 16 Des. Bekendes Wil Nie Belydenis Teken." *Rapport*, December 17. http://152.111.1.87/argief/berigte/rapport/2000/12/17/1/10.html

Teeger, Chana. 2015. "'Both Sides of the Story': History Education in Post-Apartheid South Africa." *American Sociological Review* 80 (6): 1175–1200. https://doi.org/10.1177/0003122415613078

Thom, Hendrik Bernardus. 1965. "Wat beteken die Gelofte vir ons?" Stellenbosch University. H.B. Thom Collection, Stellenbosch University Library Digital Collections. https://digital.lib.sun.ac.za/handle/10019.2/3717

Thompson, Leonard Monteath. 2001. *A History of South Africa*. New Haven: Yale University Press.

Tilly, Charles. 1994. "States and Nationalism in Europe 1492–1992." *Theory and Society* 23 (1): 131–46. https://doi.org/10.1007/BF00993675

Toit, Andries du. 2013. "Real Acts, Imagined Landscapes: Reflections on the Discourses of Land Reform in South Africa after 1994." *Journal of Agrarian Change* 13 (1): 16–22. https://doi.org/10.1111/joac.12006

Tromp, Beauregard, and Botho Molosankwe. 2008. "UFS Hostel Could Be Shut." *IOL News*, February 29. https://www.iol.co.za/news/south-africa/ufs-hostel-could-be-shut-391360

Truth and Reconciliation Commission of South Africa. 2002. "Truth and Reconciliation Commission of South Africa Report." April 12. http://www.info.gov.za/other-docs/2003/trc/

UFS Council. 2003. "Language Policy of the University of the Free State." University of the Free State. http://www.ufs.ac.za/dl/userfiles/Documents/00000/335_eng.pdf

University Council. 2014. "Integrated Report 2013." Bloemfontein: University of the Free State. http://www.ufs.ac.za/docs/default-source/all-documents/integrated-re port-ufs-2013-2540.pdf?sfvrsn=4

Van der Merwe, Johan Matthys. 2012. "Die Herdenking van Die Gelofte van 16 Desember 1838 Op Versoeningsdag: 'n Nuwe Uitdaging Aan Die Kerk." *Journal of the Church History Society of Southern Africa* 38 (95): 1–10.

Van Jaarsveld, Floris Albertus. 1979. *Die evolusie van apartheid en ander geskiedkundige opstelle*. Kaapstad: Tafelberg.

Van Rooyen, Johann. 2000. *The New Great Trek: The Story of South Africa's White Exodus*. Pretoria: Unisa Press.

Van Wyk, At. 1991. *The Birth of a New Afrikaner*. Human & Rousseau.

Verdeja, Ernesto. 2009. *Unchopping a Tree: Reconciliation in the Aftermath of Political Violence*. Philadelphia: Temple University Press.

Verslagspan—Team Report. 2012a. "Bloedbad: Tot 20 Sterf Toe Hulle Polisie Aanval." *Volksblad*, August 17. http://152.111.11.6/argief/berigte/volksblad/2012/08/17/ VB/1/HB_2043.html

Verslagspan—Team Report. 2012b. "Minute Lyke in Lonmin Moles Ruk SA/ Internasionaal Opslae." *Die Burger*, August 17. http://152.111.1.87/argief/berigte/die-burger/2012/08/17/SK/1/SK001-hoofkop.html

Verwey, Cornel, and Michael Quayle. 2012. "Whiteness, Racism, and Afrikaner Identity in Post-Apartheid South Africa." *African Affairs* 111 (445): 551–75.

Vestergaard, Mads. 2001. "Who's Got the Map? The Negotiation of Afrikaner Identities in Post-Apartheid South Africa." *Daedalus* 130 (1): 19–44.

Villiers, Ockert de. 2015. "GALLERY: Protesters Chain Themselves to Paul Kruger Statue." *News24*, April 8. https://www.news24.com/Multimedia/South-Africa/GAL LERY-Paul-Kruger-statue-protest-20150408

Vincent, Louise. 2006. "Virginity Testing in South Africa: Re-Traditioning the Postcolony." *Culture, Health & Sexuality: An International Journal for Research, Intervention and Care* 8 (1): 17. https://doi.org/10.1080/13691050500404225

Vincent, Louise, and Simon Howell. 2014. "Embracing Racial Reasoning: The DASO Poster Controversy and 'Race' Politics in Contemporary South Africa." *Journal of Southern African Studies* 40 (1): 75–90. https://doi.org/10.1080/03057070.2014.877651

Visser, Jaco. 2014. "South African Platinum Strike Talks Resume as Rand Slides." Bloomberg. January 27, 2014. http://www.bloomberg.com/news/2014-01-26/south-african-platinum-strikes-enter-third-day-after-rand-slides.html

Vos, Ügen. 2012. "Marikana-Geweld 'Het Dalk Politieke Motiewe.'" *Beeld*, August 21. http://152.111.1.88/argief/berigte/beeld/2012/08/21/B1/1/ufamcu.html

Waal, C. S. van der, and Steven Robins. 2011. "'De La Rey' and the Revival of 'Boer Heritage': Nostalgia in the Postapartheid Afrikaner Culture Industry." *Journal of Southern African Studies* 37 (4): 763–79.

Walker, Cherryl. 2005. "The Limits to Land Reform: Rethinking 'the Land Question.'" *Journal of Southern African Studies* 31 (4): 805–24. https://doi.org/10.1080/03057070500370597

Walker, Cherryl, Anna Bohlin, Ruth Hall, and Thembela Kepe, eds. 2010. *Land, Memory, Reconstruction, and Justice: Perspectives on Land Claims in South Africa*. Athens: Ohio University Press.

Wasserman, Herman. 2009. "Learning a New Language: Culture, Ideology and Economics in Afrikaans Media after Apartheid." *International Journal of Cultural Studies* 12 (1): 61–80. https://doi.org/10.1177/1367877908098855

Wasserman, Herman. 2013. "National Braai Day." *Media in the South* (personal blog). September 24. https://hermanwasserman.wordpress.com/tag/national-braai-day/

Wasserman, Herman, and Gabriël J. Botma. 2008. "Having It Both Ways: Balancing Market and Political Interests at a South African Daily Newspaper." *Critical Arts* 22 (1): 1–20. https://doi.org/10.1080/02560040802166193

Weber, Eugen. 1976. *Peasants into Frenchmen: The Modernization of Rural France, 1870–1914*. Stanford: Stanford University Press.

Wilkinson, Kate. 2017. "ANALYSIS: Why Calculating a Farm Murder Rate in South Africa Is Near Impossible." *Africa Check*, May 8. https://africacheck.org/2017/05/08/analysis-calculating-farm-murder-rate-sa-near-impossible/

Wilson, Richard A. 2001. *The Politics of Truth and Reconciliation in South Africa: Legitimizing the Post-Apartheid State*. Cambridge: Cambridge University Press.

Wilson, Richard, and Brandon Hamber. 2002. "Symbolic Closure through Memory, Reparation and Revenge in Post-Conflict Societies." *Research Papers*, March. http://digitalcommons.uconn.edu/hri_papers/5

Wimmer, Andreas. 2012. *Waves of War: Nationalism, State Formation, and Ethnic Exclusion in the Modern World*. Cambridge: Cambridge University Press.

Wimmer, Andreas. 2013. *Ethnic Boundary Making: Institutions, Power, Networks*. New York: Oxford University Press.

Witz, Leslie, Gary Minkley, and Ciraj Rassool. 2017. *Unsettled History: Making South African Public Pasts*. Ann Arbor: University of Michigan Press.

Wolpe, Harold. 1972. "Capitalism and Cheap Labour-Power in South Africa: From Segregation to Apartheid 1." *Economy and Society* 1 (4): 425–56. https://doi.org/10.1080/03085147200000023

Wright, John. 1995. "Beyond the Concept of the 'Zulu Explosion': Comments on the Current Debate." In *The Mfecane Aftermath: Reconstructive Debates in Southern African History*, edited by Carolyn Hamilton, 107–22. Bloomington: Indiana University Press.

Wright, John. 2009. "Reflections on the Politics of Being 'Zulu.'" In *Zulu Identities: Being Zulu, Past and Present*, edited by Benedict Carton, John Laband, and Jabulani Sithole, 35–43. New York: Columbia University Press.

Wyk, Pauli van. 2012a. "Dít Is Kriteria Vir Optrede: Polisie 'Was Waarskynlik

Binne Regte.'" *Volksblad*, August 18. http://152.111.11.6/argief/berigte/volks
blad/2012/08/18/VB/5/pvwoptog_1827-508.html

Wyk, Pauli van. 2012b. "Polisie 'Tree Op Binne Sy Regte Met Reaksie.'" *Die Beeld*, August
18. http://152.111.1.88/argief/berigte/beeld/2012/08/18/B1/4/pvwoptog.html

Wylie, Dan. 2000. *Savage Delight: White Myths of Shaka*. Pietermaritzburg: University
of Natal Press.

Yuval-Davis, Nira. 2011. *The Politics of Belonging: Intersectional Contestation*. London:
Sage.

Zielinski, Jakub. 2002. "Translating Social Cleavages into Party Systems: The Significance of New Democracies." *World Politics* 54 (2): 184–211.

Zuern, Elke. 2011. *The Politics of Necessity: Community Organizing and Democracy in
South Africa*. Madison: University of Wisconsin Press.

Zuydam, Lali van. 2013. "Kleinfontein: Pretoria's Own Orania." *Independent Online*,
May 21. http://www.iol.co.za/news/south-africa/gauteng/kleinfontein-pretoria-s-
own-orania-1.1519319#.VGJGcvTF_Uc

Genootskap van Regte Afrikaners (Society of True Afrikaners), 167
Gordimer, Nadine, 98
Government of National Unity, 6–7
Great Trek, 29, 30–31, 121, 126. *See also* Day of the Vow
grilling. *See* braais
Group Areas Act of 1950, 37

health professionals, emigration by, 210n15
Heritage Day (Braai Day), 138–39, 207n5
Hertzog, J. B. M., 35
history and historical narratives: by Afrikaner people, 28, 29, 30–31, 150–51; as goal of Truth and Reconciliation Commission, 42, 46, 56, 65–68, 189–90; and nation-building, 10–12; by Zulu people, 28, 29–30, 31
Hofmeyr, Steve, 53
holidays, national: and ignoring the past, 11; role of, 118, 137–40. *See also* Day of the Vow
homelands, 36–37, 38, 40
homes and neighborhoods: homelands, 36–37, 38, 40; informal settlements, 151–52; land reform, 144–48; mixing in, 142, 151–52, 190–91; securitization of, 142, 152–58, 161–62, 164–65; segregationist communities, 158–65. *See also* land
honor, 59
human rights: and "cultural communities," 214n7; freedom of movement, 35, 97, 143, 149–50; freedom of residence, 143; and state of emergency (1985), 40; and Truth and Reconciliation Commission, 46, 55; and virginity testing, 127, 130
Human Rights Commission, 214n7
Human Rights Violations Committee, 46, 55

identity: and economic inequality, 8–9; and exit from political activity, 71, 80–93; and gender roles, 107, 109, 110;

and land, 16, 28, 144, 148; and languages, 167–73; national, 27–36; race as primary social identity, 7–8, 99–103; and segregationist communities, 165. *See also* Afrikaner identity and culture; festivals; performance, rituals, and ceremonies
IFP (Inkatha Freedom Party), 16–17, 79, 84
incomes, 81, 83, 171–72, 211n5
Indian flag, 11
Indian people: resistance movements, 37, 39; voting patterns, 71
indigenity, 16, 28
information loss and nation-building, 10–11, 12
Inkatha Freedom Party (IFP), 16–17, 79, 84
Inkatha Movement, 16, 40
instrumentalism, 10
Interim Constitution, 7, 41
interpersonal relationships: and economics, 103–7; mixing in, 52, 101–2; policing of, 96, 97–98; post-apartheid, 98–107; sexual harassment and violence, 211n2; in transition era, 96
interviews: and future research, 192; guide and index, 197–201; methodology, 18–20
Isandlwana, 20
isiZulu. *See* Zulu language
iSolezwe, 21, 176–82

kaffir, as term, 211n6
Kenya, media in, 174
"Kill the Boer" (song), 51, 93
Kleinfontein, 160, 161, 164
Klopjag (band), 61
Kombuis, Koos, 117
Krog, Antjie, 61
Kruger, Paul, 143
KwaMuhle Museum, 17

labor: and apartheid, 97, 205n9; and disenfranchisement, 33; domestic labor, 97, 102; Marikana massacre, 168,